California Real Estate:
The 1980s And 1990s

These articles were originally published in the following publications: *Albuquerque Journal, The Desert Sun, The Los Angeles Times, The Press Democrat, The San Bernardino County Sun, The San Francisco Examiner, The Signal,* and the *Times-Advocate.*

Hardcover ISBN 978-1-947635-22-7
Ebook ISBN 978-1-947635-27-2

Printed in the United States of America
First Printing February 2020
Published by Inman Books

California Real Estate:
The 1980s And 1990s

Brad Inman

Contents

Introduction

The housing market in California continues to be one of the most expensive in the country. Cost and demand have both been rising for decades, resulting in an affordable housing crisis that concerns and impacts policymakers, citizens, and companies across the state. But how did we get here? And how do we solve the problem?

The following articles, written for a variety of publications between 1985 and 1990, discuss a range of factors that shaped the housing market in California. These factors include public policy topics such as infrastructure, environmental quality, affordable housing, second housing units, disaster insurance, property tax lawsuits, NIMBYism (Not In My Backyard) and, later, technology.

In reviewing my work from this time period, one theme was consistent: how do policymakers muster up the courage to increase housing supply? All of the topics I wrote about decades ago are more or less the same issues today. The solutions to the problem have also remained the same: build more housing, build more affordable housing, allow second units, permit dense housing developments and embrace modular housing (aka mobile homes).

An Aha Moment

One unmistakable trend stands out — the beginnings of the current affordable housing mess. It has been in the works for 40 years and can be squarely put at the doorstep of three main groups: homeowners, environmentalists and gutless politicians.

This unholy marriage of economic self-interest and environmental rules to restrict growth dismantled a system of producing enough housing to meet California's growing demand.

Income disparity cannot be underestimated in the affordable housing equation. But the supply/demand imbalance is equally fundamental, contributing to the affordability problem and exasperating the income divide. High housing costs gobble up a working person's economic balance sheet.

Looking back at the 1980s and 1990s, there were individuals who tried to turn the tide in favor of more affordable housing. Former Mayor of Hayward, California Ilene Weintraub was a strong supporter of more affordable housing (and housing generally) in her community. But she had to fight the NIMBY activists, moneyed homeowners who clamored about environmental concerns, whining about traffic, noise pollution, open space and quality of life generally. The bottom line was they did not want affordable housing near them.

The affordable housing crisis was decades in the making; it will take decades to fix. Long-term solutions will require commitment to the good of the community as a whole rather than to self-interest by individuals and policymakers. In looking back over these articles, I see the same California market that we are familiar with today: rising costs, increasing demand, and a lack of policies to curb these trends. I hope my future articles will highlight new and better trends for California.

No military solution to expensive housing

"VERY COMFORTABLE, affordable and convenient." That's how Navy Junior Enlistee Emanuale Alforque describes his new apartment in Oakland. Alforque and his family settled into their new quarters last month — a move made easier and less expensive by a pilot community project designed to aid military personnel.

Alforque's apartment is one of several city-owned properties being rehabilitated and offered to Navy personnel through the Bay Area-based Urban Housing Institute, with the help of no-interest loans from World Savings.

Yet despite innovative programs of this kind, thousands of military families in California still struggle to find affordable housing. Though military salaries have been upgraded considerably in the past few years, the increases haven't been large enough to keep pace with the state's housing costs.

A shortage of housing on or near military installations isn't a new problem, but only recently has it come into the public eye. In an especially tragic example last year, the son of a soldier in the Monterey area committed suicide to ease the strain on his family's budget, a large portion of which was devoted to housing. This incident was an extreme example of the economic squeeze some military families face in California's expensive housing markets.

The military makes some attempt to compensate for the high cost of shelter. All personnel receive a "basic allowance for quarters," and a "variable housing allowance" provides an additional subsidy for those stationed in high-cost areas. But monthly housing allowances total only $429 in San Francisco, $399 in San Diego and $465 in Long Beach.

Salaries don't do a great deal to augment what an enlistee or junior officer can pay for housing. An E-4 Junior enlistee in the Navy earns $810.30 a month, while a lieutenant brings home a little more than $1,750 per month. Based on the typical income and housing allowance, a junior enlistee can afford to pay about $600 per month rent in San Diego, $630 in San Francisco, and $665 in Long Beach. Home-ownership, of course, is Just about out of the question.

At these price levels, the single sailor or soldier can manage to get by, but for those with families it's a different story. As one Navy officer explains, sometimes the only real choice is to leave your family back home and create "geographical bastards."

One reason the military is so hard hit by California's housing costs is that more than 80 percent of its housing needs statewide are in the urban coastal areas, where housing is the most expensive. The Navy puts its estimated housing requirement at 33,000 units in San Diego, 10,000 units in the San Francisco Bay Area and 3,300 units in Long Beach. But based on existing Navy projects and available market-rate housing, the Navy comes up 15,000 units short in these three regions.

Historically, the military has relied on the local market to solve its off-base housing problems —a solution that simply isn't working in California. The military now is experimenting with other ways to solve the problem, such as establishing housing referral services and buying existing off-base properties.

The Navy is even attempting to develop new off-base housing itself. Construction has just been completed on two San Diego projects totalling 158 units. In 1986, more than 200 units are scheduled for construction in Chula Vista, 282 units for the Marine Corps at the El Toro Marine Base, 100 units in Twenty-Nine Palms and 44 units in Warner Springs.

In the San Francisco Bay Area, 126 units at Moffett Field and 300 additional units in other locations are slated for development in 1987.

Unfortunately, the number of units being produced is meager relative to the need. But it won't be easy for the military to expand such programs, given the reaction they sometimes get from the public. The stereotyped image of ramshackle barracks filled with transient soldiers has fueled public opposition to proposed Navy housing developments, including a recent project in San Diego and a land swap to enable a housing development in San Francisco's East Bay.

To overcome these obstacles, the military has had to depend on local community solutions to the problem. In San Diego, the San Diego Association of Governments has completed an inventory of all housing units to identify appropriate building sites, and has been instrumental in building community support for new Navy construction projects in San Diego.

The Navy has also relied on purchase of existing housing units as a means to skirt controversy. Though this approach worked well in 1981 and 1982, when builders were left with unsold inventory due to high interest rates, in today's market it b both expensive and unreliable. The last major project purchased was a 130-unit development bought in San Diego in 1982.

In the San Francisco Bay Area, the Navy is also working with the Urban Housing Institute to find interim facilities for personnel relocating to California. For example, with UHI's assistance the Navy is negotiating with UC Berkeley for the use of dormitory space during the summer months.

These programs are all worthwhile steps toward solving the military's housing problem. But for the foreseeable future, the Alforque family can consider themselves luckier than most.

Special to the Examiner: Interest Rates

LOWER INTEREST rates have improved the affordability picture dramatically for Bay Area and California home buyers. The monthly income required to qualify for a home in the state dropped 31 percent from last month, despite a significant rise in the median home price. The amount of income needed to buy in the Bay Area fell 18 percent.

The Examiner's monthly affordability gap in the Bay Area fell $270 to $1,228 from $1,498 last month; statewide, the gap dropped $357 to $794 from $1,151.

The interest rate average for all conventional loans in the Bay Area was 12.14 percent — more than one percent lower than the level reported in last month's affordability report.

The decline in interest rates offset the impact of a 2.84 percent increase in Bay Area home prices and a one percent rise statewide. The price increase for May follows a three-month trend hi which home prices have been rising. This is a reversal from a three-year period in which prices were flat.

Interest rates have played a major role in price increases, but the inflation rates are also a function of seasonal activity. Typically, there is a greater demand for housing in the spring and summer. Therefore, home prices will continue to increase through the duration of the summer. If interest rates continue to fall, prices could be climb even higher.

Next month's affordability gap will include new annual median family income figures. The new figures are expected to show that family income in the Bay Area and California have risen, which will improve the affordability picture even more.

California's new mortgage gold mine

HISTORICALLY, CALIFORNIA home buyers have had the dubious honor of paying higher interest rates than the rest of the country. But in 1985, the average San Diego home buyer borrowed at a lower interest rate than the typical buyer in Philadelphia. Thanks to several complex changes in the financial marketplace, California mortgage costs are becoming more competitive.

"In the past, the West was a capital-deficit area," says Ken Rosen, UC Berkeley real estate professor. "We had to attract capital here and therefore had to charge higher interest rates."

According to Rosen, a simple economic theory governs the situation: the greater the supply of money, the lower the interest rate.

Local economic conditions, savings rates and population characteristics combine to make a region "capital rich or capital poor." For example, Florida is a money-exporting state due to the size of the elderly population and the high savings rate. California, on the other hand, has had to import capital because of the high demand for mortgages and the short supply of local money.

Today, there is a whole new ball game, and California is on the winning side. More importantly, the state is on an even playing field now.

According to the Federal Home Loan Bank Board, the national mortgage rate for all loans (fixed and adjustable) in May was 12.09 percent. Both Los Angeles at 11.78 percent and San Diego at 11.80 percent showed lower averages than the national figures. At 12.14 percent for all loans, the San Francisco Bay Area average is only slightly higher, but the fixed-rate average was 1/4 of a percent lower than the national average.

This trend may be the conscience of several developments in mortgage finance. First is the presence of large out-of-state mortgage banking firms. "The big mortgage houses in the country are now major players in California real estate," Rosen says.

Michael Salkin, a Bank of America vice president and economist, agrees: "As heavy hitters get more active in the state, there is no reason for regional variations in interest rates."

Another explanation for the increased supply of dollars may result from a change in conventional lending practices. Traditionally, banks or savings and loans held onto mortgages until they were paid off or until the house was resold. Now, lenders package and sell the loans to institutional investors, creating a secondary market for the mortgages. This vehicle has indirectly linked the home buyer with Wall Street; loans are put into the form of securities arid sold like stocks and bonds. The original lender becomes only a conduit for the mortgage payment.

Some executives aren't so bullish about the role of the secondary market. Anthony M. Frank, chairman of San Francisco-based First Nationwide Savings and Loan, contends that the secondary market has not standardized mortgage lending.

"There are only certain kinds of loans that can be homogenized and sold into the secondary market," says Frank. For example, he notes, loans have to be less than $115,000 to be passed on; otherwise, they must remain in the lender's portfolio.

Moreover, even when the opportunity exists, many lenders do not want to give up traditional methods for handling mortgage loans. Frank says First Nationwide, for instance, puts greater emphasis on portfolio lending — making loans that the financial institution keeps — than participating in the secondary market.

Regulations governing mortgage lending also create disparities in interest rates. For example, the variation in foreclosure laws from state to state affects a lender's cost of doing business. That means lower or higher interest rates also depend on the different set of rules.

New mortgage instruments are another variable in the interest rate equation. Lenders caught holding low-yielding fixed-rate mortgages during the last interest cycle have turned to adjustable-rate mortgages, which have changing rates based on a standard index.

Initially, consumers perceived adjustable-rate mortgages as more of a gamble than an opportunity. But lower adjustable loan rates have broken down the initial resistance. "More than a million families are getting a reduction in the cost of their mortgage," says Frank.

Joel Singer, an economist and vice president of the California Association of Realtors, isn't convinced, though that rates on adjustable loans made over the last two years are going to drop dramatically in California. Singer blames "teaser rates" — very low interest in the initial years of the mortgage — for what he regards as a misconception that future rates on adjustables will be reasonable.

Disagreements aside, it is still difficult to predict the future performance of mortgage rates for Californians relative to the rest of the country. At times, there will be variations in the rates for San Francisco to Detroit, but they will rarely exceed a percentage point or so. And even if the differences are rubbed out, California home buyers will not necessarily find their homeownership costs shrinking.

Ultimately, the ebb and flow of national economic, fiscal and monetary conditions will dictate how affordable California mortgages are. Those are circumstances that all American home buyers share.

Pension funds are mortgage gold mine

First of two Parts

"ONE TRILLION dollars in pension funds by the '90's, can you believe it?" Mark Adams is admittedly intrigued by the number. Adams, a real estate investment broker, is one of many individuals working to unlock the public pension fund treasure for investment in California real estate. But their work has met with mixed success.

The retirement and pension benefits of government workers as a source of investment capital has grown by leaps and bounds. The size has made them a target for a wishful thinking housing industry, as well as for activists who dream of redirecting capital into socially redeeming causes.

In the early 1980s, this coalition forged precedent-setting legislation in California — a law that directed public pension funds to invest 25 percent of their portfolios in California housing. And now the constituency has broadened.

Samuel Pierce, Secretary of Housing and Urban Development, has made it his personal crusade to attract pension fund investments to housing. California Republican .George Deukmejian has gotten on the bandwagon, having signed a bill last year that created a new mortgage investment vehicle for pension funds.

But broad-based support hasn't led to wholesale investment in housing. Nationally, it is estimated that $31.9 billion in pensions were put into mortgages last year, a 3 percent increase in housing invest-ments from the year before. But during this same period, the size of pension funds increased by more than 11 percent. As a result, the proportion of pension funds assets invested in mortgages slipped from 5.7 to 5.3 percent.

In California, pension fund value exceeds $100 billion. Of that total, $66 billion is invested in gov-ernment funds, and a considerable portion is in the Public Employees Retirement System (PERS) and/or the State Teachers Retirement System (STERS). A report released by the auditor general estimates these funds have more than $1.5 billion invested in residential realty, a significant sum.

But according to the report, "Public pension funds are not complying with statutory requirements for investing in California residential realty." Of the 83 funds examined by the auditor general, only 18 were in compliance with state legislation requiring investment in real estate. The report estimated that another $170 million should be placed in California mortgages.

The largest funds in the state, PERS, STERS and the Los Angeles County Public Employees Retire-ment Fund are complying with the law. There may be a lesson in their success.

Jim Smith of PERS boasts of their fund's history of real estate investment, which began in 1964. "Originally, we were buying strictly FHA and VA mortgages, then GNMAs in the early '70s," says Smith. PERS began to buy directly from lenders in the mid-70s.

By everyone's standards, PERS has set the pace for pension fund investment in real estate. Before the legislation, PERS had 27 percent of its portfolio in mortgages. Today, it has more than a third of its assets invested in housing.

Smith is unwilling to draw a link between PERS' involvement in housing and the mandate in the legislation. "The legislation had no real effect on us; we just continued to make a good investment," he says.

Most pension managers are nervous about political decisions affecting where they invest their money. The administrator's job, according to Smith, is to protect the interests of the pension beneficiaries by making sound investment choices that maximize yield and minimize risk — real estate is just one of the options.

That attitude is fine for funds complying with the law. But many smaller funds are not meeting the legislative requirements, asserts Bart Doyle, president of the California Mortgage Access Corp. He complains there is "no legislative overview, and reporting has not been very good," which is confirmed in the auditor general's report.

To address the problem, the auditor general has recommended changes in reporting procedures for public funds. But since the report was issued late last year, nothing has been done to implement the recommendations.

Declining enthusiasm by the housing industry may be one explanation for the lack of follow up. In 1982, when the bill was passed, real estate interests were very concerned about the condition of the mortgage market. But according to Krist Lane, Senate Housing consultant, an improved housing market has reduced the pressure on the legislature to act.

Despite no strong constituent pressure, the Senate Housing Committee plans to follow up on the auditor general's suggestions. "As a result of the report, committee staff will investigate ways of enhancing and improving the reporting of the retirement system's real estate investment decisions," says Lane.

Some experts argue the bill wasn't sensitive enough to the investment practices of public pension funds to begin with. On the other hand, it may just take time to convince pension funds as to the value of expanding their real estate holdings. Ultimately, cracking the pension gold mine may depend on the quality of ideas presented to fund managers.

Prodding pensions into real estate

Second of two parts

THIS FALL 70 families will have new townhouses in the Amancio Ergina Village housing development in San Francisco. The families are more fortunate than most California home buyers because the homes are affordable, selling for $70,000 to $110,000.

But the price isn't the only unusual ingredient in this innovative project; in a sense, these homeowners have the longshoremen and warehouses partly to thank. The International Longshoremen and Warehouses Union pension fund along with Pacific Maritime Association pension fund participated in this project with more than $3 million in construction financing.

The union's participation is only one example of how pension funds are using their vast resources to finance mortgages, rental housing construction, condos and single-family homes. Explaining their interest in California real estate is simple; they see it as a good investment.

But many of the deals are the result of prodding, brokering and marketing by a diverse group of institutions and individuals, including trade and construction unions, community housing groups and builders. They all have been successful in bringing pension fund money into housing, albeit for different reasons.

In the case of Amancio Ergina Village, located in Western Addition, it was a hardworking community group in cooperation with the city that brokered the involvement of the longshoremen pension fund. Without the union's participation, the housing would not have been built.

Finding a niche for pension funds in real estate has not been easy. This is in part due to federal laws that restrict where and how pension funds invest. For example, regulations forbid investments made solely for social or political causes and investments with discount interest rates or favorable terms.

But even with the limitations there is a fit for pension funds with real estate. The longshoremen pension received a competitive rate of return on their loan for the San Francisco townhouses and filled a critical gap in the construction financing.

Another opportunity for pension funds is in single-family fixed-rate home loans. A Southern California group has arranged state public pension fund investment in privately originated home loans — loans that may not have been made without a pension fund as an investor.

"There is a lot of mortgage money around, but there is a shortage of mortgage money for fixed-rate loans over $115,000," says Mark Adams, a real estate investment broker.

Banks and savings and loans are reluctant to make fixed-rate loans that exceed $115,000 because they cannot sell the loans in the secondary market. Pension funds, however, are willing to buy the loans, so lenders are willing to make them. "If there is hope for the fixed-rate loan in California it will be due to pension funds," says Adams.

And the market to sell fixed-rate mortgages to pension funds is no longer a secret. Great Western Savings is aggressively seeking out pension funds, with the result of more fixed-rate mortgages and increased choices for the consumer. "We have a more volatile cost of funds due to changing interest rates on deposits," says Sam Lyons, executive vice president of Great Western. "The only way we'll make the loans is if we can sell them in the secondary mortgage market. Pension funds have a stable source of funds and are looking for long-term Investments like fixed-rate mortgages."

It's not surprising that builders also have set their sights on fixed-rate mortgages for pension fund investment. In 1983, the California Mortgage Access Corp. (CALMAC) was created by the California Building Industry Association for the purpose of attracting money into housing. In 1984, the builders received a commitment from the Public Employees Retirement System (PERS) for $25.5 million in fixed-rate mortgage loans.

But turning the agreement into loans is easier said than done. CALMAC has placed only 15 percent of the PERS commitment, a disappointment that Bart Doyle, CALMAC president blames on lower interest rates. When PERS entered the agreement with CALMAC interest rates were 13 percent to 15 percent. Rates are now in the 11 percent to 12.5 percent range, making the PERS interest rate higher than market rates.

Doyle also is discouraged by the conservative investment policies of the Public Funds. "They only want to look at gold-plated loans," he says.

Underwriting isn't the only problem; consumer preference can muddle the equation as well. "We can't compete with the attractive adjustable mortgage rates that have been so popular in the last couple of years," says Cecil Harris, executive director of the Development Foundation of Southern California. The Foundation, a collection of major construction trade unions, arranges loans for home buyers and builders. They have received no applications for residential mortgages in the last 8-10 months.

But the Foundation has not been idle. Its forte is in construction and permanent financing of large residential, commercial and industrial developments. Since 1980, they have placed over $494 million in loans, and more than half are funded and complete.

Energy savings can cost plenty

WHEN MY HOUSE was built in the 1920s, it t didn't include ceiling or wall insulation, a solar water heater or weather stripping. Today, every new house in California has these energy-saving features.

But it wasn't out of the goodness of the builders' hearts that 350,000 energy-efficient homes were built in California during the last 18 months — state law required it.

The law requiring that newly constructed homes be energy-efficient followed a series of national and international episodes we all remember. The oil embargo, long lines at the gas station and rising energy prices suddenly forced Americans to be energy conscious.

California was at the forefront of developing energy standards for new housing development. With little fanfare, the state Energy Commission developed energy guidelines for residential construction in 1978. But a bitter debate erupted when the commission proposed strict guidelines for all development in 1980. Despite the good intentions of the Energy Commission, a recession-ridden housing industry was opposed to adding more costs to the price of housing. It wasn't until 1983 that a compromise was reached and the regulations were put into effect.

Enough time has now passed to measure the success of the law. At first glance, the results are impressive: Every new house built in the state is energy efficient. But this sweeping change hasn't occurred without a difficult transition.

The complexity of the regulations has been part of the problem. The requirements are impossible for the average citizen to understand and confuse even the state's best builders and architects.

When a developer decides to build a home in California, there are two choices guiding compliance with energy laws. The developer can install all of the specific equipment required by the Commission, like a solar water heater, insulation and weather stripping. If the builder installs everything that is prescribed, the homes are in compliance.

But the task can be more difficult than it sounds, because the rules don't fit every situation. For example, the commission says houses must face south, which increases the amount of sunlight and reduces energy output. But not every house in a development can be designed to face south, and, therefore, the developer cannot meet the letter of the law.

When the specific requirements cannot be met, there is a way out. In this case, the developer can design the house with any combination of energy-savers so that the total energy used in the house does not exceed the level established by the commission.

The regulations lay out 16 different climatic zones in the state. Each zone has a maximum energy output budget that puts a ceiling on how many BTUs of energy the average house will use with a typical family. The Palm Springs' zone has the largest budget in the state because of the extreme heat and air conditioning requirements. Because of its moderate climate, the San Diego area has the smallest budget.

The zone concept probably is the best way to accommodate the varying weather conditions in the state. However, it also can create a problem for builders who must adjust their master plans to meet the energy output standard each time they build in a different zone. This adds to the cost of the home and presents another problem regarding local interpretation of the rules.

Local government enforces the energy laws, but few local government personnel have been trained in energy standards. The result is widely different interpretations of the rules.

A more basic concern is whether the residential standards are the best way to attack the energy problem. Regulating new construction is one systematic way of insuring more efficient energy use in new homes, but it will not reduce energy use in all homes. Ninety percent of the housing in the state was constructed before 1980 — before energy standards were adopted. How energy-saving is promoted for this much larger share of our housing stock is the big challenge.

Even when homes are decked out with the latest energy-saving devices, habits greatly influence energy consumption. The window weather stripping is irrelevant if shades and drapes aren't used properly. Government and private education programs, designed to teach the public how to become more energy aware, abounded in the early 1980s. But when the energy crisis abated, many of these programs were abandoned.

Finally, one must ask if energy regulations as public policy still make sense. The Energy Commission claims every requirement can be paid for through direct energy savings. But it admits the savings are earned over the life of the house.

For that reason, the law has to be measured against its effect on the national and statewide energy problem, and not against the consumer's pocketbook. And when that's the standard, California can be applauded for looking ahead. As one housing industry representative says, "A dozen experts in a room would agree the energy problem is not behind us."

Incomes improve housing affordability

Special to the Examiner

GREATER EARNING power, lower interest rates and a decline in home prices lowered The Examiner's affordability gap from last month. In the Bay Area the affordability gap dropped 20 percent to $245.

Lower interest rates were a critical ingredient in reducing the monthly income required to buy a home. The regional interest rate average fell to 11.84 percent from 12.14 percent for all loans. Statewide, the interest rate average slipped to 11.72 percent from 11.90 percent.

These drops are consistent with a six-month trend of declining interest rates.

A significant rise in median family income also improved the lot for Bay Area and California home buyers. Annual median family income rose 12 percent in 1985 to $33,933 from $29,585 in the Bay Area. Statewide, the median family income increased 9 percent to $28,830 from $26,002.

(This month, the affordability gap used a new measure of family income. Previously, the gap was based on income figures from the Department of Housing and Urban Development, which defines family as four related individuals. The new income averages are prepared by Urban Decision Systems, which defines family as two or more related individuals. This definition of family is more representative of the typical California family.)

The final factor influencing affordability is a drop in the median home price for California and the Bay Area. In the Bay Area the median price slipped to $134,198 from $136,629; statewide, the median price dropped to $114,989 from $115,011.

A softening in home prices in June follows three months of price increases. Stable interest rates and slower economic activity help explain the downturn. In addition, demand has tapered off after a springtime seasonal upswing.

California Trends

Subsequently, the state Department of Real Estate released a study painting a considerably different housing picture. Prepared by Kenneth Rosen, a housing economist and professor at UC Berkeley, the study confirmed the need for state policies that encourage a high level of new production. Such contradictions are not unusual.

On a project level, local officials also look to housing data to substantiate the need for the number and type of units proposed. Among questions asked by the local decision-maker are: How do the prices of this project compare to the average home price of the community? How many units have been approved this year and how many of the units approved last year have actually been built? What are the current vacancy rates?

Proponent and opponents alike attempt to use available data to support their positions. It's up to the official to determine the interpretation that makes sense in each circumstance.

Policy and policy-related decisions rely most heavily on four data categories: permits, starts, vacancy rates and prices and sales. Very few planning departments maintain local records of this activity. For the most part, four industry groups have assumed the responsibility for collecting this information statewide.

Security Pacific National Bank publishes California Construction Trends, a monthly account of single and multifamily permits issued by local governments. Bank of America takes it from there with its reporting of housing starts, albeit on a statewide level only. Vacancycies.

For example, when prices are on an upward trend, the Legislature may embrace discount financing programs designed to help first-time home buyers afford homes.

At the local level, higher prices may lead to policies that allow smaller units and more densely developed projects. Brokers and developers also utilize information on price, the length of time that homes are on the market and number of sales to make marketing decisions.

CAR admits problems with its data collection. The most limiting is the absence of data for key markets — San Francisco for one.

The Federal Home Loan Bank of San Francisco (FHLB) is another key source of housing information. For more than six years the bank has been in the business of reporting single and multifamily vacancy rates for metropolitan areas. In general, low vacancy rates are associated with low rates of population growth, few recent moves and relatively high home values.

Conversely, a high rate can indicate population growth potential, mobility in the marketplace and lower home values.

Caution must be exercised, however, in drawing conclusions based on vacancy rates only. As Connie Vicory points out in a recent FHLB publication. "The interrelationship of vancancy rates with other housing and population characteristics. . does not make vacancy rates a proxy for other measurements of housing conditions or a sole indicator of market tightness "

The pros and cons of redevelopment

IN THESE TIMES, paring down government social spending is a mainstream political theme, and expensive housing programs are a popular target for cutbacks. In some cases, where federal and state expenditures have been reduced, local resources have been shaken loose to solve housing problems. One activity aiding local communities in this enormous task is redevelopment — a local strategy with a history of success but with its share of controversy as well.

Redevelopment is a complicated scheme used to stimulate development in urban areas. Through their power to control and levy property taxes, cities and counties generate vast sums of money to rebuild large portions of the state.

Redevelopment began in response to decay in our urban centers. California Community Development Law states that "redevelopment is to be used for the elimination of blight, the expansion of housing, and the creation of jobs." It has involved hundreds of millions of dollarsand thousands of acres of land in most cities throughout the state.

Sixty-one percent of California cities have redevelopment agencies, and more than 450 individual projects are under way. Projects range from 2 acres to 13,000 acres in size, generate more than $375 million annually in revenue, and include office buildings, museums, hotels, shopping centers, housing projects and industrial warehouses.

Some modern California landmarks built through the redevelopment process include: Embarcadero Center in San Francisco, Bunker Hill in downtown Los Angeles and Horton Plaza in San Diego. A major project planned for development is the Desert Fashion Plaza in Palm Springs.

But redevelopment is not free from controversy, glitches and/or abuse. For example, in the past some cities have declared everything within their city limits as a redevelopment area — prompting critics to question their definition of blight. Other cities demolished entire residential neighborhoods without providing adequate replacement housing.

Abuse led the state legislature to reform redevelopment law in 1976. Local government is now required to do a better job of providing replacement housing and to set aside a portion of their revenues for a housing fund. In 1984, legislation further changed redevelopment law, requiring 80 percent of the land in a redevelopment project area to be urbanized — preventing abuse by over-eager cities. At first glance, the results of reform are impressive.

According to a report by the California Debt Advisory Commission, more than 15,000 net new housing units have been built in the state through redevelopment.

But there is more to the story. Although new housing has exceeded the number of demolished units, the agencies have had problems producing very low-income housing: 11,000 housing units for very low-income people were destroyed, and only 6,000 were built.

In response, the legislature mandated redevelopment agencies to set aside 20 percent of their revenues for housing. The revenue, called tax increments, is generated from increased taxes on the higher property values resulting from development. About $45 million could be raised from the 20 percent set aside for housing, according to an estimate by the state Department of Housing and Community Development.

However, there is a dispute over how well the requirement is working.

In Los Angeles, City Councilman Ernest Bernani isn't convinced it is. He has been a thorn in the side of the Los Angeles Community Redevelopment Agency, demanding a greater commitment to housing for the most needy and negotiating an agreement with the Agency requiring it to set aside $1.4 million annually for the homeless. Bernani defends his position by pointing to new downtown sky-scrapers in the redevelopment area that have displaced poor residents.

Abuse led the state legislature to reform redevelopment law, and local government is now required to do a better job of providing replacement housing

The local disagreements have brought the legislature back into the debate in 1985. Los Angeles Assemblywoman Teresa Hughes is pushing through a bill requiring a greater share of redevelopment projects to set aside 20 percent of their tax increments for housing. Existing law applies only to projects planned after 1977. The Hughes legislation would require pre-'77 projects to follow the rule as well. This change would greatly increase the amount of money for housing — many projects are not covered by existing law.

Another bill working its way through the legislature would create more rigorous standards for replacement housing. The bill initially required redevelopment agencies to replace every very low-income housing unit demolished with a new unit. The bill, as amended, requires 75 percent of very low-income units lost to be replaced.

Milt Farrel, Executive Director of the Association of Redevelopment Agencies, claims the requirement may be too onerous. "The cost of land and construction makes it very difficult to bring down housing costs affordable to very low-income individuals," Farrel said.

Any attempt to change redevelopment law will be controversial. The forces that build and redevelop California cities are powerful, and groups seeking to make redevelopment serve a larger public purpose are increasingly vocal and united. Regardless of the political players, the very nature of redevelopment will always put it in the middle of conflict — being part of the solution can at times make it part of the problem.

S&Ls that invest in affordable housing

THE SAVINGS Associations Mortgage Co. doesn't try to make big splashes — it prefers to work quietly behind the scenes. But that low-key approach hasn't undermined its success; more than 3,400 California families have benefited from SAMCO financing.

SAMCO is a collection of statewide savings and loans, organized to undertake "socially-oriented" housing investments. It is an unusual private corporation with a public purpose, and its track record is impressive: more than $104 million in loans for affordable housing.

Seventy senior citizens in San Francisco's Chinatown, 58 first-time home buyers in Hayward, 56 tenants in Novato, and 72 recovered alcoholics in the Bay Area are just some of the people who have or will find housing in developments financed by SAMCO.

SAMCO is an unusual private corporation with a public purpose and its track record is impressive

SAMCO's role in affordable housing finance is simple. The board of directors of SAMCO, headquartered in San Jose, reviews loan proposals submitted by non-profit and private developers. Once the project is approved, SAMCO members — 38 savings and loans throughout the state — are asked to make a loan on a portion of the total project.

A good example is the case of a San Francisco non-profit housing corporation that needed a loan to acquire and rehabilitate a run-down 66-unit residential hotel in Chinatown. To purchase and improve the building a $900,000 loan was required — a loan with enormous social value but little appeal to the average lender.

After reviewing and approving the application, SAMCO agreed to the terms and interest rate on the loan. A subscription letter then went out to SAMCO members seeking their participation.

It works like a modern business enterprise for which a group of lenders come together to help finance the venture. Like the business deal, SAMCO lenders each take a portion of the loan: one for $50,000, another for $100,000 and so on, until the total loan amount is secured.

"These are loans that, individually, lenders are unwilling to take the risk on. If the loan goes sour, losing $50,000 isn't as serious as a one million dollar loss," says Don Maddox, vice president of Los Angeles-based Executive Savings and Loan and chairman of SAMCO.

But what motivates a group of profit-making lenders to do high-risk, low-return social investing? The spector of government regulation partially explains their enthusiasm.

In the middle 1970s federal and state laws required savings and loans and banks to look more favorably at loans in urban locations. The laws responded to increased community concern over the lack of loans being made in certain city neighborhoods.

It was during these turbulent times that a small group of savings and loans decided to join forces to solve the problem, and SAMCO was formed. Initially, SAMCO concentrated on home mortgage loans, originating them and selling them to its members. Between 1971 and 1975, 21 mortgage pools were created totaling over $30 million in loans. But success did not come easy.

SAMCO learned a few hard lessons: loans in some urban locations differ from others in that they carry varied risks and more strict servicing requirements. Early mistakes came close to ruining the future of the corporation. According to one of the founding members, the residential mortgage portfolio was a mess; delinquency rates reached 20 percent, a bad loan rate unheard of in the industry.

Part of the problem was unfamiliarity with the higher risk urban market, and SAMCO wasn't structured to spread out the risk on bad loans. After its shaky beginning SAMCO began to share the risk, and individual institutions became more involved in scrutinizing SAMCO's lending practices.

Today, SAMCO has a reputation for making sound and prudent investment decisions. SAMCO Executive Vice President, Doris Schnider, boasts that the delinquency and foreclosure rate now stands at less than 2 percent. "Despite the social nature of the investment, SAMCO operates in a businesslike fashion, which means good underwriting and aggressive loan collection," says Jim Yacenda, vice president of the Federal Home Loan Bank of San Francisco, the central bank and chief regulator for California savings and loans.

Once improvements were made to its business practices, SAMCO shifted it's focus from mortgage loan pools to permanent financing for affordable development and rehabilitation projects. Projects now receive close scrutiny and must meet three rigorous tests: one, the project must be economically viable; two, it must provide sound security to SAMCO members; and three, a minimum of 51 percent of the living units must be made available to low- and moderate-income households (families with incomes of less than $22,550 annually in California.)

According to Maddox, SAMCO has become a specialized company that understands the affordable housing market. It has funded or committed to the financing of 30 projects with a value of approximately $40 million and totaling 1,252 units of housing.

SAMCO has also become an expert in working with a wide range of public and private groups including local and state government, churches and community organizations. It has used these relationships to match private dollars with grants and loans at the state, federal and local levels.

Despite its history of trial and error, SAMCO thrives successfully in a market most institutions ignore. But considering the magnitude of the housing affordability problem in California, SAMCO's good deeds are really only a drop in the bucket. It's unfortunate SAMCO stands alone.

Rise in home prices hurts affordability

Special to the Examiner

AFTER A two-month run in which the affordability of California and Bay Area houses improved, home prices are on the rise again, widening the gap for the average family.

The Examiner's monthly affordability gap rose 6.8 percent to $892 from $835 statewide and 4.3 percent to $1,025 from $983 in the Bay Area.

The gap — a broad measure of how much monthly income is needed to buy a median priced house — widened in August despite a drop in interest rates. The interest rate drop was offset by rising home prices.

In August the median home price reached its highest mark in 1985, topping off at $119,358 in California and $138,075 in the region. That's a 3.7 percent hike statewide from July and a 2.8 percent increase in the Bay Area.

The increase in the median home price in California was a 5.2 percent rise from the like period in 1984.

The increase in housing prices follows a year-long trend. Housing demand, fueled by lower interest rates, and a declining inventory have contributed to higher home prices.

In the Bay Area, the regional interest rate average fell to 11.57 percent from 11.84 percent for all loans, adjustable and fixed rate. Statewide, the interest rate average dropped to 11.41 percent from 11.72 percent. However, the drop in interest rates was not enough to improve affordability because the gain in prices was too great.

Housing sales have been on the upswing in 1985, but the recent surge in transactions is attributable to seasonal activity. Sales are historically higher in the spring and summer, contributing to greater demand and higher rates of home price inflation.

Late last month, the California Association of Realtors noted that July resales pushed prices higher. San Francisco's median home price of $138,075 was a 3.6 percent increase from a year-ago.

Berkeley program may signal new attitude among planners

In one Bay area planning director's office the walls are adorned with nearly a dozen awards from state and national organizations. All are for environmental planning and design. More extensive than most such collections, this symbolizes a planner's professional achievements. In the development community, these awards also might symbolize the often uneasy relationship between builders and environmentally-minded planners.

Most developers talk less about obvious bias on the part of local planners than about a subtle, ingrained bent toward environmental considerations at the expense of residential and economic growth. Rather than criticizing individuals, they criticize the entire planning profession.

But if one of the nation's leading planning schools can be taken as a portent of things to come, the profession is undergoing fundamental change. At UC Berkeley's Department of City and Regional Planning, being a planner involves a different set of skills, ideas and goals than it did a few years ago.

"These days, planners are feeling a lot of pressure to come up with some positive strategies for housing development. It's no longer enough to sit back and react to development proposals," observes David Dowall, associate professor in Berkeley's planning department. "Real estate skills are getting much more emphasis than in the past."

As a result, new courses have been introduced stressing land economics and development skills, and planning students take more courses in the business school. This pragmatic tone is a real shift from the late '60s and early '70s when Berkeley planning students were riding on a wave of environmental awareness.

"I think we were long on sensitivity, short on practicality," says '77 graduate Rick Holliday. "Not only was development an unpopular goal, the school's curriculum wasn't really conducive to that goal."

Holliday likes to recall one particular discussion about career interests. "First, the professor asked who wanted to go into consulting, and about three-fourths of the class raised their hands. Next he asked who wanted to work for a federal agency, a state agency, or a local agency. That took care of almost everybody else. Finally, one student asked, 'What if you want to be a developer?' The conversation stopped dead as everybody turned around, dumbfounded, wondering who on earth would want to do a thing like that."

Holliday went on to become a nonprofit housing developer and is now vice president of BRIDGE, a regional developer of affordable housing. Today's graduate planning students are getting in class some of the hard skills he got through experience.

In large part, this is because recent years have brought a new breed of planner to Berkeley's teaching staff. Faculty members such as David Dowall, Michael Teitz, and Roger Montgomery have a strong technical and practical orientation. This is reflected in the courses they teach and in the issues they raise with students. "We still talk about the effects of development on neighborhood character," says Dowall, "but we also discuss how local regulations impact housing costs."

Ken Rosen, who heads the University's Center for Real Estate and Urban Economics and is a professor in the School of Business, also has done much to enhance the image of development as a profession. Several of the courses offered by the business school's real estate program are routinely taken by those in the master's degree planning program.

Dowell and Rosen structured a joint program that will further strengthen the connection between planning and business. Another boost to the program's development aspect came in the form of a $50,000 grant from the Urban Land Institute. It funds new studies in land economics.

Not only are Berkeley planning graduates of the '80s likely to have more professional development skills than their earlier counterparts, they seem to have a greater sympathy — in some cases, even a strong commitment — to housing development. The revamped curriculum mirrors a shift in attitudes and aspirations among planning students.

As planning students talk about goals and careers, it seems their perspective has changed, but not their motivations. They have a different view of development but not because they're more interested in making money. It is because housing and economic development have become recognized as compelling social issues. To today's Berkeley grads, development is one of the tools for social change.

"The other planning students I know have come from activist backgrounds," agrees Benji Golvin, a recent graduate of the Berkeley's master program.

"They've come to Berkeley to get a broader perspective, plus the development skills."

To be sure, this new perspective has evolved over a period of years. The classes of the '70s did produce such outstanding housing professionals as Rick Holliday; David Lyons, vice president of the Rand Corp. in Los Angeles; Richard Look, a housing developer in Edmonton, Canada; and Dowell Myers, a housing professor at the University of Texas.

Each pursued a career in housing despite the prevailing mores. Recalls Dan Lachman, another '77 graduate who is now executive director of the nonprofit Diablo Valley Housing Corporation, "Traditionally, planners saw for-profit development as something you either had to stop or make better somehow; but I've never believed that planners and developers have to be adversaries."

It may seem optimistic to suggest that what goes on in classrooms at Berkekey today will have a profound effect on housing tomorrow. But the school has produced many people who run planning deparments in California. The maze of local housing regulations now in place may be the legacy of an earlier missionary mindset that placed new housing opportunities below other values.

As today's graduates get out into the job market, gain experience and help local governments act on their commitments to housing, we should see the difference.

A growing elderly population poses new problems for state

California is getting older — more than 400 people reach 65 every day, joining the three million others over 65 already living in the state. The expansion of the elderly population is dramatically changing California consumption patterns, social trends, and public policy. It is also beginning to revolutionize how we provide shelter. This three-part series examines the state's elderly housing situation — its problems and solutions.

The aged population is growing at a staggering pace. By the year 2000, four million people over 65 will live in California — a 39 percent increase over today's figure. Most counties throughout the state are predicted to experience a surge in their aged population: 55 percent in Riverside and San Diego Counties; 43 percent in Kern County and 19 percent in Los Angeles. Only one county is likely to experience a slight decline — San Francisco. Every other county in the Bay area will see an average rise of 30 percent.

The graying of America is a national trend, but it will affect California in the unusual way — the demise of our youthful image. Today, the state's median age, 30 years old, is identical to the national average — an upward shift from just five years ago. The Bay area has the highest median age at 32.2 years and San Diego County the youngest at 28.8 years. And the state's median will continue to rise throughout the next two decades.

"The age of the population will directly affect the types of housing units needed, the choice to rent or own, and the income available to pay for housing," explains Steven O'Heron of the Federal Home Loan Bank of San Francisco. For example, when baby boomers reached home buying age, smaller units and more dense development followed, and financing schemes such as graduated payment mortgages were unveiled. Recently, the housing industry has taken aim at the upscale, moveup yuppie home buyer, who craves new amenities and 15-year short-term loans. Although difficult to predict, an older population is likely to trigger a new set of market responses.

Understanding the unique dimensions of this population is the first step in designing solutions for their problems. We have learned that not everyone over 75 is a good-natured Grandma or a feeble old man who belongs in a nursing home. There is more to it than that. The elderly differ according to income, health, age and level of activity.

There are at least three distinct income groups within the elderly population. First in the upscale, well-housed elderly. They are largely homeowners who have substantial equity in their homes that they own free and clear. They also qualify for the one-time $125,000 federal and state tax free exclusion on te resale of their homes — giving them considerable mobility. Many in this group have lucrative pensions and earn income from part- and full-time jobs. They are old, rich and healthy.

This group's numbers will grow as retirees continue to migrate into the state. California runs second only to Florida in appealing to older movers — attracting 8 8 percent of all elderly moves in the country.

A second group is house-rich and cash-poor. They are homeowners, but have no pensions and live on social security stipends. Discouraged by the disparity in property tax assessment created by Proposition 13, they are slow to abandon their older homes.

The most repressed group is both cash- and house-poor. On fixed incomes with few assets, they often suffer from health problems and are physically and emotionally isolated. They are pathetically pushed into the worst neighborhoods in the state, such as the Tenderloin in San Francisco, downtown Los Angeles and the most depressed parts of Hollywood. The story of one new subsidized housing project in Pasadena indicates the magnitude of need within this group: a 90-unit elderly project had 5,000 qualified applicants.

Income is not the only factor distinguishing the elderly from the rest of the population. Age and health are also important to consider. "Because of the miracles of modern medicine, the characteristics of our elderly population are changing radically. Unfortunately, housing policy and production have not kept pace," says Steve Graham, executive director of services for Seniors in San Francisco.

The healthiest and youngest group is the active retirees who take early retirement and move to resort or retirement communities like southern California's Rossmore Leisure World. They have a range of options including: apartment and condo living; rural or urban settings; and resort or typical communities. And most important of all, they require no special services.

Next are the retirees with health problems or emotional stress due to losing a spouse. They are less active, but have an intense drive to maintain their own households and hold on to independence.

We all learn to accept the inevitability of growing older, and as individuals we treat this fact of life very seriously. But as a society we are not sensitive to the housing needs of our elderly population. As the population as a whole ages it will behoove all of us to reconsider housing policies and programs for the state's elderly residents.

From empty nests to golden eggs

This is the second of three parts on the housing needs of California's elderly. This week: affluent senior citizens and those that own their home.

IN A recent conversation, an older California homeowner was emphatic about where he chooses to live: "I don't care what else is out there — co-ops, senior-condos or Sun City — I want to stay in this house, in this community and in this neighborhood."

Such strong feelings are not uncommon for the elderly; they like where they live and want to stay put. "Only five percent live in nursing homes, while another five percent a year move to a new community," says Sylvia Lewis, editor of Planning Magazine, in a recent report on senior citizens.

But there is an important prerequisite for being able to stay at home without complications: money. And the experts say there is no shortage of affluent seniors.

"This bracket of the American population has immense financial clout," says architect Jim Babcock. "They are becoming one of the most formidable . . . financial blocs in the nation," he says.

Many in this group opt to "age in place." Staying in the home they have enjoyed since middle-age, these seniors can afford to pay for their health care and personal services.

It's also a sizeable group in California: 73 percent of the over-65 group own their homes.

Homeownership itself translates into a certain degree of wealth; the house bought prior to 1970 in urban coastal California has tripled in value, creating, on the average, $100,000 in equity. "The empty nest has become the golden egg," says Patrick Hare, a planning specialist on the elderly.

The golden egg has little value, however, if circumstances change for the senior. For example, if the senior's health fails, the desire to stay at home may be threatened. Historically, the only choice available has been to move into housing where services are provided.

But leaving their homes and neighborhoods is not the only option today. House-sharing is one alternative. Most single-family homes exceed the physical needs of the "empty nester." A room or group of rooms can be rented out, creating security (if not companionship) for the homeowner and renter.

The idea is catching on. Non-profit senior citizen groups promote matching as a solution to the problems brought on by physical isolation and the high cost of housing. More than 50 organizations in California help put senior homeowners together with tenants. Some of the groups include: Options for Women Over Forty in San Francisco, Project Share in Berkeley and the Human Investment Project in San Mateo.

'This bracket of the American population has immense financial clout. They are becoming one of the most formidable financial blocs in the nation.'

For those seniors concerned about their privacy or the trauma of living with a stranger, there is another opportunity: converting a portion of the home to a separate rental unit. The apartment generates income and provides security for the homeowner.

(A two-year-old state law man dates a change in local zoning restrictions in which California cities are required to permit the addition of second units in single-family neighborhoods. However, controversy still surrounds the legislation and implementation has been spotty.)

A house also falls short as a golden egg if the equity can't be tapped. For many homeowners, finding a cost-effective way to tap their home equity is difficult if not impossible.

The Reversed Annuity Mortgage (RAM) program is one solution; it gives the homeowner cash flow from a loan on their equity. The San Francisco Development Fund, a Bay Area non-profit group, has worked to market the RAM concept in California. The program has met with mixed success but should become increasingly popular as more and more senior citizens seek ways to capture the value in their homes.

House-sharing, secondary units and the RAM program are a few of the experiments being advanced to meet the needs of the large senior homeowner population.

In the future, more attention will be focused on the suburbs, where there are fewer services available for seniors. "The aging phenomenon (in the suburbs) has created a need for day care for the elderly, senior centers and a variety of other services," according to the report in Planning Magazine.

Remaining in the nest, however, doesn't work for everyone. Many senior citizens tire of homeownership responsibilities and seek a change. Others move because of poor health or a wish to avoid an isolated lifestyle. But relocating today doesn't mean a move into a nursing home.

The alternative is an independent living setting that includes personal, intermediate and skilled nursing care and a congregate lifestyle. Residential facilities offering living units with multiple levels of care are called life-care centers. A reasonable income and net worth, however, are required to qualify for a unit in a life-care facility; it can be an expensive option that only the middle- to upper-income senior citizen can afford.

Life-care centers servicing this group have been dominated by non-profit church groups — 61 life-care facilities in the state are run by benevolent organizations. Episcopal Homes Foundation, American Baptist Homes of the West and California Presbyterian Homes are three of the largest church groups involved in California life-care.

It's no surprise that private investors and developers are quickly moving into the life-care market. "It is estimated that during the next five years $33 billion will be raised and spent to create over 1,800 life-care communities, averaging 300 residents a piece," says Babcock, the architect.

The bugs will have to be worked out, however, before private life-care takes off. "There is nothing new about condos and co-ops in the real estate industry, but in the retirement housing market where health care is also included, it's a new idea," says Paul Gordon, an attorney and legal specialist on life-care development.

Questions the experts are asking include: What is the best way to finance life-care developments? How should they be designed to meet changing consumer preference?

California Trends: For many seniors, 'empty nest' provides 'golden egg'

One older California homeowner is emphatic about where he chooses to live; "I don't care what else is out there — co-ops, senior-condos, or Sun City — I want to stay in this house, in this community and in this neighborhood."

Such feelings are not uncommon for the elderly — they like where they live and want to stay put. "Only 5 percent live in nursing homes, while another 5 percent a year move to a new community," says Sylvia Lewis, editor of Planning Magazine, in a recent report on senior citizens. But money is a prerequisite for choosing to stay at home without complications.

Experts say there is no shortage of affluent seniors. "This bracket of the American population has immense financial clout," says architect Jim Babcock. "They are becoming one of the most formidable financial blocs in the nation," he says.

Many in this group opt to "age in place." Staying in the home they have enjoyed since middle-age, these seniors can afford to pay for their health care and personal services.

Homeownership itself translates into a certain degree of wealth; the house bought prior to 1970 in urban coastal California has tripled in value creating, on the average, $100,000 in equity. "The empty nest has become the golden egg," say planning specialist on the elderly, Patrick Hare. It is a sizable group in California; 73 percent of the over-65 group own their homes.

"The "golden egg" has little value, however, if the equity can't be tapped or if circumstances change for the senior, either of which may require a reexamination of the alternatives. For example, if the senior's health fails, the desire to stay at home may be threatened. Historically, the only choice has been to move into housing where services are provided. But today, leaving their homes and neighborhoods is not the elderly's only option.

House-sharing is one of the alternatives. Most single-family homes exceed the physical need of the "empty nester." A room or group of rooms can be rented out, creating security (if not companionship) for the home owner and renter. The idea is catching on.

Non-profit senior citizen groups promote matching as a solution to the problems brought on by physical isolation and the high cost of housing. More than fifty organizations in California help put senior "homeowners together with tenants. Some of the groups include: the 'Human Investment Project in San Mateo, Senios Allied in Living in Sacramento, Options for Women Over Forty in San Francisco, Project Share in Berkeley, Alternative Living for the Aging in Los Angeles, Housing Sharing Assistance in Santa Monica and the Shared Housing Programs in Chula Vista and El Cajon.

A catalyst for the service is a state program that provides financial am to non-profit groups assisting with senior shared-housing.

Some of the elderly however, are less sanguine about losing their privacy or confront the trauma of living with a stranger. There is another opportunity; converting a portion of the home to a separate rental unit. The apartment generates income and provides security for the home owner. Due to a state law mandating a change in local zoning restrictions, California cities are required to permit the addition of second units in single family neighborhoods.

For many home owners, finding a cost-effective way to tap their home equity is difficult if not impossible. The Reversed Annuity Mortgage (RAM) program is one solution — giving the home owner cash flow from a loan on their equity. The San Francisco Development Find, a Bay Area non-profit group, has worked to market the RAM concept in California, The program has met with mixed success but should become increasingly popular as more and more senior citizens seek ways to capture the value in their homes.

House-sharing, secondary units and the RAM program are a few of the experiments being advanced to meet the needs of the large senior home owner population. Other efforts should be more targeted. For example, social scientists look to the changing characteristics of the suburbs, "the aging phenomenon (in the suburbs) has created a need for day care for the elderly, senior centers, and a variety of other services," according to the report in Planning Magazine.

Remaining in the next, however, doesn't work for everyone. Many senior citizens are tired for homeownership responsibilities and seek a change. Others move because of poor health or a wish to avoid an isolated lifestyle. But it doesn't mean a move into a nursing home.

One alternative is an independent living setting that includes personal intermediate and skilled nursing care and a congregate lifestyle. Residential facilities offering living units with multiple levels of care are called life-care centers. A reasonable income and net worth, however, are required to qualify for a unit in a life-care facility, it can be an expensive option that only the middle-to upper-income senior citizen can afford.

Life-care centers servicing this group have been dominated by nonprofit church groups sixty-one life-care facilities in the state are run by benevolent organizations. Episcopal Homes Foundation, American Baptist Homes of the West, and California Presbyterian Homes are three of the largest church groups involved in California life-care.

It's no surprise that private investors and developers are quickly moving into the life-care market. "It is estimated that during the next five years $33 billion will be raised and spent to create over 1800 life-care' communities, averaging 300 residents a piece," says Babcock.

The bugs will have to be worked out, however, before private life-care takes off. "There is nothing new about condos and co-ops in the real estate industry, but in the retirement housing market where health care is also included, it's new idea," says paul Gordon, attorney and legal specialist on life-care development.

Questions the experts are asking include: what is the best way to finance life-care developments? How should they be designed to meet changing consumer preference? How-deep is the market? How will the IRS treat entrance fees for proprietary life-care? In the meantime, the elderly should be cautious before tend other questions are answered.

The new and growing senior population is creating- competition among builders, hospitals, real estate investors and even a major hotel chain — they all see opportunity in the growing and affluent senior housing market. Their success will depend on how accurately they behavior and needs development of the elderly. For the well-healed are asking senior citizen, it adds up to a wider range of choices.

A new source of funds for housing

HALF OF A billion dollars can go a long way.

Thanks to the Federal Home Loan Bank's Community Investment Fund, savings and loans will make $500 million in loans available this year for community and economic development projects in California, Arizona and Nevada.

A brain child of the Federal Home Loan Bank Board, the regulator for savings and loan institutions, the fund has a successful seven-year history in California. Through its credit advance program, the Federal Home Loan Bank loans money to savings and loans; a small portion of the loans is set aside for the Community Investment Fund. In exchange for a low interest rate savings and loans agree to use CIF funds to lend on community projects which have difficulty getting financed.

Considering the high cost of funds, it's not a surprise CIF's carrot approach has worked: Since 1978, one billion dollars have been invested in California. The funds have financed the development of rental and senior housing projects, first-time homebuyer mortgages and retail shopping centers in depressed urban areas.

For 62 families in Santa Monica CIF means getting a new home. This fall, they will move into limited equity cooperatives partially financed through the investment fund. Other new and existing homeowners have benefited. First Federal Savings of Bakersfield, for example, tapped community investment funds and made single-family mortgage loans in cooperation with the Farmers Home Administration. Pomona First Federal made home improvement loans with the funds.

Great American Savings and World Savings used CIF to provide construction loans for new housing. A Great American loan financed a 275-unit elderly housing development in San Diego. The project was processed quickly and designed to save on construction costs; together, these techniques helped make the rents more affordable. World Savings made a loan on an Oakland self-help housing development.

Housing isn't the only opportunity for Community Investment Funds; Cal Fed financed the development of a commercial retail center in Watts. Imperial Savings made a loan on a mixed-use development which combines ground floor retail space with elderly rental housing in the upper stories.

The Community Investment Fund began as an experiment. Its purpose was to provide financial institutions with a better understanding of the borrowing needs of their local communities —markets sometimes ignored by lenders. Entire neighborhoods begin to starve for Capital, and deterioration sets in. As in the case of the retail shopping center in Watts, the funds can help bring back already depressed areas.

The fund has been successful in introducing lenders to new and unfamiliar markets, according to Jim Yacenda of the Federal Home Loan Bank of San Francisco.

"CIF teaches the lender what to look out for in these kinds of projects — how to measure security and risk," says Yacenda. "A loan for a new and innovative manufactured housing development in Palm Springs may never have been made without CIF. The next time around, the savings and loan may use what it learned to finance a similar project with their own funds."

Sour real estate loans are crippling the earnings of many savings and loans. The delinquency and foreclosure rates on CIF loans, however, have been very low. Highly motivated borrowers help to explain the excellent performance, according to Yacenda. These borrowers (local governments, nonprofits and local merchant builders) are prudent and cautious when approaching conventional lenders, he says.

"They add more equity to the deal or find other ways to reduce the risk — going the extra mile to make the lender feel secure," he says.

A $500 million FHLB commitment for 1986 will go beyond the initial goal of educating the lending community, "The CIF loans will finance local development projects that people give up on due to cutbacks in federal assistance," says Yacenda.

The Santa Monica co-op is a good example. Historically, affordable co-ops have depended on government support and have been ignored by conventional lenders. CIF is the financial vehicle that makes this project work.

Like all good ideas, CIF is vulnerable to abuse. Lenders could accept the cheaper money and then ignore the quid pro quo of making a redeeming community investment. Although the investment guidelines are flexible, FHLB officials are confident that there are adequate safeguards against such abuse.

California Trends: CIF sets aside $500 million for unique community projects

A half billion dollars can go a long way. Thanks to the Federal Home Loan Bank's Community Investment Fund (CIF). $500 million in loans will be made available for community and economic development projects in California, Arizona and Nevada. A brain child of the Federal Home Loan Bank Board, the regulator for savings and loan institutions, the fund has a successful seven year history in California. The goal is to provide savings and loans with financial incentives for lending on unique community development projects.

Through it's credit advance program, the Federal Home Loan Bank loans money to savings and loans; a small portion of the loans are set aside for the Community Investment Fund. In exchange, savings and loans agree to lend on community projects which have difficulty getting financed. A lower interest rate provides the incentive for participation in the program.

Considering the high cost of funds, it's not a surprise the carrot approach of CIF has worked; since 1978, one billion dollars have been invested in California. The funds have financed the development of rental and senior housing projects, first-time homebuyer mortgages and retail shopping centers in depressed urban areas.

For 62 families in Santa Monica it means getting a new home. This fall, they will move into limited equity co-ops partially financed through CIF. New and existing homeowners have also benefited. For example, First Federal Savings of Bakersfield tapped community investment funds and made single-family mortgage loans in cooperation with the Farmers Home Administration, and Pomona First Federal made home improvement loans.

World and Great American Savings Banks used CIF to provide construction loans for new housing. A Great America loan financed an innovative-275unit elderly housing development in San Diego. The project was fast-tracked and designed to save on construction costs; together, these techniques were effective in making the rents more affordable. World Savings made a loan on an Oakland self-help infill housing development.

Housing isn't the only opportunity for Community Investment Funds; Cal Fed financed the development of a commercial retail center in Watts. Imperial Savings made a loan on a mixed-use development which combines ground floor retail space with elderly rental housing in the upper stories.

The Community Investment Fund began as an experiment. It's purpose was to provide financial institutions with a better understanding of the lending needs of their local communities — markets sometimes ignored by lenders. Without access to capital, entire neighborhoods are starved and deterioration sets it. As in the case of the retal shopping center in Watts, the funds can help bring back depressed areas.

Introducing lenders to new and unfamiliar markets in part of the success of CIF according to Jim Yacenda, of the Federal Home Loan Bank of San Francisco. "CIF teaches the lender what to look out for in these kinds of projects — how to measure security and risk," says Yacenda. "A loan for a new and innovative manufactured housing development in Coachella Valley may never have been made without CIF. The next time around, the savings and loan may use what it learned to finance a similar project with their own funds," he says.

Today, sour real estate loans are crippling the earnings of some savings and loans. The delinquency and foreclosure rates on CIF loans, however, have been very low. Highly motivated and scrupulous borrowers help to explain the excellent performance. These borrowers (local governments non-profits and local merchant builders) are prudent and cautious when approaching conventional lenders, according to Yacenda. "They add more equity to the deal or find others to reduce the risk — going the extra mile to make the lender feel secure," he says.

A $500 million FHLB commitment for 1986 will go beyond the initial goal of educating the lending community. "The CIF loans will finance local development predicts that people give up on due to cutbacks in federal assistance," says Yacenda. The Santa Monica co-op is a good example. Historically, afford-able co-ops have depended on government support and have been ignored by conventional lenders. CIF is the financial vehicle that makes the project work.

Like all good ideas, CIF is vulnerable to abuse. Lenders could accept the cheaper money and then ignore the quick pro quo of making a redeeming community investment. Although the investment guidelines are flexible, FHLB officials are confident that there are adequate safeguards against such abuse. First, the Bank monitors all CIF investments. Second, because many of the loans are part of a package involving public funds, there is an atmosphere of public scrutiny.

Counting the critics is one way to measure the success of an idea. With no visible detractors it appears the Community Investment Fund Program is doing a good job.

Innovative funding for housing budget

GOVERNOR DEUKMEJIAN and low-income housing advocates rarely see eye to eye. But when the governor signed SB 478 last month, their relationship took a turn for the better.

The bill creates the California Housing Trust Fund and provides for a "permanent" source of money for housing low income Californians. According to its supporters, the Trust Fund is the first of its kind in the country.

"The Trust Fund has the potential of offering a significant short term boost to meeting the demand for additional low income housing . . . and does not create an additional burden on the state general fund," says Christine Diemer, the governor's housing deputy. Apparently the governor saw an opportunity for housing, and most importantly he liked the price tag.

Since his inauguration in 1983, Deukmejian has been holding the line on state spending, and in the last two years housing assistance has felt the effects of his budget pencil. Last year, Deukmejian vetoed $41 million in housing proposals.

The trust fund, however, uses a source of money that does not require a general fund appropriation, an approach that appealed to the administration. "The governor supported creation of the Housing Trust Fund because it utilizes an innovative approach of financing . . . which recognizes the overall desire to maintain the state's fiscal health," Diemer says.

Finding resources without tapping the general fund is no easy task. But the legislation's sponsors discovered a new pot of gold in tidelands oil leases. Since the early 1970s, the state has leased the right to drill offshore oil. The leases are based on oil prices, and the revenue is dedicated to specific public purposes, like school projects and the construction of government buildings. SB 478 adds the Housing Trust Fund as a $20 million beneficiary.

On the surface, the fund is an idea with very few drawbacks. But in spite of the soundness of the idea, turning the concept into a signed bill was easier said than done.

A history of ill will between housing advocates and the administration didn't help. One point of contention included Deukmejian's veto of housing assistance bills in the 1984 legislative session. And the administration didn't welcome an attempt by advocates to hold the state housing budget hostage over a controversial homeless report. All of this has hurt cooperation on matters such as the Trust Fund proposal.

Against this backdrop of tension, a grass roots campaign was mounted to convince the legislature and the governor that SB 478 was a good idea. "We are not a very well-organized constituency and don't have the political clout to get enough housing aid through direct appropriations, so we had to do everything we could to convince the governor of the merits of this proposal," says Marc Browne of the California Rural Legal Assistance Foundation.

Housing advocates flooded the governor's office with letters and calls of support. Editorial endorsements and support from within the administration also helped, according to Brown.

The strategy worked; the legislature approved the measure, the governor signed the bill and a new housing initiative was launched.

Turning the legislation into a workable program, however, still faces a number of hurdles. The first is reaching agreement on how the Trust Fund fits into an overall state housing plan. "We feel it should supplement existing programs or create new approaches, not replace future appropriations for existing projects," says Brown.

The administration has not proclaimed the Trust Fund program to be the only answer to state housing programs, but the governor has made it clear that he will continue to fight to control the cost and size of state government. Therefore, housing programs will continue to face a fiscal test that all state proposals are measured against; $900 million in appropriations from the 1983-1984 legislative session was competing for only $93 million in the general fund.

No doubt the push and pull over spending for housing assistance will continue for years to come. A more immediate question is how next year's Trust Fund allocation will be spent. The legislation requires the governor to submit a proposal to the legislature by the first of the year. Housing groups and the administration have already held meetings to discuss the possibilities. Surprisingly, there are signs of agreement.

Housing advocates want the Trust Fund to serve the needy, a position consistent with the governor's philosophy of targeting all state assistance. The administration would like to design efficient programs that leverage private capital. Housing advocates agree because they want the biggest bang for their buck. And both sides want rental housing to receive the largest piece of the pie.

Nevertheless, not everything is solved by this new consensus. Deukmejian did veto several housing bills in the latest legislative session, including measures for school fees on home construction and the disposition of public lands for housing. In addition, there will continue to be conflict over issues like rent control.

But in the final analysis, the present truce, however temporary, is good news for people needing housing in the state.

California plays decisive role in Realtors' agenda

There's an explanation for all of the news this past week about housing: The annual meeting of the National Association of Realtors (NAR). Whenever the largest trade association in the world gets together, real estate news follows.

In public opinion polls Realtors aren't very popular, but despite citizen sentiment NAR has a long history of shaping the national housing agenda, and Californians play a decisive role in its direction, philosophy and effectiveness.

There are 100,000 realtors in the state — one in every 250 Californians — making it the largest contingent in the 700,000-member national association. The Sacramento Board of Realtors has more real estate agents, brokers and sales people than all of the realtors in the State of Nebraska and twice that in the state of Maine.

Numbers aren't the only explanation for the state's influence; the leadership in NAR speaks for itself. Clark Wallace, a San Francisco Bay Area Realtor, is incoming president of NAR, and 84 of the 475 NAR directors are from California. In addition, Californians chair the three most powerful committees: real estate finance, professional standards, and legislation.

Mobilizing NAR on federal housing issues is one by-product of California's power — making changes that benefit the California real estate industry and in some cases homeowners and home buyers.

For example, in 1982 the California Association of Realtors (CAR) was instrumental in amending legislation that deregulated the savings and loans industry — changes preventing abolition of loan assumptions (the ability of home sellers to pass on their low-interest mortgages to new buyers). At the time, interest rates were very high and 65 percent of home sales were seller financed — usually at lower mortgage rates. CAR persuaded NAR to make the issue a legislative priority. The new law permitted buyers to assume loans for three more years.

"California has always been at the forefront of real estate finance issues," says Clark Wallace. "And NAR has made it an increasing priority because of our work in California," he said.

Imputed interest is another good example. A 1984 law would have required home sellers that provide financing to charge market interest rates for many transactions; this is called imputed interest. California Realtors lobbied members of the state's congressional delegation to change the law. Taking his lead from CAR, Congressman Robert Matsui of Sacramento pushed through a moratorium on imputed interest and worked out a compromise in the 1985 tax bill that modified the rules.

"Because California home prices are 50 percent higher than the national average, affordability issues always make California Realtors jump," says Wallace. "That's why CAR moved to successfully change the rules for higher secondary-market mortgage loan limits," he says. Before CAR acted, loan limits were based on national home prices and as a result didn't serve high-cost areas like California, according to Wallace.

On these issues, California Realtors build coalitions with other high-cost states like Colorado, Florida and Arizona.

California's role on the national scene, however, is not always well planned, and many times a trend that begins in California isn't welcomed by real estate interests in other parts of the country. Pressure to increase the Realtor's responsibility with disclosure during a home sale is one controversial example. Regulatory changes demanding greater disclosure began in California and are now spreading around the country.

Higher fees rankle the home builders

EXPECT A SHARP reaction when you mention government fees to a home builder. Nothing rankles a builder more, particularly when the fees are going up, and that's the direction they are headed.

Development fees are not new. Local government has always had the authority to charge builders for public expenses incurred in the development process. The price and type of fees levied, however, are changing dramatically.

There are two kinds of fees that builders must contend with. First are those paid to local government for the review of development plans and the inspection of construction progress. Evaluating development proposals for compliance with a myriad of local and state planning regulations is expensive for municipalities. Laws for Seismic safety, community plan conformance, health and safety rules and zoning laws are complicated and difficult to interpret.

Nevertheless, the price of these particular fees has not risen as fast as inflation, according to a study by the Construction Industry Research Board. In 30 California communities surveyed between 1975 and 1984, planning fees increased 84 percent and engineering fees rose 40 percent. Those increases are less than the hike in the consumer price index for the same period.

But these fees are only one way to charge the builders. Major capital projects like schools, parks, flood control, sewer and water systems are big ticket items, and the costs to develop them have risen rapidly in the last 10 years. Fees for infrastructure — a fancy name for large-scale community projects - rose more than 500 percent between 1975 and 1984. For home guilders, this is an unwelcomed trend.

"Builders are increasingly being asked to finance everything in or near their housing developments," says Tom Bannon, legislative advocate with the California Building Industry. "They can absorb part of the costs, but the rest goes right into the price of the house," he says. Some experts estimate fees push up home prices 7 to 10 percent.

"Expensive demands on residential development place the burden at the front-end for home buyers," says Bob Morris of the San Diego Building Industry Association. "We use to spread these costs out over several years and distribute the obligation to everyone in the community through bonds — but not anymore," he says.

Much of the change can be attributed to the passage of Proposition 13. Under Prop 13, local government lost its statutory authority and the resources necessary to readily provide streets, roads, parks and other Community amenities.

Prop 13 hits cities and counties two ways: Tax revenues were cut sharply, and the landmark tax initiative eliminated alternative approaches for funding new infrastructure.

For example, Prop 13 made local general obligation bonds a useless tool. "Communities have to rely on special purpose bond issues instead of general obligation bonds," says Connie Barker, lobbyist for the California league of Cities. "They are more expensive, a smaller group of taxpayers pay the price tag, and they don't meet all of the cities' needs,"

To solve the problem, the legislature has put a measure on the June ballot to restore general obligation bonds, but they can only be used when they are approved by two-thirds of the voters. "It's not a final solution because it will still be hard to get citizen support," says Barker.

"Local governments are in a pinch, forcing them to look at other options for solving the problem," says Bannon. "There are two alternatives: state assistance or fees. When that's the choice, they turn to the builder to pay the bill," he says. That's because the state has budget problems of its own and has not made infrastructure funding a top priority, according to Bannon.

A school fee bill that Governor Deukmejian vetoed this past session is a good example. California builders consider school fees to be the most onerous. To bring some relief, the building industry drafted legislation designed to mitigate rising school fees. The bill created rules governing how school districts could levy fees, limited the amount of locally generated school exactions and appropriated $500 million from the school construction program.

According to the Governor's veto message, the measure was vetoed because of its fiscal impact.

The federal government is even more reluctant to jump in and solve the problem. Federal funding for water treatment projects has been eliminated, for instance. Without the aid, financing large-scale projects is a nightmare for local government.

Considering how tight state and federal budgets are, local governments and builders will have to work out their own solutions. In the meantime, building fees will continue to rise and affect the cost of housing. That's the price paid until a new approach is found.

Housing Finance Agency's birthday

ONE OF the largest housing lenders in the state has no stockholders and no private owners and never makes a profit. That lender is the California Housing Finance Agency, a government institution that made more than $400 million in mortgage loans last year, aiding nearly six thousand California families.

"It is true we play a big role in the mortgage business in California," says Karney Hodge, Executive Director of CHFA.

The agency does it, however, in an unusual way; CHDA is designed to help those who are not served by the private mortgage market. "The public purpose is what makes us unique and different from every other bank or savings and loan," says Hodge.

By issuing tax-exempt bonds, CHFA offers interest rates two to three percentage points below the market. This modest advantage helps many home buyers purchase their first house. The below-market rate financing is also used by apartment builders. In exchange for lower interest rates, developers set aside a portion of their new apartments for low- and moderate-income tenants.

Celebrating its tenth anniversary, CHFA has left a meaningful mark on housing finance in the state. Between 1976 and 1985, 32,000 housing units were funded — 20,000 single-family mortgages and 12,000 apartments — representing $1.4 billion in loan value.

But the agency has had ups and downs in the last ten years. Even before it was born, it was controversial.

Legislation creating CHFA came out of an unusual special session of the legislature called by then Governor Jerry Brown. After years of inaction, the session was convened for the sole purpose of developing a state housing finance agency.

A couple of years previously, similar bills had reached Governor Reagan's desk; they were all vetoed. "It was considered a Republican program everywhere else in the country because it didn't use direct subsidies," says Frank Patitucci, the first permanent director of CHFA and now a private businessman in Palo Alto. "But in California it faced considerable resistance from conservatives."

The battle was so heated, intriguing and controversial that it prompted a book, "Politics Backstage," an account of the politics behind the creation of CHFA. Among the strong opponents of the proposal was George Deukmejian, then a state senator.

Opinions have changed since then, however, including Deukmejian's. "The California Housing Agency is an integral component in our state's strong housing market and continues to provide leadership in the production of housing . . . ," the Governor said in a recent report on the agency.

But part of the controversy persists today. "The legislature had a lot of impatience and unreasonable expectations when CHFA was formed," says Patitucci, "They expected immediate results in terms of who and how many people would be served.'

This pressure is all too familiar today. For example, there is concern about whether lower income groups are getting their fair share of CHFA's public benefits. "The agency likes to think of itself as a bank, yet it is a bank with a Social responsibility," says Renne Franken, former legislative housing consultant and now a housing expert with the state treasurer's office.

Tony Frank, chairman of First Nationwide Savings and former CHFA chairman, says there has to be a balance between two goals of housing the poor and the agency's ability to operate. "The finance agency is at the mercy of the bond market," he says. "Lending money you don't get back results in poor bond ratings and a loss of financial support; then you can't do business at all."

Bond raters are looking for security and yield, and low-income housing doesn't always satisfy those investment criteria.

'Walking this tightrope means it (CHFA) does not have the ability to provide very low-income housing, but it can provide housing to those two or three percentage points below what it takes to get in through the private door," says Frank. "It may be a thin slice of Californians, but even a thin slice means thousands of families in the state."

Executive Director Karney Hodge thinks the agency has matured to a point where it can use its powers to reach lower-income Californians. For example, most housing finance agency officials in other states are complaining about proposed federal rules that will target tax-exempt bonds for the poor. Hodge disagrees.

"We are using tax-exempt money and accordingly there should be a clear public purpose; further defining and articulating that purpose makes sense.'

Consistent with this philosophy, Hodge has developed a new program that will provide apartments for low-income Californians. Eighty percent of the apartments will go to families earning between 50 and 80 percent of the median income, and 20 percent will go to families making less than half of the median family income.

Despite this new thrust, there are other criticisms. For example, advocates oppose the "gold plating" of agency developments: project amenities that increase construction costs and rents. Others criticize CHFA's emphasis on smaller units when there is increasing demand for family housing. And there are questions about what the agency plans to do with its $50 to $100 million reserve fund. Should it be used to lower rents in CHFA developments or remain in a reserve fund protecting the agency against unexpected losses?

But when all is said and done, it would be difficult to find anyone concerned or affected by housing problems that wouldn't wish CHFA a warm and happy birthday.

Clearing the way for disabled housing

RENTAL HOUSING developers want to be free of onerous and costly regulations and the disabled want barrier-free housing. Both are laudable goals, but until recently the two sets of demands have been in conflict.

Last month, a long and controversial debate ended when the state hammered out handicapped regulations for new rental housing construction. Neither the builders nor the disabled are completely happy with the outcome, but agreement was reached. "Three years of negotiations . . . have resulted in a successful balance between the concerns of builders about controlling new construction costs and the needs of the handicapped for suitable housing," says a spokesperson for the State Department of Housing and Community Development.

The balance struck: 40 percent of all new rental housing in the state will be built adaptable for the disabled, according to one estimate, and the builders' costs will not exceed $750 per rental unit.

However, the jury is still out on the likely success of the new rules.

State legislation in 1968 required all commercial and government buildings to be accessible to the state's 90,000-100,000 wheelchair users. It wasn't until 1978 that statewide handicapped standards were proposed for new residential buildings. And the final rules didn't take effect until September of this year.

The newly adopted standards have over 75 separate requirements for rental projects exceeding four units. They include rules on both the accessibility and the adaptability of new apartments.

Bureaucratic jargon like "accessible" and "adaptable" are important terms in both the intent and the effect of the regulations. The State Department of Housing and Community Development defines an *accessible* housing unit as "the combination of various elements in a building which allows access, circulation and the full use of the building by the handicapped." An *adaptable* unit is one that can be "adapted at a later date to fit the needs of mobility-impaired persons." An example is requiring support backing for grab bars in the bathroom but not the grab bars themselves.

"Adaptable is a lesser standard," says Walter Park, an advocate for the disabled and Director of Independent Housing Services. The rules only make future changes possible and, therefore, "they (the regulations) are more flexible and a less stringent approach."

The result is they do not entirely meet the needs of the wheelchair population, Park asserts, although the rules will aid the growing senior citizen population, particularly the frail elderly.

At the center of the debate over handicapped regulations are construction costs. The builders argued that the regulations first proposed in 1982 would have increased their costs by up to $3,000 per apartment. "A share of these costs would have been passed on to the consumer in the form of higher rents," says Bob Raymer of the California Building Industry.

"When the Brown administration proposed these requirements, the disabled advocates estimated the additional costs would only be $200 per unit," Raymer says. But, he says, they used a model apartment project for their calculations "that included only small units with one bathroom, which is not typical for a standard California apartment. They also recommended a closet be removed to accommodate the larger bathroom. This, they erroneously argued, would save money for the builder."

Concerns about higher construction costs prompted the building industry to appeal the proposed 1982 rules when first proposed. That led to a series of negotiations between the housing industry and the disabled community, with the Department of Housing and Community Development moderating the talks. After two years of give and take, a compromise was reached.

On the question of costs, a $750 cap was placed on the amount a builder is required to spend on each unit in to meet the requirements.

To further obviate the builder objections, a number of regulatory exceptions were agreed upon: the regulations only apply to rental units; projects of four units or less are not covered by the rules; and units are exempt if a project is on a site that slopes more than 15 percent. Finally, 12 separate exceptions were written for the 75 individual regulations.

Builders and regulators agree that they will need experience with the new law before its effectiveness can be determined. "People are always afraid of what they don't know," says Park. "I think that the builders will see the marginal costs are very small. But most importantly, we are going to see some adaptable housing built in the state."

While builders are willing to give the new building standards a try, Raymer says his association has left the door open for future amendments. "We are going to monitor the regs and see if what is required makes sense; if they aren't working, we'll try to modify them."

A temporary truce is good news. With a consistent set of rules, everyone involved can move off the theoretical policy debate and try to see what works. All sides will benefit from some practical experience.

California Trends: Housing Market Forecast for 1986

(EDITOR'S NOTE: *Following is part one of a two-part series forecasting California housing trends for 1986.*)

Nineteen eighty-five will be a hard year to beat. It was good for both the California housing industry and the state's home buyers. Interest rates continued their descent, housing construction was strong, homeownership became more affordable, rental housing construction boomed, and $20 million in state money was freed up for affordable housing.

But a few dark clouds loom on the 1986 horizon: tax reform proposals remain on the table, California home prices are still 75 percent higher than the national average, federal housing assistance faces the budget axe, and the rent control debate roars on.

In these two parts, I look at issues and events that are likely to shape the 1986 California housing picture. For insight into the future, I have turned to some of the most respected housing experts in the state, as well as renters, home-buyers, and homeowners. Some are optimistic, while others are cautiously concerned. Nevertheless, together the individual predictions weave an insightful look into the future of housing in California.

"I predict a very bright picture for mortgage interest rates in 1986. My original forecast was for a slight increase next year — fixed rate mortgages at 13 percent and ARMs at 10-11 percent. But with the passage of the federal budget deficit measure by Congress I am more optimistic and revising my predictions.

"The expectation is that with the Federal government getting its fiscal house in order there will be downward pressure on rates. I think the expectation will turn into reality with fixed-rate mortgage rates somewhere around 11 percent and ARMs at 9 percent or lower. The trend will definitely be lower mortgage interest rates in 1986."

— Michael Salkin, Bank of America, San Francisco.

"The California resale market in 1986 will continue to be quite buoyant but will slow somewhat in the second half of the year. In total, we think resales will be down 5 percent from 1985, but it will still be the second best year since 1980.

"Most real estate economists have virtually reached a consensus on their views for 1986; that in itself makes me nervous."

— Joel Singer, California Association of Realtors, Los Angeles.

"I sold my house in Connecticut last year and moved to San Francisco and couldn't be happier — except for the cost of housing. It's outrageous. In 1986, I have no other choice but to buy a home because my 18-month capital gains fuse is running out. But what can I afford to buy . . . any ideas?"

— Suzanne Sarra, Renter, San Francisco.

"Home prices will rise at least 8 percent next year — faster than the rate of inflation and bucking the trend of the last few years when everything was flat. We also think the overall rate of inflation will accelerate. Home prices led the inflationary parade in the late 70's, and when they took it on the chin in the early 80s the economy soon followed. Home prices are usually in advance of the rest of the economy."

— Larry J. Kimbell, UCLA Business Forecasting Project, Westwood.

"Tax reform in a monumental form will not take place. It will be piecemeal and will be enacted over a number of years. As a result, it will continue to create some uncertainty in the market place. But continued talk in the real estate community about uncertainty, which is inevitable, can only become a self-serving prophecy. The smart real estate investors let everybody else talk about it while they plan for it and act accordingly."

— Brian Banmiller, Host KCBS Real Estate News Magazine, San Francisco,

"There will be a modest increase in single-family housing permits on the order of 6 percent. This is in response to lower mortgage interest rates. We are expecting a 33 percent decline, however, in multi-family housing permits. In the multi-family area, a lot of activity was borrowed from this year (1985) that would have been built next year.

"There are three factors that explain the rush this year: first, anticipation of tax reform and impact on rental housing: second, a substantial increase in bond financing; and third, the change in the state building code for handicapped standards which took effect in September."

— Ben Bortolotto, Construction Industry Research Board, Los Angeles.

"In the next couple of years, housing demand will be lackluster. Female participation in the work force has peaked out; household income won't be pushed up by wives getting jobs — because they are already working.

"We might see an uptick in the birth rate as opposed to baby boomers postponing the decision to have kids — demographers call it the baby boom echo. This could affect the type and amount of housing space needed."

— David Dowall, U.C. Berkeley, Berkeley.

"I don't expect to see very much appreciation in my condo in 1986 so I plan on staying where I am until 1987. Then I can hopefully sell my unit and get into a real house."

— Ron Bush, Condo Owner, Redondo Beach.

More predictions on what 1986 holds

Second of two parts.

THE NEW Year arrives next week and with it a strong California housing market. It's difficult to see what might derail what has been a robust housing scene. But things can quickly change; today's good news can quickly become tomorrow's problems. Here's what the experts think about growth control, state politics, rental housing production trends and other issues facing housing in 1986.

Rental housing

"The free market is thriving and working; it is almost a textbook situation. With all of the pent-up demand, rental housing construction is booming and probably will not stop in 1986, at least in areas like San Diego County. The boom means the tenant is getting all kind of choices; so it is good news for renters.

"The biggest constraint will be the supply of land zoned for rental. Those that have the land are commanding high prices. There are always political, philosophical and physical constraints on land, making land in short supply. There is a lot of out-of-state interest in parts of California. Some big builders from Portland and Texas would love to build in San Diego, but they can't' find the land."

George Carlson John Burnham Co., San Diego

On renting

"Our apartment building just sold, and so we are expecting a rent increase. But we might move anyway because we don't have heat, my roommate sleeps with her ski cap on; the fireplace doesn't keep us warm enough."

Anonymous renter Santa Barbara

Rent control

"Don't expect much (on statewide rent control legislation) to happen in an election year. And despite the dire need for providing incentives for increasing the supply of rental housing, the current political makeup of the state Senate will probably preclude the opportunity for statewide rent control standards.

"At the local level, my score card shows rent control initiatives slowing down, but if we experience rising rents in the state the pressure could mount overnight."

John Seymour State Senator

California growth

"Growth areas are going to be the high desert and the central valley, Advanced telecommunications allow growth to occur in outer low-cost areas. The cost of doing business in urban areas is too high, plus they are being choked toy traffic and congestion."

David Dowall Institute of Urban Land and Regional Development, U.C. Berkeley

Growth control

"It has become clear in the last year that the suburban office boom is creating a new wave of city and county growth management efforts. Traffic is the focus for many of these actions, and citizens and local government leaders are increasingly turning to the ballot box to resolve them. The big challenge will be how these community-by-community decisions will fit into the overall welfare of the surrounding metropolitan area."

Larry Orman People for Open Space

Elections and housing

"Elections won't affect the marketplace next year, but the '86 elections could ultimately affect housing in the state. I don't think any electoral decision has an immediate impact, but in the long term there are repercussions when new people get into power. How the assembly, senate and governor's races line up in '86 could shape attitudes about housing production and growth generally, as well as policies for the financing of infrastructure. All in all, I think a positive political attitude towards housing will carry through the remainder of this decade."

Robert Rivinius California Building Industry Association

National housing

"Recent decisions on the federal budget do not bode well for the poor who need housing. The Gramm-Rudman-Hollings Balanced Budget legislation is going to put increased pressure on the remaining federal funding for housing assistance. "Things like social security are exempt from the deficit reduction law, but housing is not; therefore, there is no protection for housing programs. We are expecting severe attacks on all poverty programs along with low-income housing assistance. The only good news is that localities are not ready for these cuts; they did not vote for them and they don't want them. Local grass roots frustrations with actions by the President and the Congress will sharpen the debate."

Barry Zigas National Low-Income Housing Coaltion, Washington D.C.

State housing aid

"The highlight for 1986 will be on the transition. Due to changes at the federal level, we have to focus on adjustments to state housing programs which have historically been designed to leverage and maximize federal money. This also applies to the private market. For example, stricter national underwriting guidelines on mortgage loans make it harder for people to qualify for a home loan. They will turn to the state for assistance."

Susan DeSantis Calif. Dept. of Housing and Community Development

Affordable housing

"The federal retreat from housing will continue in 1986 and is frustrating to all of us concerned about housing costs in California. Without a coherent and sensitive national housing policy we're left to grapple with shelter problems by ourselves. But this is not the time to withdraw' and give up. Instead we need to look at new resources and new ways of doing business."

I. Donald Terner Bridge Housing Inc.

Real degrees

Second of three parts

SOME CONSIDER it a fad, others call it a trend. Colleges and universities all over the country are making real estate work more professional with new advanced education offerings.

In large part, turning out real estate wizards is a response to the industry's need. Everything from building a house to making a mortgage loan is getting more complicated and requires an increasingly sophisticated work force.

But inside the walls of academia, there are disagreements. Some top MBA programs like Harvard's and Stanford's have decided to ignore the trend. They point out that while their graduates will have been able to take few specialized courses in real estate, they are prepared to run almost any business enterprise someday. When it comes to top jobs, the students are grabbed up by employers from all types of industry, including real estate. "We gave up on degrees by industry a long time ago," says Kirk Hanson, a professor at the Stanford Business School.

Many universities don't offer MBAs in specific industries. Instead, they confer degrees in disciplines described as marketing, accounting or finance.

Olena Berg, a Harvard MBA, said that at first she regretted not having a specialized degree when she became vice president of Gerson Bakar and Associates and manager of the firm's inventory of Northern California rental property. Now as president and chief operating officer, she appreciates her Harvard education and praises its "management focus" and "overview" approach.

'As you move up, you need the management skills that a program like Harvard provides," says Berg. "Along with other skills, you have to know how to hire and motivate people," she says.

When choosing an educational program, students should consider where they want to land after graduation, says San Francisco real estate consultant Stephen Roulac. He gives Harvard and Stanford high marks for turning out "managers" and credits the more specialized MBA program like Berkeley's with putting out the "professional staffers." (With an MBA from Harvard, a PhD from Stanford and a Berkeley law degree, Roulac is carefully loyal to each of his alma maters.)

But even schools with a real estate emphasis are finding that a general approach to a real estate education may not be specialized enough. As a result, they intentionally favor one side of the business whether it's development, mortgage finance or land planning.

MIT's new one-year masters degree in development is a good example. The first of its kind, the MIT program focuses exclusively on real estate development, drawing on four MIT departments: business, architecture, engineering and planning.

"Most traditional MBA programs don't teach students about laying sewer lines and roads, or drawing up a site plan, but if you want to develop today, you had better understand some of these Issues," says James McKellar, director of the MIT program. Columbia, USC and Texas A&M are following the MIT lead and will soon offer their versions of it.

Other schools like Berkeley and Penn's Wharton have excellent reputations in real estate finance. The Universities of Wisconsin and North Carolina have become experts in land planning, and Central Florida University will soon be offering a major in corporate real estate management.

Some experts predict that many of the new real estate programs won't last. One measure of their longevity is student interest. Their ability to generate resources and make a commitment to research is crucial. Several universities have established real estate research centers, which publish reports and collect data on the market.

Launching a research center takes more than just a good idea, it takes bucks. The new MIT program is funded by 94 companies that have a stake in the real estate business, each has put up $5,000 to $10,000 to see the Center through. At Wharton, retail developer Arthur Fischer gave $1.5 million to his alma mater for a building that will house the new center.

Loyalty, big egos and social con science all help motivate real estate tycoons to fund these academic enterprises. But according to MIT's McKellar, in some cases there may be a keener self interest at work.

"They see the research center as a window into the future, giving them a larger view of trends that might affect their business down the road," he says.

Fifty-two firms and individuals help support UC Berkeley's Center for Real Estate. But the center also receives 20 percent of its operating budget from the state through real estate broker license fees. In addition to public support, some universities are getting a boost from the Urban Land Institute, a Washington, D.C.-based trade association, which will give $60,000 this year to help start up real estate centers and improve existing ones.

Even their strongest advocates such as MIT's McKellar admit specialized programs "aren't yet competing with the more traditional MBA program." But whatever the approach, the professionalization of real estate will ultimately mean better planned buildings and improved real-estate services. That should be good news for everyone.

California trends: Specialized real estate degrees new college 'fad

Special to the Sun: Second of three articles on real estate education. Today's topic: The debate over the best graduate programs at universities and colleges.

Some call it a fad and others call it a trend. But however you describe it, colleges and universities all over the country are getting into the act of professionalizing real estate with the latest version of an advanced degree in real estate.

In large part, turning out real estate wizards is a response to industry's need for better-trained employees. Everything from building a house to making a mortgage loan is more complicated and requires a sophisticated work force. But inside the ivory walls of academia, no one seems to agree on what is the best way to teach it.

Some top MBA programs like Harvard and Stanford have decided to ignore the trend — almost dismissing it as a "fad." They point out, however, that along with getting a few specialized courses in real estate, their graduates are prepared to someday run almost any business enterprise. And when it comes to top Jobs, the students are grabbed up by employers from all types of industry — including real estate.

"We gave up on degrees by industry a long time ago," says Kirk Hanson, professor at the Stanford Business School. Like Stanford, many schools don't offer MBAs in specific industries like securities, electronics, insurance, or real estate. Instead, they offer a business degree in disciplines like marketing, accounting, and finance.

Harvard MBA Olena Berg regretted not having a more specialized degree when she first became vice president of Gerson Bakar and Associates and manager of the firm's vast inventory of Northern California rental property. But now as president and chief operating officer, she appreciates her Harvard education and applauds their "management focus" and "overview" approach. "

As you move up, you need the management skills that a program like Harvard provides," says Berg. "Along with other skills, you have to know how to hire and motivate people," she said.

When choosing a program, students should consider where they want to land after graduation, says noted real estate consultant Stephen Roulac. He gives Harvard and Stanford high marks for turning out "managers" and credits the more specialized MBA program like Cal-Berkeley with putting out the "professional staffers". With an MBA from Harvard, a Ph.D from Stanford, and a Cal-Berkeley law degree, Roulac is a careful loyalist to each of his alma maters.

But even schools with a real estate emphasis are finding a general approach to real estate education may not be specialized enough. Consequently, they deliberately favor one side of the busijoins ness whether it's development, mortgage finance, or land planning.

MIT's new one-year Masters in Development degree is a good example. The first of its kind, the MIT program focuses exclusively on the development side of real estate, drawing on the expertise of four MIT departments: business, architecture, engineering, and planning.

"Most traditional MBA programs don't teach students about laying sewer lines and roads, or drawing up a site plan; but if you want to develop today, you had better understand some of these issues," said James McKellar, Director of the MIT Program. Columbia, USC and Texas A&M are following the MIT lead and will soon offer their versions of the Masters in Development.

Other schools like Berkeley and Penn's Wharton have carved out a niche with excellent reputations in real estate finance. The University of Wisconsin and University of North Carolina have become experts in land planning, and Central Florida University will soon be offering an emphasis in corporate real estate management.

Some experts predict that many of the new real estate programs will not last. One measure of their longevity is student interest, but their ability to generate resources and make a commitment to research is also very important. Several universities use private and public funding for the establishment of real estate research centers that put out reports and collect data on the market.

But launching a research center takes more than just a good idea; it takes bucks. The new MIT program is funded by 94 companies who have a stake in the real estate business and have put up $5,000 to $10,000 each to see the Center through. At Wharton, retail developer Arthur Fischer gave $1.5 million to his alma mater for a building that will house the new center.

Loyalty, personal grandiosement, big egos and social conscience all help motivate real estate tycoons to fund these academic enterprises. But according to MIT's McKellar, in some cases there may be a keener self interest at work. "They see the research center as a window into the future — giving them a larger view of trends that might affect their business down the road," he says.

At Berkeley's Center for Real Estate, 52 firms and individuals help support it. But they also receive 20 percent of their operating budget from the state through real estate broker license fees. In addition to public support, some universities are getting a boost from the Urban Land Institute, a private development trade association, which will give $60,000 this year to help start up real estate centers and improve existing ones.

Despite all of the resources and enthusiasm, even the strongest advocates, like MIT's McKellar, admit specialized programs "aren't yet competing with the more traditional MBA program."

The best teacher

Third in a three-part series

N 1968, Standard Oil Co. of California wanted to sell 600 acres in Richmond for housing. Bucking the popular wisdom, Stanley Dorst, then president of its land development subsidiary, thought the site was better suited for a regional shopping center.

The company, now Chevron Corp., went along with Dorst's plan, and today the 1 million-square-foot development is near completion.

Scores of lawyers, bankers and corporate mucky-mucks participated in the decision to turn this hilltop oil tank farm into a regional shopping mecca. But like many mega-development deals, it was one person with a contrary idea that saw it through.

Today some college and universities are offering new advanced educational offerings in real estate, turning out a new cadre of business graduates trained in that field. But according to many real estate experts, formal college training has little to do with one's ability to spot a good real estate deal. Experience, a willingness to take risks and common sense may be more important than an MBA from a top university.

"The main advantage of an MBA is that you are a few years older, which means more maturity and experience," says Preston Butcher, president of Lincoln Properties Co.

But there may be a more intangible skill that comes into play: the developer's intuition. "There definitely is a sixth sense," says Gerson Bakar, chairman of San Francisco-based Gerson Bakar and Associates, which pioneered the concept of garden apartments and built more than 20,000 apartments.

Bakar sees development as a creative process. "When you see a good deal, you can feel it," he says. "I pass up a lot of proposals that look good on paper because I don't have a good feel for them," he says. "Some people have it and some don't."

Bakar says he has never used a market study to test the feasibility of his projects, but he concedes that it is impossible to define the successful developer's "sixth sense."

Not everyone, however, buys into the idea of a gut feeling about what will be a worthwhile development. "The intuitive is overblown," says William Zucker, director of the new Wharton School of Real Estate. Zucker questions whether anyone has the ability to "gaze into a magical crystal ball" and see a good deal. He attributes romanticism about the sixth sense to "developer war stories without a balance of tales about the deals that went sour."

Zucker says the successful developer is less of a seer than a quintessential entrepreneur. "They have a firm belief in themselves and can tolerate all kinds of ambiguity," he says. The entrepreneurial profile does not include "an innate gift at birth," but does include skills that are earned from trial and error in the market place, he says.

But more importantly, "they know where and how people want to live and work — they know the marketplace," he says. "Ultimately, development is a people business: getting people to move into your buildings."

"Occasionally, I'm called creative and intuitive," says Butcher, "but that has nothing to do with it; success comes from many years in the business."

Butcher adds, "A few pros like Gerson Bakar probably have the sixth sense, but most developers have such big egos that they think they are intuitive, when they really aren't. You need common sense, logic and a willingness to learn from mistakes."

Experience from a multitude of good and bad development proposals teaches the developer what to watch out for, according to Dorst. "It's like the medical profession; based on 1000 case studies, you know which treatment works and which doesn't"

"But even when all of the Information has been considered, someone has to decide whether to move forward with the project," says Dorst.

He says real estate decisions are also similar to oil exploration. Geologists have reams of scientific data that point to where oil might be located, but there is no assurance that the oil is there. Someone has to make the choice to drill or not.

"It is a myth, however, that the developer entrepreneur is a careless risk taker," says Wharton's Zucker. "Otherwise their bodies would be strewn all over the place."

According to Zucker, the well- i positioned entrepreneur minimizes risk by using other people's money, someone else's research and the tax laws.

Examining real estate development risk is not simply looking at the financial rewards that a project can yield, according to Butcher. "I look at the downside first — everything that can go wrong with a deal — then I look at the profit side."

In today's overbuilt real estate market, understanding when and where to take a risk is more important than ever, according to William Caldwell, president of Detroit-based Caldwell American Industrial Corp. "You have to be very disciplined about building today."

Caldwell, who is also the 1986 President of the Urban Land Institute, a Washington based development trade group, adds, "You have to be selective and flexible, keeping your options open as the market changes."

As design, financing and development of real estate become more complicated, developers can no longer rely exclusively on their intuition. "A lot of people can smell a good deal; but making it work comes from experience and having people around you who understand complex projects," says Caldwell.

Nevertheless, having a little bit of the sixth sense certainly can't hurt.

California trends: Spotting a good deal: Is it '6th sense' or skill?

Special to the Sun

In 1968, Standard Oil of California wanted to sell 600 acres in Richmond for housing. Bucking the popular wisdom, Stanley Dorst, then president of their land development subsidiary, thought the site was better suited for a regional shopping center. The company went along with Dorst's plan and today the one million square-foot development is near completion.

Scores of lawyers, bankers, and corporate mucky-mucks participated in the decision to turn this hilltop oil tank farm into a regional shopping mecca. But like many mega-development deals, it was one person with a contrary idea that saw it through.

According to many real estate experts, formal college training has little to do with one's ability to spot a good real estate deal.

Experience, a willingness to take risks, and common sense may be more important than an MBA from a top university. "The main advantage of an MBA is that you are a few years older, which means more maturity and experience," says Preston Butcher, president of Lincoln Properties.

But there may be a more intangible skill that comes into play: the developer's intuition. "There definitely is a sixth sense," says Gerson Bakar, chairman of Gerson Bakar and Associates, who pioneered the concept of garden apartments and built more than 20,000 apartments. He sees development as a creative process "When you see a good deal, you can feel it," says Bakar. "I pass up a lot of proposals that look good on paper because I don't have a good feel for them," he says. "Some people have it and some don't."

Bakar has never used a market study to test the feasibility of his projects but concedes that it is impossible to define the successful developer's "sixth sense." Not everyone, however, buys into the idea of a gut feeling about what will be a worthwhile development.

"The intuitive is overblown," says William Zucker, director of the new Wharton School of Real Estate. Zucker questions whether anyone has the ability to "gaze into a magical crystal ball" and see a good deal. He attributes romanticism about the sixth sense to "developer war stories without a balance of tales about the deals that went sour."

Zucker says the successful developer is less of a seer than a quintessential entrepreneur.

"They have a firm belief in themselves and can tolerate all kinds of ambiguity," says Zucker. The entrepreneurial profile does not include "an innate gift at birth," but does include skills that are earned from trial and error in the market place, he says. But more important, "they know where and how people want to live and work — they know the market place," he says. "Ultimately, development is a people business — getting people to move into your buildings."

"Occasionally I'm called creative and intuitive," says Butcher. "But that has nothing to do with it; success comes from many years in the business." Butcher says "a few pros like Gerson Bakar probably have the sixth sense, but most developers have such big egos that they think they are intuitive, when they really aren't," says Butcher. "You need common sense, logic and a willingness to learn from mistakes."

Experience from a multitude of good and bad development proposals teaches the developer what to watch out for, according to Dorst. "It's like the medical profession; based on 1,000 case studies, you know which treatment works and which doesn't."

"But even when all of the information has been considered, someone has to decide whether to move forward with the project," says Dorst. He says it is similar to oil exploration. Geologists have reams of scientific data that point to where oil might be located, but there is no assurance that the oil is there. Someone has to make the choice to drill or not.

"It is a myth, however, that the developer entrepreneur is a careless risk taker," says Wharton's Zucker. "Otherwise their bodies would be strewn all over the place," he says. According to Zucker, the well-positioned entrepreneur minimizes risk by using other people's money, someone else's research, and the tax laws.

Examining real estate development risk is not simply looking at the financial rewards that a project can yield, according to Butcher. "I look at the downside first — everything that can go wrong with a deal — then I look at the profit side," he says.

In today's over-built real estate market, understanding when and where to take a risk is more important than ever, according to William Caldwell, president of Detroit-based Caldwell American Industrial Corporation.

"You have to be very disciplined about building today," says Caldwell, who is also the 1986 president of the Urban Land Institute, a development trade group. "You have to be selective and flexible — keeping your options open as the market changes," he says.

As design, financing, and development of real estate become more complicated, developers can no longer rely exclusively on their intuition. "A lot of people can smell a good deal; but making it work comes from experience and having people around you who understand complex projects," says Caldwell.

Nevertheless, having a little bit of the sixth sense may still go a long way.

Landlord liability

NO ONE likes to get sued, and landlords are no exception. But in California the fear runs deep.

Because of a 1985 State Supreme Court case, Becker v. IRM Corp., apartment owners can find themselves in a legal hot spot when a tenant is injured in their apartment. There has never been a question about landlord liability when the owner is negligent in the maintenance of the building. But in the Becker case, the court said the building owners were liable regardless of what they knew about the safety of the apartment.

George Becker seriously injured his arm after slipping and falling against a glass shower door in his Moraga apartment. He sued IRM, the landlord, but the case was dismissed. He then appealed to the State Supreme Court, which overturned the lower court's decision. Becker settled with the builder and the shower door manufacturer for $150,000 while he continued to press his case against the landlord.

In its ruling in favor of Becker, the high court applied the abstruse legal principle of strict liability. The "purpose of strict liability Is to insure that the cost of injuries resulting from defective products are born by the manufacturers who put such products in the market rather than by injured persons who are powerless to protect themselves," the majority of the court said.

The strict liability notion also assumes "all of those who are part of the overall producing and marketing enterprise should bear the costs of injuries from defective products." And, according to the ruling, landlords are part of that "stream of commerce" and are responsible for the safety of their buildings.

Because the apartments were constructed in 1962 and purchased by IRM in 1974, the court held that they had no on-going relationship with the previous owners or the builder. Consequently, IRM was considered the first link in the chain of "buying and selling a product" and was liable for the building's defects.

According to the testimony, IRM didn't know that the complex had untempered shower doors when it bought the property or when Becker rented the unit. A tempered shower door is made of plastic, does not shatter upon impact and reduces the risk of injury. In legal terms, the untempered shower door was "a latent defect."

The court ruled, however, that IRM was still liable.

Landlords and property managers came unglued when the ruling was handed down and are pushing legislation to soften its impact. They point to the dissenting opinion of the Court that states, 'Any landlord, even one renting the family home for a year, will now be insurer for defects in any wire, screw, latch, cabinet door, pipe or other article on and in his premises at the time they are let despite the fact that he neither installed the item nor had knowledge or reason to know of the defect"

The legislation, AB4254, was introduced by Assemblyman Larry Stirling, R-San Diego. It says a landlord would be exempt from strict liability rules when the owner completes "a reasonably competent and diligent inspection of the property and makes necessary repairs." Real estate lawyer Alex Creel says the bill has two benefits. "As landlords conduct routine inspections and make repairs, they will get relief from strict liability, and the quality of all rental housing will improve," he says.

Squaring off against the legislation are the California Trial Lawyers Association, the California Rural Legal Assistance Foundation and the Western Center on Law and Poverty. One of their gripes is how much protection the inspections will actually provide. "A latent defect by definition is not visible, so an inspection will do nothing to detect the problems," says Marc Brown, staff attorney for the California Rural Legal Assistance Foundation.

"There is also a philosophical issue about how to balance the losses when a tenant is injured by a latent defect," Brown says. "The alternative to one tenant getting stuck with the costs is the landlord getting insurance against losses from all defects and for all tenants. The landlord is in a better position than the renter to get insurance and to sue the manufacturer."

Brown concedes "this may mean increased insurance costs and slightly higher rents, but it is better public policy to spread the costs among all tenants."

The legislation has stalled in an Assembly judiciary subcommittee, which one lobbyist says is tantamount to "a slow death."

Similar to many landlord-tenant squabbles, this issue comes down to who should pay. The housing industry argues that the strict liability rule makes sense for large corporations when they put out faulty products, but the law shouldn't apply to responsible landlords.

Tenant advocates see it differently. Brown argues, "Landlords say they aren't General Motors and can't pay the costs like a manufacturer, and we say tenants aren't GM either."

California trends: Landlords seek relief from liability decision

Special to the Sun

Everyone is paranoid about getting sued, and landlords are no exception.

But in California the fear runs deep. Due to the 1985 State Supreme Court case Becker Vs. IRM Corporation, apartment owners can find themselves in a legal hot spot when a tenant is injured in their apartment. If landlord groups have their way, however, this ruling will be modified by the state legislature.

George Becker seriously injured his arm after slipping and falling against a glass shower door in his Moraga apartment. He sued IRM, the landlord, but the case was dismissed. He appealed to the state Supreme Court which overturned the lower court's decision. Becker settled with the builder and the shower door manufacturer for $150,000 while he continued to press his case against the landlord.

The court applied the legal principle of strict liability for ruling in favor of Becker. The "purpose of strict liability is to insure that the cost of injuries resulting from defective products are born by the manufacturers who put such products in the market rather than by injured persons who are powerless to protect themselves." said the majority of the court.

The strict liability notion assumes "all of those who are part of the overall producing and marketing enterprise should bear the costs of injuries from defective products." According to the ruling, landlords are part of that "stream of commerce" and are responsible for the safety of their buildings.

Because the apartments were constructed in 1962 and purchased by IRM in 1974, the court held that they had no ongoing relationship with the previous owners or the builder. Consequently, IRM was considered the first link in the chain of "buying and selling a product" and was liable for the building's defects.

There has never been a question about landlord liability when the owner is negligent in the maintenance of the building. But in the Becker case, the court said IRM was liable regardless of what they knew about the safety of the apartment.

According to the testimony, they did not know that the complex had untempered shower doors at the time that they bought the property or at the time that Becker rented the unit. "This is considered a latent defect," the court decided. A tempered shower door is made of plastic, does not shatter upon impact, and reduces the risk of injury.

Landlords and property managers came unglued when the ruling was handed down. They point to the dissenting opinion of some justices which states, "Any landlord, even one renting the family home for a year, will now be insured for defects in any wire, screw, latch, cabinet door, pipe or other article on and in his premises at the time they are let despite the fact that he neither installed the item nor had knowledge or reason to know of the defect."

Despite opposition from trial lawyers and tenant advocates, real estate groups sponsored legislation to find relief from the court's ruling. AB 4254 Introduced by Assemblyman Larry Stirling of San Diego says a landlord would be exempt from strict liability rules when the owner completes "a reasonably competent and diligent inspection of the property and makes necessary repairs."

Real estate attorney Alex Creel says the bill has two benefits. "As landlords conduct routine inspections and make repairs, they will get relief from strict liablity and the quality of all rental housing will improve," he says.

Squaring off against the legislation are the California Trial Lawyers Association, the California Rural Legal Assistance Foundation and the Western Center on Law and Poverty. One of their gripes is how much protection the inspections will actually provide. "A latent defect by definition is not visible, so an inspection will do nothing to detect the problems," says Marc Brown, staff attorney for CRLA.

"There is also a philosophical issue about how to balance the losses when a tenant is injured by a latent defect," says Brown. "The alternative to one tenant getting stuck with the costs is the landlord getting insurance against losses from all defects and for all tenants," he says. "The landlord is in a better position than the renter to get insurance and to sue the manufacturer."

Brown concedes "this may mean increased insurance costs and slightly higher rents, but it is better public policy to spread the costs among all tenants."

The legislation is currently stalled in an Assembly judiciary subcommittee, and according to one housing industry lobbyist that is tantamount to "a slow death." Similar to many landlord/tenant squabbles, this issue comes down to who should pay. The housing industry argues that the strict liablility rule makes sense for large corporations when they put out faulty products but the law shouldn't apply to responsible landlords.

But tenant advocates see it differently. "Landlords say they aren't General Motors and can't pay the costs like a manufacturer and we say tenants aren't G.M. either," says Brown.

Homeowner joys

FOR SEVENTY-FIVE years, the mantra for the 700,000-member National Association of Realtors has been private property rights. But this spring they renamed their annual week-long celebration called "Private Property Week" to "American Home Week."

According to Clark Wallace, NAR president and a Bay Area developer, a NAR committee came up with 18 recommendations and selected the "American Home" theme because" it's like apple pie, motherhood, Chevrolet and hot dogs."

Wallace says NAR's decision to drop the "Private Property Rights" slogan doesn't signal a reduced commitment to defending the Fourth Amendment to the Constitution. "If we drop our longstanding and deep support for private property rights, there would be nothing left for this organization to do that is important to its members," he says.

To Russia with love

Realtors aren't alone in boosting the ideal of home ownership. In a guest column for the Washington Post, Yelena Bonner, wife of Soviet Union exile Andrei Sakharov, hails the American quest for home ownership. "No matter their place on the social ladder, their salary, capital, inheritance, winnings in the lottery or the stock market . . . Americans want a house of their own," says Bonner.

"The desire to own a house is not a class ambition . . .," she continues. "It is an expression of a national desire for privacy." Bonner adds that she regrettably has never owned a house: "I've never had a corner to call my own."

'Helping Hands'

Houston has the highest apartment vacancy rates of anywhere in the country, and it is good news for tenants who are enjoying falling rents, landlord giveaways and shrinking security deposits.

It has also spawned a unique approach to aiding low-income renters. Dubbed the "Helping Hands Program," Houston landlords donate the use of one or more of their apartments for at least one year for poor tenants who only pay utilities and 15 percent of their income on the rent.

Robert Sherman, president of the National Apartment Association, is calling on landlords all over the country to start up programs similar to Houston's. Sherman says that it is an opportunity for landlords to make a worthwhile contribution to their community and that it makes good economic sense in a soft rental market.

Rent control debate

Only a few states have a raging debate about rent control, California included. In most other states it is an alien concept. Nevertheless, the National Multi-family Housing Council, a national trade group of large apartment owners and developers, has pushed through legislation in 10 states prohibiting local jurisdictions from even considering rent control.

State legislatures in Arizona, Colorado, Florida, Georgia, Minnesota, Louisiana, Oregon, South Carolina, Texas and Washington have taken away the power of local government to adopt rent regulations; and Illinois, Virginia and North Carolina are considering similar measures. With the exception of Minnesota, none of these states has been faced with rent control proposals; this explains why the legislation wasn't controversial.

In California, however, rent control has been the hottest political issue in the real estate field for eight years. Fourteen cities have enacted local rent control laws, and repeated attempts by the housing industry to gain support for statewide preemptive laws have failed.

Games builders play

Construction game creator Foreal Systems was denied a booth at last week's Pacific Coast Builders Conference. Foreal produces the clever card game "Construction Chase," which simulates the trials and tribulations of building a house, from getting a red flag from the building department to laying the foundation.

Colene Rowell, the maternal partner of the mother-and-son enterprise at Foreal systems, says in denying their application for a booth at the West Coast builder gala, PCBC told them: "Builders don't play games."

Building permits vary

Fueled by lower interest rates and heavy demand, California housing construction is booming. Nevertheless, the picture isn't rosy in every part of the state. According to the Construction Industry Research Board, seven regions in the state have experienced a slowdown in new building permits for the first four months of 1986.

The biggest declines were registered in Santa Rosa and Stockton, where construction fell off 40 percent. Other areas experiencing a drop include Chico, Fresno, Sacramento, San Luis Obispo and Yuba City.

But according to Ben Bartolotto of the research group, statistics can be deceptive. Bartolotto says the overall statewide gains reflect a blip in the market because of the surge of rental housing that was financed through mortgage revenue bonds. Builders rushed to use tax-exempt bonds before the threat of tax reform killed the financing mechanism.

When the year-end figures are in, Bartolotto predicts that total building permits will be off 6 percent from last year.

California trends: Group pushes laws to stop rent control

Special to the Sun

Only a few states have a raging debate about rent control — California included.

In most other states it is an alien concept. Nevertheless, the National Multi-family Housing Council, a national trade group of large apartment owners and developers, has pushed through legislation in 10 states that prohibit local jurisdictions from even considering rent control.

State Legislatures in Arizona, Colorado, Florida, Georgia, Minnesota, Louisiana, Oregon, South Carolina, Texas, and Washington have taken away the power of local government to adopt rent regulations; and Illinois, Virgina, and North Carolina are considering similar measures.

With the exception of Minnesota, none of these states has been faced with rent control proposals; this explains why the legislation wasn't contoversial.

In California, however, rent control has been the hottest political issue in the real estate field for eight years. Fourteen cities have enacted local rent control laws, and repeated attempts by the housing industry to gain support for statewide pre-emptive laws have failed.

Fueled by lower interest rates and heavy demand, California housing construction is booming. Nevertheless, the picture isn't rosy in every part of the state. According to the Construction Industry Research Board (CIRB), seven regions in the state have experienced a slow-down in new building permits for the first four months of 1986.

The biggest declines were registered in Santa Rosa and Stockton, where construction fell off 40 percent. Other areas experiencing a drop include Chico, Fresno, Sacramento, San Luis Obispo, and Yuba City.

But according to Ben Bartolotto of the CIRB, statistics can be deceptive. Bartolotto says the overall statewide gains reflect a blip in the market because of the surge of rental housing that was financed through mortgage revenue bonds. Builders rushed to use tax-exempt bonds before tax reform legislation killed the financing mechanism.

When the year-end figures are in, Bartolotto predicts that total building permits will be off 6 percent from last year. According to his forecast, single-family housing will make moderate gains but rental housing will fall off dramatically.

The American dream of homeownership is the envy of the world and Realtors aren't alone in boosting the ideal of homeownership. In a guest column for the Washington Post, Yelena Bonner, wife of Soviet Union exile Andrei Sakharov, hails the American quest for homeownership.

"No matter their place on the social ladder, their salary, capital, inheritance, winnings in the lottery or the stock market. . .Americans want a house of their own," wrote Bonner. "The desire to own a house is not a class ambition. . .it is an expression of a national desire for privacy," she said.

Bonner says she regrettably has never owned a house: "I've never had a corner to call my own."

Houston has the highest apartment vacancy rates of anywhere in the country, and it is good news for tenants who are enjoying falling rents, landlord giveaways and shrinking security deposits.

It has also spawned a unique approach to aiding low-income renters. Dubbed the "Helping Hands Program," Houston landlords donate the use of one or more of their apartments for at least one year for poor tenants who only pay utilities and 15 percent of their income on the rent.

Robert Sherman, president of the National Apartment Association, is calling on landlords all over the country to start up programs similar to Houston's. Sherman says that it is an opportunity for landlords to make a worthwhile contribution to their community and that it makes good economic sense in a soft rental market. Unfortunately, this is one idea that may depend more on market conditions than benevolence.

Construction game creator Foreal Systems was denied a booth at this week's Pacific Coast Builders Conference in San Francisco. Foreal produces the clever card game "Construction Chase" which simulates the trials and tribulations of building a house — from getting a red flag from the building department to laying the foundation.

Colene Rowell, the maternal partner of the mother-and-son enterprise at Foreal systems, says PCBC denied their application for a booth at the West Coast builder gala because they said "builders don't play games."

California Trends: Request made to Legislature would aim condominium owner associations

Condominum owner associations are under the gun to clean up their act. Management, legal and insurance problems have eaten away their assets and damaged their credibility with individual condo owners and prospective buyers. They are taking steps to turn things ground, however, including a request to the California Legislature that would make it easier to collect unpaid condo dues.

"Condominium fees — the bread and butter of homeowner association — range from forty up to several hundred dollars a month. They pay for maintenance of the common grounds, fire insurance, central utilities and other shared amenities.

"It's the lifeblood of associations, and their ability to collect dues affects their long-term fiscal health," says Tom DeLapp, consultant to the Community Association Institute (CAI), a condo association trade group.

When homeowners get in a financial pinch, condo dues are the first Obligation to be ignored, according Je DeLapp. "When they're in a bind, they pay off debts that spoil their credit rating or something that might cause them to lose their home," he says.

The headache for the association is trying to collect the delinquent rules. When gentle persuasion fails, associations use whatever leverage they have — like threatening to cut off the water or disconnecting the cable television. But according to association managers, these tricks meet with mixed success. "We can't say you aren't allowed to swim in the pool or threaten not to paint your unit. There is no real reduction in services when you don't pay your dues," says DeLapp.

When coercion doesn't work, associations turn to the courts. Small claims is the least expensive recourse, but "the judgment is only a piece of paper without enforceability," says one association manager. A municipal court injunction has more teeth, but obtaining a ruling can be a costly and long drawn out process

The ultimate legal threat is to place a lien on the property and initiate foreclosure proceedings. By forcing a sale of the unit, the association can hope to recover their losses from the proceeds of the sale. But this isn't always the case.

Once the association tries to foreclose, the lender holding the first mortgage jumps in. "By law, our lien is subordinate to the lender's note; and if the bank forecloses there isn't enough money to pay us, so we get wiped out," says Los Angeles property manager Mark Goldberg.

According to CAI officials, the problem is getting worse. In the soft condominium market there is very little equity to pay off the mortgage and to cover the unpaid condo fees when the unit is sold or foreclosed on. The association is left holding the bag.

"We have buldings where thirty percent of the owners ar delinquent, says Goldberg. "You can live with five percent bad debt, but not much higher," he says. No one collects reliable statistics on the average rate of delinquencies, but CAI estimates it to be 7-12 percent, though some real estate experts claim this figure is high.

Associations place the blame on' lenders, "In a foreclosure situation, the bank is the owner, but in some cases they are unwilling to pay the; dues that cover the costs of mowing the lawn, painting the outside of the building and cleaning the swimming pool," says DeLapp.

A way out of the bind is to make1 homeowner's dues a debt that runs' with the land like a mortgage or property taxes. But this would require state legislation — an idea that scares lenders and realtors.

AB 4376 introduced by San Diego Assemblyman Larry Stirling says, that financial institutions would be' required to pay up to six months of delinquent homeowner's assessments out of the proceeds of the foreclosure. On average, this would amount to $1,000 per case, according to Goldberg.

Ron Kingston of the California Association of Realtors says, "If passed, the bill would discourage lenders from making condo loans. If there are mysterious liens ahead of the lender's, then their mortgage could be in trouble."

Kingston also questions the gravity of the situation: "CAI couldn't prove that there is a problem out there," he says. "And if there is, California already has several legal options for recovery."

With heavy opposition from state bankers, realtors, and savings and loans, the legislation failed to get out of the assembly judiciary committee. Nevertheless, the committee chairman urged all parties to work out a satisfactory compromise.

Condo owner groups are now earning several alternatives. One idea is to require condo buyers to establish impound accounts and prepay six months in dues upon purchasing their unit. If foreclosure begins at a later date, delinquent dues could be paid out of the impound account.

In the meantime, since a quick fix is not at hand, buyers should think ahead. "Many people bought condos as a cheaper option — an apartment with equity — and thought the association would take care of them," says DeLapp. "But they learned that they are responsible for themselves and if one of their neighbors goes belly-up, they may be responsible for them as well."

California trends: Her job: Giving first aid to ailing S & L's

Special to the Sun

In the last 15 years, Roslyn Payne has worked on some sticky real estate deals, but never so many troubled ones at once.

As president of the newly created Federal Asset Disposition Association (FADA), Payne is helping ailing savings and loans get out from under sour real estate ventures — up to $15 billion, according to some estimates.

Deregulation, over-built real estate markets, volatile interest rates and poor management have splattered many s & l's with red ink. In a few cases, the Federal Savings and Loan Insurance Corporation (FSLIC) has had to step in and take control of the institutions. Once in charge, the FSLIC is discovering that the real estate loan portfolios are in mayhem.

Delinquent construction loans, vacant rental and condo projects and foreclosed commercial buildings have drained the life out of otherwise healthy savings and loans. FSLIC realized that they weren't prepared to manage or liquidate the holdings. Consequently, FADA was created to do the job.

"It is a very unique attempt to harness the private sector for solving a big public problem," said Tony Frank, Chairman of First Nationwide Savings and Loan. Frank concedes that it is an awesome task with a lot of people looking over FADA's shoulder. But he says, "If it can be done, Roslyn Payne can do it."

A Harvard MBA with 15 years of executive real estate experience, Payne is cautious about predicting future success. She compares her $250,000 a year job to launching a new business and exhudes the confidence of an eager entrepreneur. Her response to questions follows:

What is the problem and how did it get so bad?

Troubled savings and loans share certain characteristics. For example, they rushed to grow too rapidly. They also frequently used new investment powers to invest in areas they lacked expertise — like commercial and construction lending. And finally, their sources of funds caused them trouble. They were brokered funds that demanded a higher interest rate and greater risk ... As a result, some in the industry are worse off than they ever have been.

Why was it necessary to create a whole new institution to solve the problem? Couldn't the FSLIC simply sell the assets?

In the 30s, when there were widespread problems in the mortgage market, Congress created the authority for FADA. Since then, the financial system has done very well. But in the last few years things have gotten bad enough that this step was necessary . . . The difficulties have not been interest rate problems but asset qualities — the type of loans the institutions choose to make. . .

We bring a private real estate market approach to this problem. FSLIC is not used to dealing with the real estate community — they don't know how to bid, negotiate and pull all of the elements together ... They are under civil service rules and can't attract the kind of real estate specialists necessary to do the job.

Do you operate as a business or a government agency?

We have a foot in both camps — public and private. A government agency, the Federal Home Loan Bank Board, created FADA and gave us special powers to operate in the private sector. For example, we don't have to follow the rigorous federal government bidding procedures. We can go out in the market and find experts in areas like negotiation, disposition, and construction.

Will FADA actually own the properties?

We do not take title to the assets; the institutions (savings and loans) keep title. FSLIC is the underlying receiver and they hire personnel to deal with the problems — just like a receiver would in a typical bankruptcy.

The receiver looks to us to work on the non-performing assets: bad loans, foreclosed properties ... We help them manage the holdings and in some cases dispose of the assets, but we never own them outright.

What exactly will you do to aid the receiver?

We look at the asset, go through the file, figure what we have and decide what needs to be done. Next we present a game plan: what is the asset worth and how should the property be managed or how can it best be sold.

Then we look globally at the asset — if we do all of these things what happens? The receiver needs to know the answer so they can see how it fits in with overall creditor claims. These are effectively bankrupt situations and so you have to decide who gets paid.

What kind of properties are you dealing with, and where are they located?

When we wrap all of this up, I think we will find 90 percent of the assets are real estate or real estate related and 10 percent will be other assets like energy loans, consumer oriented or commercial companies. The institution's problems will correlate to the type of business they were in. They are concentrated in the West Coast and energy-related states.

How do you measure success and how long will it take?

If we succeed we will have saved the financial system an enormous amount of money.

We have a 10-year plan, but I don't think it will take that long. On the other hand, we have a three-year lease on our office space, but I think it will take longer than that.

Women agents start own 'old boy' network

WHEN Bay Area real estate broker Nancy Luce was working on a $35 million foreclosure sale in Phoenix, she needed reliable legal advice on Arizona real estate laws. Through a contact in the Association of Women in Commercial Real Estate, she quickly found Anne Hanyak, a Phoenix attorney, who gave her the necessary counsel.

This wasn't the first or the last time that a woman has teamed up with another woman to make a real estate deal. In major cities throughout the country, independently-organized AWCRE groups have become a network for women in real estate.

At a recent San Francisco luncheon meeting, "networking" was a big part of the agenda. In addition to a formal business session, the women were busy trading business cards, setting up appointments and intently discussing their latest real estate projects.

At the meeting, Roslyn Payne spoke on her new rule as president of the Federal Asset Disposition Association. Payne piqued the interest of the 150 women there with her insights into how foreclosed properties can he located, how deregulation may affect real estate loans, and how lax reform will change investment decisions.

Payne's only reference to the male-dominated real estate bank-inn business was a comic description of FADA's new hoard of directors. "None of them look like me," she said.

AWCRE members don't complain about it, but other real estate trade groups have been slow in promoting women into the leadership ranks. It wasn't until two years ago that the California Association of Realtors elected its first woman president, though they have had a very active Women's Council of Realtors for decades. This year, the National Association of Home Builders elected its first woman to a leadership post — as secretary treasurer.

"Women are playing a more prominent role in our group and a greater role in the industry in general," says Henry Chamberlain, vice president of the Building Owners and Managers Association.

According to Chamberlain, there are 18 women on HOMA's 91-member Board of Governors and two women serve on the nine-member management committee. Nevertheless, a woman has never been elected president of BOMA.

Luce carefully points out that the creation of AWCRE is not an ideological statement or an attempt "to only do business with other women. We don't view this as a reactionary move, but instead as a complementary move," she says. "We don't even pretend to think that we can be in the real estate business without working with men.

Though none have applied, men are eligible to join AWCRE. In San Francisco, the group's president Claudia Kelly says, "It is unlikely they will, but they can if they have an interest in our goal of promoting women in commercial real estate."

AWCRE's membership foes are $100 a year. To qualify, a person must derive half of his income from commercial real estate and have two years of experience in the business.

AWCRE activities are similar to those of traditional real estate industry associations with a focus on encouraging education, professionalizing the trade and furthering member business contacts. "The old boy network' is a role model for what we are doing," says Luce.

The organizations also bring their members up to speed on new developments in real estate law, finance, and construction. The San Diego Chapter of Women in Commercial Real Estate, for example, sponsors eight public seminars a year. Recent workshops have focused on trends in shopping center development and an up-close look at different San Diego real estate markets.

AWCRE leaders boast, however, that their organization has a broader focus and greater diversity of interests. Their membership includes professionals in architecture, lending, real estate law, brokerage, pension investing, leasing, acquisitions and other types of commercial real estate.

Newsletters are a popular member benefit. The recent edition of San Francisco's "Bottom Line" profiles women appraisers, includes a schedule of upcoming events, describes major estate deals and lists employment openings. The "Job Hank" has opportunities for an asset manager, a leasing agent, a property manager, an income property producer, a real estate accountant and a development project manager; starting salaries range from $25,000 to $75,000 plus a year.

AWCRE groups from all over the country have recently come together to form a national federation. According to Linda Greenberg of the San Diego chapter, the federation has assisted women in locating buyers and finding financing in other market areas. "There is a lot of money shipped around the country to finance real estate," says Greenberg. "For instance, a San Francisco pension fund may be looking for an investment in San Diego."

Members say the association is a practical investment of their time. "It has opened doors for me that wouldn't have ordinarily been there." says Greenberg. When asked if she had made any business deals as a result of her AWCRE association, she replied, "Definitely. That's what it's all about." .

California trends: Affordable housing victim of Fed's rule

Special to the Sun

Six years ago, Congress changed the rules in a popular federal program that provides builders incentives to construct affordable apartments in rural areas.

But only now — as renters face staggering rent increases — is the full import of their actions being felt.

The legislative maneuver allowed thousands of developers who participate in the Farmers Home Administration's Section 515 program to prepay their cheap federally-subsidized mortgages without penalty.

It's an economically efficient system that helps the government recapture its investment when the loans are paid off, but it has had some painful side effects for renters. Once the government stops providing cheap mortgage money, they can no longer force the owner to keep the rents low. Consequently, the new owners — without other forms of subsidy — will charge whatever the market will bear.

"Following mortgage prepayment, rent increases are substantial," states a report by the State Department of Housing and Community Development. In some cases it has meant rent hikes in excess of 50 percent. For example, the average increase for a one-bedroom apartment was $150 and $176 for a two-bedroom.

The state study estimates that steep rent increases could force up to 90 percent of the tenants in projects they surveyed to move out.

Though the 1980 law only applies to those developments built before 1979, more than 1,000 units in California have already been converted to market-rate housing and another 6,000 are threatened with conversion. Newer projects — those financed by the Farmers Home program after 1979 — are subject to federal rent controls for 20 years.

The recent squeeze on rural renters has not gone unnoticed. In August, Federal Judge E. J. Garcia issued a temporary injunction that prohibits the prepayment of a Farmers Home loan on the 104-unit Sunset Apartments project in Rocklin. The judge also required the Farmers Home Administration to continue providing rental assistance to very low-income tenants in the project.

Ordinarily, the supplemental rental assistance feature of the Section 515 Program is terminated when the federal mortgage is paid-off. Though tenants dislocated by the action are put on a priority list for renting in other Farmers Home projects, "generally there is no alternative housing developments with vacancies that are affordable," says Susan Peck of the California Coalition for Rural Housing.

Ticked off by the displacement of 72 elderly tenants in a FmHA loan prepayment in his own district, Rep. Richard Lehman of Fresno has gotten Congress back into the act. He has introduced legislation that would slap a one-year moratorium on those prepayments which may contribute to renter eviction. The legislation would also require the Farmers Home Administration to continue paying rental assistance for those loans prepaid one year before the effective date of the bill.

"I am proposing an interim measure because I feel strongly that the Congress must thoroughly assess this matter and develop a comprehensive and long-term policy to address these prepayments," said Lehman when he introduced his bill, HR 5463, in August. A House hearing was held on the bill in Washington last Tuesday.

Up in arms over Lehman's proposal are the National Association of Home Builders and the Council of Rural Housing and Development. "We are sympathetic to the plight of the tenants, but doesn't the government have some responsibility to honor a contract?" asks Charles Edson of the council.

"It sounds corny to talk about justice, but that is part of the issue," says Edson. "Changing the rules in the middle of the (game) is unreasonable," he says. "We are dealing with investors who expect to get the benefits that they contracted for when they went into a syndication agreement," says Patrick Sablehaus, a board member with the California Rural Builders Council, a private group that has remained neutral on the Lehman bill.

"Once the tax benefits are exhausted, they expect to sell the project." Lehman's bill would make that sale difficult, if not impossible, in many cases.

Sablehaus says some builders would be hurt by the bill but "we don't think we should oppose it because we recognize there is a real problem out there."

A broader concern is that the legislation will scare builders away from getting involved in future federal housing programs. "You are not going to get people to come in and build low-income housing if they think the Congress will change the rules every time," says Edson.

But housing-activist Peck says the renters' predicament should be the highest priority, and she predicts a more promising scenario for future builder participation. "I am not concerned that this program will fall on its face," she says. "There will always be builders attracted to federal programs that offer lower interest rates and tax benefits."

In the final analysis, this entire debate may be irrelevant if the Reagan Administration gets its way. As part of its budget austerity drive, it is doing everything it can to cut back the Farmers Home Administration housing ventures. The administration says the $420 million public price tag has been too high.

And not surprisingly, one thing that both builders and tenant advocates agree on is that the administration is making a big mistake.

Supreme Court to hear property case

Property rights activists never tire in their mission to convince the U.S. Supreme Court that land-owners should be compensated if local regulations deprive them the use of their property.

In the case of First English Evangelical Lutheran Church v. County of Los Angeles, the church had a camp for underprivileged children that was wiped out by a fire. When they wanted to rebuild, the county turned them down because the general plan prohibited development on the site. With no relief from the county, the church turned to the courts for help.

This is the fifth time in six years that the High Court has considered the issue of just compensation. But each time, the court has turned back the question because they found procedural problems with the cases brought before them. For example, in other cases, the court has said that the aggrieved property owners had other forms of administrative or legislative recourse and should have exercised those avenues before they turned to the courts.

According to land-use attorney Kenneth Bley, this one is ripe for the court to rule in favor of just compensation. "The church has exhausted all remedies; there is no relief valve," says Bley. Bley filed a legal brief in support of the church on behalf of the National Association of Home Builders, a leading supporter of private property rights.

CITY DEPOSITS TARGETED TO AFFECT MORTGAGE LENDING HABITS — The City of San Diego is flexing its financial muscles with local banks and savings and loans. The city is using its power as a major depositor to influence the mortgage lending habits of those institutions that make home loans.

Out of concern about the availability of mortgage credit in poor neighborhoods, the San Diego City Council has launched an experimental program that restricts which banks or S&Ls get a share of $500,000 in deposits from the City's cash reserves.

According to the plan, the city treasurer will not deposit its funds in those lending institutions that fail to make an "average" number of home loans in specified poorer neighborhoods.

Considering the city has $600 million in total assets, the $500,000 investment is modest. But according to Jim Yacenda of the Federal Home Loan Bank, "It is not just a symbolic gesture, lenders do take notice of such actions," he says.

CHEAP MINI-TERM SECOND MORTGAGES — If you want to take out a second mortgage on your house and are seeking one of the lowest interest rates in the country, look no further.

The Money Store, an indepedent mortgage company, is offering interest rates at 7.5 percent (prime rate) on second trust deeds, but not without a hitch: you have to pay off the loan in six months. "I don't know of anyone that is lending at prime rate to the public; lower rates are usually only available to large corporations," says Money Store's Executive Vice President William Templeton.

If you want a longer term loan, the New Jersey-based Money Store — with operations in 19 states and seven offices in California — will offer rates of 8.5 percent for a three-year loan, 9.5 percent for a five-year loan and 11 percent for a 15-year loan. The longer-term loans are only slightly more competitive than the rest of the market.

But qualifying for the six-month loans can be rough: it requires a 40 percent downpayment and the monthly house payment cannot exceed 20 percent of monthly income. For longer-term loans, the Money Store eases up on its qualifying requirements.

According to Templeton, the six-month loan is not a gimmick. "It is striking a chord," he says. "It is attractive to the short-term borrower — like the small businessman — who needs an infusion of cash."

CASINOS GETTING INTO THE AFFORDABLE HOUSING ACT — Casinos are experts at taking people's money. But in Atlantic City, Bally's Park Place Casino has figured out an innovative way to give some of their winnings back — in the form of an affordable housing development.

In cooperation with state and city officials and local housing groups, Bally's participated in a unique plan to develop 72 moderately-priced condominiums. Bally's donated land valued at $1.7 million for the project and also purchased $5.9 million in tax-exempt county bonds. The two-and three-bedroom condos will sell for $60,000 and $65,000 respectively.

Bally's interest in affordable housing isn't entirely altruistic. As part of the State of New Jersey's Casino Reinvestment Act, all Casinos are obligated to invest in community housing projects.

Court's ruling on assumable loans had big impact

Last of a three-part series on the California Supreme Court and its decisions affecting housing.

When I bought my first home, it couldn't have been at a worse time: it was 1982 and interest rates and home prices were at their peaks.

But thanks to the 1978 California Supreme Court decision of Wellenkamp v. Bank of America, the seller's 10 percent mortgage was assumable — making my purchase much easier.

My story is not unique. No single action of the California Supreme Court has had a greater impact on housing and real estate than the now-famous Wellenkamp decision. According the the California Association of Realtors, 750,000 home loans were passed on from seller to buyer between 1978 and 1985 — the period between the court's decision and the passage of federal laws that closed the door on many loan assumptions.

The Wellenkamp decision diverted millions of dollars from lenders to homebuyers, making it immensely popular among consumer groups and real estate agents and equally bad news for banks and savings and loans.

In 1975, the Mans Family sold their home to Cynthia Wellenkamp who assumed their 8 percent Bank of America mortgage. When B of A was notified of the sale, they told Wellenkamp that she could assume the loan, but only if she was willing to pay the prevailing interest rate of 9.25 per cent. When she said no to their terms, the bank enforced a clause in the loan that permitted it to call the full amount of the loan due.

Wellenkamp sued the bank. According to the Supreme Court which ruled in her favor, the "due-on-sale" provision restrained the owner's ability to sell the home.

The decision became controversial when thousands of home-buyers rushed to dodge paying higher rates by assuming sellers low-interest loans.

The formula worked for everyone but the hard-hit savings and had big loans business. The industry was struggling to cover their losses from a mismatch of paying higher interest rates on deposits while continuing to earn mortgage interest at lower rates. For them, Wellenkamp posed a serious threat.

Consequently the banking industry fought the decision on every front. They sponsored state and federal legislation to overturn the ruling and continued their legal battle in the courts. Some institutions went so far as to change their regulatory charter from state to federal in order to get out from under the Wellenkamp ruling.

"The court's decision was a great, mistake," says Loyola law professor Gilian Kanner. According to Kanner, the decision courted with "economic disaster" by drying up loan portfolios, pushing up mortgage rates in general and bumping up home prices.

In a report put out by the Supreme Court Project on the Wellenkamp decision, its author Richard McDonald accuses the court of "economic policy making." "The decision broke new legal ground in a variety of ways and created serious problems, both legal and economic, that could have been avoided," says the report.

According to McDonald, in addition to "misapplying prior California case law," the Court disrupted the California mortgage market. Specifically, the report claims the decision "made mortgage contracts in California less certain and, therefore, more costly."

Real property legal expert and law professor John Hetland disputes these claims. He says the decision was consistent with a long line of cases dating back to 1972.

Further, he says "it was an emotional issue; the dollars and cents weren't that important to lenders, but they were to home-buyers. "If you look at the growth of the California savings and loan industry between 1978 and 1982, Wellenkamp didn't hurt them; they prospered."

The decision was so important to propping up home sales during that period that the California Association of Realtors put the full weight of their trade group's research, legal and legislative muscle behind preserving the Wellenkamp edict.

Today the court's decision is irrelevant because new banking rules have virtually wiped out loan assumptions on fixed-rate mortgages. And with lower home-loan rates, the popularity of loan assumptions have run their course in the market place. But no one can dispute that the "Wellenkamp window" kept the California homeownership engine running.

Wellenkamp may be the most dramatic example of the California Supreme Court's impact on real estate. But like many of their actions in the last 10 years — from property rights to tenant rights — the Court has created both supporters and critics.

As long as there are debates in California about the issues of growth, development, regulation and private and public rights, the Supreme Court will find itself in the middle of these disagreements. Therefore, even if the composition of the court changes, it will remain a target for both disdain and admiration by those in the world of real estate.

Realtors' lobbyist nears retirement

Heavyweight real estate lobbyist Dugald Gillies is retiring at the end of this year.

For 19 years he has been the legislative guru of the 100,000-member California Association of Realtors (CAR). And while some of his adversaries welcome his departure, it will not be for lack of respect.

A 1986 California Journal poll of lobbyists and legislators selected Gillies the most effective lobbyist in Sacramento. The last time the poll was conducted was 1978 when he received the same honor.

The following is a question and answer interview with Gillies.

Which legislation that you have worked on in the last two decades has had the most profound effect on real estate?

For dramatic effect, it was the defeat of lender-sponsored legislation that would have overturned the Wellenkamp decision on loan assumptions. At that point in time (1980-1982), without the right to loan assumption, hundreds of thousands of buyers would have been totally frustrated. But it was also negative because it was beating someone's proposal.

Less dramatic was our hard and long fight on property tax limitation. And though the final result was achieved through Prop 13, it was our effort that helped California trends create the climate so that it could occur. Prop 13 stopped what was becoming a confiscatory policy on homeownership.

Were there other issues?

One was the enactment of laws that required greater professionalization for those that served the public in real estate transactions. In my first year at CAR (1968), we established an education pre-qualification (six units of college classes) in order for someone to get a real estate license. Today it requires 24 units which helps insure that a person entering the brokerage field is qualified to represent sellers.

How much of your job has been bringing along your own membership, the Realtors?

Half of my job is educating my constituency to the sensitivity of the legislature and their hot buttons. The other half is taking their stories from the market place to the legislature. Sometimes the Realtors want me to make a problem go away with a magic wand, and I have to explain to them that it won't fly. But you also get ideas from legislators that not only won't work but would stop the economy dead in its track. But that is our job — explaining how decisions will affect home ownership, renters and landlords.

Is it hard to represent a conservative constituency before a moderate to liberal legislature?

It's not particularly difficult. The membership has been realistic, and they have selected legislative goals that are directly related to the real estate industry, not because of their political orientation.

We have sponsored legislation that has been the delight of liberals and other legislation that has been the delight of conservatives.

Do you have regrets about some of the position CAR has taken in the past, like opposition to civil rights laws that were designed to stop housing discrimination?

I think the world has changed and perceptions within the industry have changed. I believe that in those days many within in the industry were convinced that their clients would desert them if they sold a house to a minority next door to them.

I think they thought it was in their self-interest not to. As it turned out, the laws changed public attitudes and their clients did not desert them and they learned that their fears had been groundless.

How has the amount of political contributions influenced how the legislature operates?

The fact that money is important is an irritant. As a lobbyist I would prefer to deal with legislation purely on its merits. In the final analysis, most legislation is decided on its merits.

But it isn't campaign money that has made a difference; it is the full-time legislature. Individual legislators used to be of independent means with jobs in their district and a livelihood. But today you have people who have never had a job outside of public service. Because they have nowhere else to go, getting re-elected is a hell of a lot more important.

The whole thing is out of proportion, but I don't know how you go back. Because of the complexity of society and urbanization and a higher standard of living, the legislative process has gotten more complex.

Without law, the marketing of the title for property becomes very tenuous. Without law, the financing of real property becomes impossible — because you need law to protect the security under which it is financed. Take condos, it was a market response to the new needs of homebuyers, but it required law to make them work.

What is the key to being an effective lobbyist?

The key is doing your homework, being realistic in your goals, and being honest and aboveboard. You might lose one by being honest, but in the long run you will come out better.

There is a tight circle up here and everyone knows everybody. They know if you do your homework — if you bring in reliable information. And they know whether you are honest or not. It is all related to your effectiveness.

Have you found yourself in conflicts between the private interests of Realtors and the public interest?

I don't think so. The real estate industry makes an affirmative contribution to society. We have three to four hundred thousand real estate sales a year in California, and it requires a trained body of people to make the market efficient.

To the extent that I have helped buyers and sellers function, I have acted in the public interest.

13 cities get green light on enterprise zones

Since 1980, President Reagan has hailed enterprise zones as the cure for unemployment and de cay in America's urban centers. But while federal legislative proposals are bogged down in controversy, states like California have been plodding along with their own local version of enterprise zones.

The idea sounds simple: cities designate urban areas that have high unemployment and business disinvestment as enterprise zones. Through tax incentives, government funds are used to prod private employers into locating and expanding businesses within the zones and hiring and training the unemployed.

But putting the idea into practice in California has already involved over three years of state and local government law-making, regulation promulgation and bureaucracy building. Finally, this past month, 13 communities were entitled to begin offering state tax breaks to businesses located in the enterprise zones. It is too early to tell, however, how many employers will jump at the opportunity.

With bipartisan support, California put together an interesting mix of tax credits. Employers earn credits and deductions on their state income taxes for hiring employees that are enrolled in local job training programs, and receive credits on the sales tax they pay on new machinery.

Businesses in the zone are also entitled to write off purchase expenses the first year rather than depreciate the investments over a longer period of time. And to attract private capital, lenders can deduct the interest they earn from income on loans they make to businesses in the zones.

City governments are also expected to throw in their own incentives including a reduction in the cost of development fees, road, water and sewer improvements, job training programs and redevelopment.

Since the zones weren't formally designated until Oct. 15, it is too early to predict whether the state program will make any difference.

"On the margin, it could be effective," says Kurt Chilcott, manager of Enterprise Zones for the State Department of Commerce. "If a firm has already made a decision to move to Fresno, it may choose the zone," he says.

Even if the incentives aren't enough to attract new businesses, it may help shape employment and training activities for those firms that are currently in the zones or for those that have plans to move there.

For example, Michael Jenkins, enterprise zone coordinator for San Diego, points to a planned 20-story Ramada Hotel that "has already broken ground and is looking at taking advantage of the employer and wage incentives Enterprise zones will only work if cities make it a priority."

Careless landlords could face tax problems

When landlords fail to fix a leaky roof, repair a broken toilet or correct an electrical problem, they could find themselves in trouble with the state Franchise Tax Board — they may even lose their state real estate tax write-offs.

The California Substandard Housing Abatement Program requires local fire, health and building departments to notify the state when a property owner persists in ignoring major housing code violations. Once the state confirms the charge, it can deny real estate tax deductions such as mortgage interest and depreciation.

The law is designed to help local agencies do a better job of enforcing building codes. But many local government officials are only vaguely familiar with the requirement, and others are reluctant to use it. Their inaction has spurred housing advocates and legislators to seek amendments to the 1978 law that would put greater pressure on uncooperative landlords.

The statute gives even the most stubborn landlords ample time to avoid the squeeze from the tax board. Upon receiving written notice of major code violations, property owners have six months to correct the problems. If they fail to make the improvements, they are warned that the state Franchise Tax Board will be alerted to the situation. They then have an additional 10 days to appeal before the state actually gets involved.

The state Franchise Tax Board reviewed only 965 cases and inflicted financial penalties on 409 property owners last year. This is just a fraction of the total number of properties that have major code violations. According to a 1981 state study there were more than 1.3 million housing units in need of rehabilitation or total replacement. It is impossible, however, to estimate how many of these dwelling units might meet the abatement program's test of "substandard."

To date, the critical but weak link in the abatement program is problems getting local government to turn over more cases to the state. The legislature foresaw this problem and included a provision that offers local government a financial incentive to participate. The state turns the revenue that would have normally accrued to the benefit of the property owner over to the local agency that brought the case to the state's attention. Last year, local agencies collected $146,000 from the tax board.

San Francisco is one of a handful of cities that have taken advantage of the law; it turned 169 cases over to the Franchise Tax Board in 1985 and earned more than $65,000 from its efforts. "We have been using the law since it was first enacted, and it has proved to be very valuable," says Peter Burns, senior housing inspector with the city.

The law not only punishes slumlords, it also motivates other owners to make repairs more quickly. "When word got out that we were going to report violators to the Tax Board, violations were being corrected much faster," he says.

But according to Franchise Tax Board spokesman Jim Reber, only three cities regularly make use of the program. "Almost all of the activity is occuring in Los Angeles, San Francisco and Oakland." According to Reber, these three cities have most of the substandard housing, which explains why they are so active with the program.

"We have very few situations where the property gets so bad that we need to use it," says Sylvia Ehrenthal, community and economic development director for the city of Hayward. And when it does, Ehrenthal says the city has a workable local procedure for prodding recalcitrant landlords into action.

The new San Diego housing inspection supervisor, Bonnie Contreras, says there has been a perception "that there weren't enough cases to pursue." But she "plans to look into it," and believes "it could be a valuable tool."

Some communities complain that they don't have the political support or the financial resources to develop and carry out a program for inspecting properties, tracking the cases and following-up with problem properties. "Many local jurisdictions haven't made comprehensive housing code enforcement a priority," says Bill Powers of the Western Center on Law and Poverty.

Consequently, the Western Center helped pushed through a bill that would make it easier for local government to recapture all of the costs associated with code enforcement. It was vetoed by the governor, however, because he saw it as a duplication of the existing system for reimbursing local government.

There have been several other attempts to strengthen the abatement law. One proposal would have reduced the amount of time a property owner has to correct violations from six months to 60 days. Real estate industry groups opposed the change, however, arguing that 60 days was not long enough to take out the necessary building permits, hire a contractor, and make the improvements.

Whatever changes are ultimately made, for now the rules are clear: failure to abate serious housing code violations is against the law. And in a few communities, when property owners are stubborn enough to ignore the rules, they may face an onerous financial penalty.

California trends: Neighborhood Watch - more than crime deterrent

One out of every 30 California households was burglarized last year.

Consequently, it's not surprising that hundreds of California communities have clamored to organize Neighborhood Watch programs, a grass-roots crime prevention scheme in which residents join together to fight crime.

But according to state Sen. Ed Davis, R-Los Angeles, the program isn't living up to its original purpose. "Every community in the country has adopted the name of 'Neighborhood Watch, but there is more to it than having a police officer explain how to put reliable locks on your door," says Davis, who pioneered the program in 1970 when he was the Los Angeles police chief.

"A Neighborhood Watch program should help to reweave the social fabric that has been lost in our cities; it's not just stopping burglars, it helps makes a community a better place to live."

Davis says he patterned the program after the thesis in the book 'Territorial Imperative" which described how "a smaller animal on his own turf could successfully fend off a larger animal. We applied the same theory to the Neighborhood Watch program where a group of neighbors working with police officers creates a powerful and dynamic force against criminals," says Davis.

For renters worried about community crime, there is a new twist to Neighborhood Watch: Apartment Watch.

In the San Fernando Valley, tenants are organizing crime prevention programs in apartment buildings. Modeled after the Neighborhood Watch program, tenants and landlords work together to safeguard their apartments and learn techniques for spotting would-be criminals.

"The first step is educating renters to believe that the apartment complex is their neighborhood," says Dianne Wood of the San Fernando Valley Apartment Association. Many residents had never met their neighbors before they attended an Apartment Watch meeting, according to Wood.

The developers of the "2000 Post" apartment project in San Francisco are relying on a high-tech security device for discouraging residential burglars. The building is equipped with a wireless security system that electronically tips off building security when someone tries to break in.

Developed by Mitsubishi of Japan and the Ohio-based Forerunner Company, the new system employs electronic transmitters that monitor doors and windows. When someone tries to break in, a signal is sent to the building's central computer control unit, at which time, security personnel telephone the apartment where the transmission originated. If no one answers, they contact the San Francisco Police Department.

The conventional apartment security system is "hard-wired," according to Vicki King of the Network Multi-family Security Corporation. The Dallas-based firm, which has not yet put a wireless system on the market, is one of several companies that produces apartment security devices found in thousands of California apartments.

In a 'hard-wired' apartment building, the individual units have a similar alert system, except that they are configured using wires instead of transmitters.

"The false alarm rate is about 90 percent in all security systems," says King. And she contends "the 'hard-wired' building does a better job of preventing false alarms."

According to a recent decision by the California Supreme Court, condominium associations must bear some of the responsibility for protecting residents against crime. In the case of Frances T. vs. Village Green Owners Association, a female resident was raped after the association told her to remove unapproved exterior lighting around her unit. The California high court ruled in her favor.

"We are concerned about the decision because volunteer directors of community associations will face greater exposure to civil liability," says attorney Donna May, chairman of the legislative action committee of the Community Association Institute. "This is one of several rulings that discourages people from serving on condo boards — there won't be anyone to run these communities."

California trends: Real Estate experts gaze into the future

Real estate industry groups are making some wildly conflicting statements about their statistics on what kind of mortgages California consumers want.

If you listen to the California Association of Realtors and the California Mortgage Bankers Association, you are led to believe that homebuyers are flocking to the traditional fixed-rate home loans and are snubbing their noses at adjustable-rate mortgages (ARMs).

If you listen to the California League of Savings Institutions and the Federal Home Loan Bank Board, you might conclude that homebuyers are learning to love ARMs.

Each of these groups uses different but reliable data on mortgage activity to support their claims about the home-loan market. But conflicting information is painting a muddled picture for consumers who may be influenced by what type of loan they read or hear is most popular.

Here are a few recent examples of contradictory conclusions drawn from industry research reports:

> *"The decline in interest rates . . . has allowed homebuyers to reassert their preference for traditional long-term fixed-rate financing," concludes a new report put out by the California Association of Realtors. Seventy-nine percent of all new mortgages in the first half of 1986 were fixed-rate compared to only 35.5 percent in 1984, according to CAR.*

> *". . . Adjustable-rate mortgages continue to be the most popular instrument for borrowers at California savings institutions," says a press release issued by the League of Savings. "According to a survey by the Federal Home Loan Bank Board, 67 percent of all home loans originated in California, Arizona and Nevada featured adjustable rates."*

> *There was an "unprecedented 216 percent increase" in the number of new and refinanced fixed-rate single-family loans . . . "while the origination of ARMs remained flat. This represents a strong consumer preferenceuankers Association based on statistics from their 1986 semi-annual survey of loan production.*

In each of these studies, a different survey sample is used to measure the trends   which accounts for the differences in the research results. But it is more than just a debate over who conducts the best research or who collects the most accurate statistics. Because of their particular industry interests, each of the organizations makes sweeping statements about consumer home-loan borrowing habits.

Generally, Realtors would like to see an increase in the supply of competitively-priced fixed-rate mortgages, and savings and loans would like to see a greater consumer appetite for ARMs.

"Despite what lenders are doing to push adjustable-rate mortgages and despite some of the good deals with ARMs, home-buyers aren't interested," says Colleen McFarland, real estate branch manager of Coldwell Banker's Riverside office. According to McFarland, homebuyers don't understand all of the paperwork that explains how an ARM will work and "they are left not knowing exactly what will happen to their payment with a ARM."

Pointing to the number of large California savings and loans that offer only ARMs and yet have record-level loan demand, savings and loan industry representatives argue that the public has accepted ARMs.

"We anticipate lending more than $9 billion in 1986, and we only offer ARMs," says Patricia Harden, vice president of Home Savings, the nation's second largest savings institution. According to Harden, their strict ARM lending policy has not hurt business: "We have far exceeded our 1985 loan volume."

"The people who took out an ARM and never experienced a rise in their mortgage payment are beginning to say this isn't a bad deal," says Joe Humphrey, chief economist with the Federal Home Loan Bank of San Francisco.

"If you compare the costs of a fixed-rate mortgage to an ARM taken out in 1980, homebuyers with adjustables paid less money on their mortgage payments," says UC Berkeley business professor Bob Edelstein.

Edelstein adds, however, that homebuyers are willing to pay a price for the security of a fixed-rate mortgage. "They are paying for insurance against future adjustments in their monthly mortgage payments."

Lenders admit that overcoming consumer resistance to ARMs is a big job. "Initially, our loan officers were as unfamiliar with ARMs as the consumer," says Harden. "We have gone through a comprehensive personnel training process within the institution so that our staff is better equipped to market the ARM."

But real estate brokers argue that the best way to make ARMs more acceptable is for institutions to offer an interest rate noticeably lower than fixed-rate mortgages and to reduce the cap on how high the ARM interest rate can go up in any one period and over the life of the loan.

In the meantime, borrowers looking for trends in the market place should first examine who is making the claims about what is going on.

What we can expect for 1987

First of two parts

TOUGH QUESTIONS are being asked about how well the California real-estate market will perform in 1987. Will tax reform and over-building slow down the pace of new construction? Will home prices and residential land values continue up? Will mortgage rates remain stable? Will housing become more affordable for first-time home buyers? Will the push for rent control gain momentum?

Obviously, no one has the final answers to these questions. But to shed a little light on what we might expect in the new year, I asked a dozen real-estate experts to made their predictions. Here's their forecasts.

Interest rates slip

We predict that interest rates will edge down in 1987. It looks like the Federal Reserve is willing to keep the money supply going to keep interest rates down and the economy propelled.

Because of a seasonal dip in the demand for housing, rates are weakening now. But in the spring and the summer when demand heats up for new homes and refinancing, we could see a slight rise in rates.

With stable and even rising home prices, lenders aren't likely to get tough on loan-qualifying requirements because they won't be as concerned about the borrower's future equity.

Home prices up 6%

The rate of home price appreciation is already beginning to moderate and will continue to slow down in 1987. But we expect prices to rise about six percent, which will be greater than the rate of inflation; we predict the CPI (Consumer Price Index) to be around four percent

There will be 5-to-7 percent fewer homes sold in 1987, but this will leave sales at 440,000 units, making it the third best year in the decade for home sales and twice as high as the bottom of the 1981-1982 recession.

For the average new home buyer, affordability is not going to improve substantially. Income growth and lower interest rates will help compensate for price increases, but affordability will be a bigger problem here than it is in other parts of country.

Home building up 2.9%

With 291,000 housing units receiving building permits in 1986, the pace of residential construction broke all records since 1962. Almost half of that construction was for multi-family development.

Next year we expect single-family housing to remain strong with a 2.9 percent increase over 1986. And we predict that 125,000 of total units constructed will be multi-family housing — condos, townhomes and apartments — a 19.4 percent drop from 1986.

Tax reform and the cap on tax-exempt bond financing will slow down multi-family development, and lower interest rates should keep the single-family market going.

But because of growth limitations, land costs and uncertainty about the market, single-family housing will not be as strong as it might be.

Land values mixed

My forecast on land prices is a mixed bag: It depends on what kind of land you are talking about.

The value of most raw land suitable for development of office and research buildings will continue to decline. Prices will remain stable and even rise somewhat for warehouse and distribution sites because supply and demand of warehouses are in balance in most areas. Land for retail development will vary depending on location.

Land-use policies and problems with financing infrastructure will continue to shield residential land from market pressures that have created a surplus of supply and falling prices on other lands. Consequently and unfortunately, land for housing will continue to be expensive.

In next Sunday's Examiner, predictions on rent control, appraisals and mortgage lending.

California trends: Various factors could affect real estate in '87

Special to the Sun

This year, public policies, interest rates and uncertainty about the economy will push and pull the real estate market in many different directions. In the second of two parts, here is what a few real estate experts predict will occur in 1987.

APPRAISALS

"We are going to see the industry tighten up on appraisals. Along with greater attention to meeting new federal regulatory requirements, there will be a need for more expertise and better accreditations of appraisers and more emphasis on classroom training. We will see improvements made in the computerization of the appraisal system so that it becomes easier and faster for both the lender and the consumer.

"It will continue to be tough to obtain reliable appraisals on commercial and industrial buildings because it is difficult to arrive at an accurate value for these types of projects-it is hard to get price comparable and demand is more volatile."
Michael Salkin
First Interstate Bank, Los Angeles

MORTGAGE FINANCE

"The thrift industry is schizophrenic. Most savings and loans, especially the large well-run ones, are making solid profits and adding to their net worth. Also, a huge demand for home financing has generated enormous fees.

"But several hundred associations are essentially bankrupt. The Federal Savings and Loan Insurance Corporation does not have enough money to perform its function of rescuing them or getting them out of business — except very slowly.

"Some financial institutions that are trying to get rid of real estate owned deals are making cash for trash loans: the lender offers a very low interest rate if the borrower also buys a bad property, financed at the same rate. This will be a tremendous opportunity in 1987 for the construction industry to work out troubled properties at advantageous interest rates."
Susan Giles
Laventhol and Horwath Real Estate Advisory Services

SACRAMENTO SCENE

"I think the major issue to be debated in the legislature will be residential rent control and the debate over rent guidelines — an approach that I support because it would provide relief from unreasonable rent control rules. We will also be pursuing a bill for preemption of commercial rent control. This is in reaction to commercial rent control that was enacted in Berkeley and proposed in other cities.

"Another prominent issue will be tax simplification. Legislation that is being introduced to create a flat state income tax is certain to have ramifications for real estate. For example, one onerous element would be putting a cap on the amount of mortgage interest that homeowners can deduct.

"Another issue will be liability exposure for property owners. I will pursue legislation that would overturn a state Supreme Court case that held a property owner liable for property defects that the owner had no knowledge of."
Sen. John Seymour
R-Orange County

RENT, TENANT ISSUES

"As long as the real estate industry is insisting on total rent regulation decontrol when units are vacated, I see a continuing stalemate on the rent control issue in Sacramento. But I do think we should consider statewide legislation that would exempt new construction from rent control.

"We also have to insure that any tax simplification bill doesn't take away the tax credit for renters. Tenants have always been getting the short end of the stick in the tax code, and maintaining this tax credit is a small step towards equity with homeowners who can deduct their mortgage interest payments."
Lenny Goldberg
Lobbyist for Berkeley and West Hollywood rent control boards

BUYING A HOME

"I'm in a quandary over all of this. Prices are outrageous here: 50 percent higher than where I came from in Connecticut. Plus, location adds $25,000 to the price, and a garage is worth another $25,000. So next year, I must decide whether I want to be in a neighborhood that isn't considered a prime area or go for a smaller unit with fewer amenities."
Suzanne Sarra

California trends: Uncertainty tops expectations for real estate in 1987

Second of two parts

PUBLIC POLICIES, interest rates and uncertainty about the economy are expected to push and pull the real-estate market in many different directions this year. Here is what some of the experts predict for the new year as well as some general observations.

Tighter appraisals

We are going to see the industry tighten up on appraisals. Along with greater attention to meeting new federal regulatory requirements, there will be a need for more expertise and better accreditation of appraisers and more emphasis on classroom training. We will see improvements made in the computerization of the appraisal system so that it becomes easier and faster for both the lender and the consumer.

It will continue to be tough to obtain reliable appraisals on commercial and industrial buildings because it is difficult to arrive at an accurate value for these types of projects. It is hard to get price com-parables and demand is more volatile.
—Michael Salkin

First Interstate Bank, Los Angeles

S&Ls schizophrenic

The thrift industry is schizophrenic. Most savings and loans, especially the large well-run ones, are making solid profits and adding to their net worth. Also, a huge demand for home financing has generated enormous fees.

But several hundred associations are essentially bankrupt The Federal Savings and Loan Insurance Corp. does not have enough money to perform its function of rescuing them or getting them out of business — except very slowly.

Some financial Institutions that are trying to get rid of real estate are making "cash for trash" loans: The lender offers a very low interest rate if the borrower also buys a bad property, financed at the same rate. This will be a tremendous opportunity in 1987 for the construction industry to work out troubled properties at advantageous interest rates.
— Susan Giles

Laventhol and Horwath Real Estate Advisory Services, San Francisco

The legislative agenda

The major issue to be debated in the Legislature will be residential rent control and the debate over rent guidelines — an approach that I support because it would provide relief from unreasonable rent control rules. We will also be pursuing a bill for pre-emption of commercial rent control. This is in reaction to commercial rent control that was enacted in Berkeley and proposed in other cities.

Another prominent issue will be tax simplification. Legislation that is being introduced to create a flat state income tax is certain to have ramifications for real estate. For example, one onerous element would be putting a cap on the amount of mortgage interest that homeowners can deduct.

Another issue will be liability exposure for property owners. I will pursue legislation that would overturn a state Supreme Court case that held a property owner liable for property defects that the owner had no knowledge of.

— State Sen. John Seymour Orange County

Tenants Issues

As long as the real-estate industry is insisting on total rent regulation decontrol when units are vacated, I see a continuing stalemate on the rent control issue in Sacramento. But I do think we should consider statewide legislation that would exempt new construction from rent control.

We also have to ensure that any tax simplification bill doesn't take away the tax credit for renters. Tenants have always been getting the short end of the stick in the tax code.

The timing may be right in 1987 to develop a greatly expanded housing coalition — where tenant organizations, unions and church groups join with the real estate industry to push for all types of affordable housing.

— Lenny Goldberg

Lobbyist for Berkeley and West Hollywood Rent Control Boards, Sacramento

Home buying

I'm in a quandary over all of this. Prices are outrageous here. They are 50 percent higher than where I came from in Connecticut Plus, location adds $25,000 to the price, and a garage is worth another $25,000, So next year, I must decide whether I want to be in a neighborhood that isn't considered a prime area or go for a smaller unit.

I am thankful I have a patient real estate agent; he has become my therapist through it all.

— Suzanne Sarra

California trends: Apartment, investor tax change costly to state

Special to the Sun

An arcane change to state tax law affecting real estate may be much more costly for the California state treasury than originally predicted.

In 1984, when the legislature made an esoteric change in how apartment developers and real estate investors would be taxed, state officials may have underestimated the amount of foregone state tax revenue by millions of dollars. And, according to real estate experts, the change had little to do with the recent surge in apartment construction — which was the original purpose for making the change.

When the bill was being considered by the state legislature, Department of Finance and Franchise Tax Board officials predicted that the bill would reduce the annual tax bite for all apartment developers and investors by $5 million to $15 million. And though consistent with the best projections at the time, they underestimated the number of apartments that would be developed by at least 50,000 units.

Complete reports on the lost revenue will not be available from the Franchise Tax Board until later this year. But, theoretically, the annual loss to the treasury could be $3.6 million to more than $10.8 million higher than the official estimate.

In 1984, the state was experiencing record-low apartment vacancies, spiraling rents and a virtual halt to new construction, and public officials were scrambling to find ways to stimulate the development of rental housing. By allowing speedier write-offs for the depreciation of new apartment buildings, the legislation promised to help spur the production of rental housing. The bill was also intended to bring state depreciation rules into conformity with federal law.

When the bill was being considered, Ellen Worcester, legislative analyst for the Assembly Committee on Revenue and Taxation, challenged the conventional wisdom about the rental market. In her analysis she said, "the bill's supporters asserted that construction of rental housing is 'largely now not economically viable.' "But she disputed that claim saying that "statistics . . . show a recent surge in housing construction in California."

Worcester's analysis was right on the mark: the 'surge' became a full-blown statewide boom in rental construction. From July 1, 1985 (the date the bill went into effect) through July 1, 1986, there were building permits taken out for more than 163,000 multi-family housing units. According to Ben Bortolloto of the Construction Industry Research Board, at least 75 percent of these multi-family permits were for apartments — representing 121,000 rentals for the year.

The state agencies calculated their estimates of foregone state revenue based on a forecast of 70,000 apartments — consistent with other housing forecasts but 72 percent shy of what was ultimately built.

On the surface, the record surge in apartment construction implies that the measure was successful and the lost revenue may have been worth it. But experts say that the vast majority of the apartments would have been built regardless of what the state did on depreciation. Federal tax laws, lower interest rates, escalating rents, and demand for rental housing were the critical forces behind the rental boom.

"In the projects that we were syndicating, it was never brought up as an advantage in the financing of our developments," says Rick Holliday of Bridge Housing, Inc. "Therefore, from our experience, it was never an issue," says Holliday.

"It made life easier because of the conformity question, but it did nothing to affect our decision to build new apartments," said one very large developer that didn't want to be identified.

Worcester says that the state tax rate is substantially lower than federal tax rate and, therefore, they always question whether marginal reductions in state taxes are meaningful enough change behavior. "In other cases, we have found that they are not," says Worcester.

But for projects that were on the borderline of financial feasibility, the law may have put them over the edge. An analysis performed by the Center for Real Estate at UC Berkeley said that the change "would give a significant marginal incentive to new rental construction . . ." The report predicted the change would "produce an additional 5,980 to 9,200 multi-family housing starts in 1985 . . ."

The UC Berkeley analysis also pointed out that offsetting the foregone state revenue "would be substantial revenue gain from: 1) the production of new rental housing...; 2) the recapture of depreciation on the sale of the complex; 3) the capital gains taxes from the sale of the complex; 4) income tax revenue collected from the new projects and 5) property taxes on the newly built units.

But if you assume most of the apartments would have been built regardless of the depreciation change, then the capital gains, income and property taxes would have been collected without the legislation.

Theoretically, the nominal tax savings received by developers and investors could have been passed on to the consumer through discounted rents. But in a prototypical project, the developer or investor would receive annual tax savings of $215 per unit according to the Berkeley study. And, therefore, even if the entire amount was passed on to the tenant, the rent reductions would be less than $20 per month.

With recent changes in federal tax law that again lengthen the depreciation period for rental housing, state officials are likely to reconsider their actions on this law. They may decide they aren't getting enough bang for the public tax buck.

California Trends: Last decade's back-to-the-city movement going back to suburbs

(First of Two Parts.)

In the '70s, there was speculation that the next generation of the Americans would reverse the suburban exodus and carve out a new version of the American dream in the heart of the city — trading a manicured lawn on the 18th green for a turn-of-the-century run-down Victorian or a downtown condo.

But the results have been mixed: A few urban neighborhoods have enjoyed a remarkable renaissance but most communities remain stuck in the murk of urban decay.

"The whole promise of urban revitalization was overstated as compared to what happened," says H. James Brown, director of the Harvard University State, Local and Intergovernmental Center. "There was never really a movement back to the cities — it was more myth than reality," he says.

Migration trends show that suburbia remains immensely more popular than city living. Except for a handful of booming sunbelt com. munities, every major city in the country has experienced a loss in population in the last two decades.

In the middle '70s, when a few young urban pioneers began buying older homes and fixing them up, the urban-metamorphosis theory appeared to have merit:

Increased transportation costs brought on by the oil embargo forced people to consider moving closer to their jobs.

Some of the most affordable real estate values in any community were found in inner-city neighborhoods.

Young singles and married couples purportedly possessed a different set of values including a respect for the old and the historic, greater tolerance for heterogeneity and an abhorrence for the suburban way of life.

Tax breaks, federal grants and historic preservation designations were pushed through at all levels of the government which awarded a financial boost to those choosing to live in the city.

Almost every city in the country has a prototypical revitalized neighborhood: Brooklyn Heights in New York, Rockridge in Oakland, Golden Hill in San Diego, Denver's Capitol Hill, the South End in Boston, Chicago's Wicker Park, and even the West Bluff in Peoria.

But on the other hand, the same cities have plenty of neighborhoods that haven't been transformed like the Bronx, West Oakland, Southeast San Diego, Five-Corners in Denver, the Southside of Peoria, Roxbury in Boston, and parts of Chicago's Southside.

The neighborhoods that have experienced the most profound change have a particular set of characteristics. "The change is found in the elite or historic neighborhoods — those that already have a little prestige," says Brown.

"Some areas become like a magnet and they change overnight," says San Francisco community activist Brad Paul. "But others never reach a critical mass, and in these neighborhoods you won't find boutiques or places serving cappuccino."

Population statistics demonstrate how limp the back-to-the-city movement has been. "In the 1970s there was net-out migration from our nation's cities, and it has continued into the '80s," says Kathryn Nelson, a U.S. Department of Housing and Urban Development economist and author of the forthcoming book "Will Migration Revive Distressed Cities?"

Compounding the problem are the incomes of those who have jumped ship. A greater share of higher-income people have been moving out of cities while a larger share of lower-income residents have stayed.

Urban theorists say this trend leads to a vicious cycle. When the affluent leave, the city is left with more poor people and increased pressure on city services and, consequently, higher taxes. This leads to a stronger incentive for businesse and the remaining higher income residents to flee.

Nevertheless, Nelson says there is evidence that this cycle can be cracked, and she uses Washington, D C. as an example where the out-migration of higher-income people has slowed.

So why hasn't the return-to-the-city trend ever fully materialized? There may be a sociological dimension. "The people that decided to move into the cities in the 1970s were at the tail end of the '60s consciousness; their counterparts in the '80s are the young MBAs that are more like an earlier generation and want to move to the suburbs," says Dick LeGates, urban policy professor at San Francisco State University.

There was also a clash of public policies that has cast a shadow over the merits of gentrification. Many poor and lower-middle income neighborhoods didn't welcome the idea of the new young gentry bringing on higher rents and a dramatic shift in neighborhood character.

"The poor got pushed out of the newly discovered neighborhoods into not-so-prime neighborhoods," says Harvard's Brown. "So just when the center city phenomenon began, gentrification and condo-conversion policies — sensitive to the problem of the poor — slowed it down," he says.

Despite the signs, it may be too early to judge the final outcome of the urban renaissance movement. "We don't know for sure if it is merely a blip in the long term suburban dream," says LeGates.

California trends: Back to the city: Results are mixed

Special to the Sun

This is the first of a two-part series called "Back to the city: A movement or not." The series looks at some urban areas that have been reborn and others that are still in decay.

In the 1970's, there was speculation that the next generation of Americans would reverse the suburban exodus and carve out a new version of the American dream in the heart of the city — trading a manicured lawn on the 18th green for a turn-of-the-century rundown Victorian or a downtown condo.

But the results have been mixed: a few urban neighborhoods have enjoyed a remarkable renaissance but most communities remain stuck in the murk of urban decay.

"The whole promise of urban revitalization was overstated as compared to what happened," says H. James Brown, director of Harvard University's State, Local and Intergovernmental Center. "There was never really a movement back to the cities — it was more myth than reality," he says.

Migration trends show that suburbia remains immensely more popular than city living. Except for a handful of booming sunbelt communities, every major city in the country has experienced a loss in population in the last two decades.

In the middle 70s, when a few young urban pioneers began buying older homes and fixing them up, the urban-metamorphosis theory appeared to have merit:

Increased transportation costs brought on by the oil embargo forced people to consider moving closer to their jobs.

Some of the most affordable real estate values in any community were found in inner-city neighborhoods.

Young singles and married couples purportedly possessed a different set of values including a respect for the old and the historic, greater tolerance for heterogeneity and an abhorrence for the suburban way of life.

Tax breaks, federal grants and historic preservation designations were pushed through at all levels of the government which awarded a financial boost to those choosing to live in the city.

Almost every city in the country has a prototypical revitalized neighborhood: Brooklyn Heights in New York, Rockridge in Oakland. Golden Hill in San Diego, Denver's Capitol Hill, the South End in Boston, Chicago's Wicker Park, and even the West Bluff in Peoria.

But on the other hand, the same cities have plenty of neighborhoods that haven't been transformed like the Bronx, West Oakland. Southeast San Diego. Five-corners in Denver, the Southside of Peoria, Roxbury in Boston, and parts of Chicago's Southside.

The neighborhoods that have experienced the most profound change have a particular set of characteristics. "The change is found in the elite or historic neighborhoods — those that already have a little prestige," says Brown.

"Some areas become like a magnet and they change overnight," says San Francisco community activist Brad Paul. "But others never reach a critical mass, and in these neighborhoods you won't find boutiques or places serving cappuccino."

Population statistics demonstrate how limp the back-to-the-city movement has been. "In the 1970s there was net-out migration from our nation's cities, and it has continued into the 80s,' says Kathryn Nelson, a U.S. Department of Housing and Urban Development economist and author of the forthcoming book "Will Migration Revive Distressed Cities?"

Compounding the problem are the incomes of those who have jumped ship. A greater share of higher-income people have been moving out of cities while a larger share of lower-income residents have stayed. Urban theorists say this trend leads to a vicious cycle. When the affluent leave, the city is left with more poor people and increased pressure on city services and, consequently, higher taxes. This leads to a stronger incentive for businesses and the remaining higher-income residents to flee.

Washington DC, Nelson says, is an example that this cycle can be cracked.

So why hasn't the return-to-the-city trend ever fully materialized? There may be a sociological dimension. "The people that decided to move into the cities in the 1970s were at the tail end of the 60s consciousness; their counterpart in the 80s are the young MBAs that are more like an earlier generation and want to move to the suburbs," says Dick LeGates, urban policy professor at San Francisco State University.

One discouraging feature to city life has been the condition of the public school system. "The real question that the back-to-the-city movement always faced was whether it would continue after families began to have children and were forced to make decisions about putting their kids through an urban education," says Robert W. Burchell, Ph.D., director of research at the Center for Urban Policy Research at Rutgers University.

There was also a clash of public policies that has cast a shadow over the merits of gentrification. Many poor and lower-middle income neighborhoods didn't welcome the idea of the new young gentry bringing on higher rents a dramatic shift in character.

"The poor got pushed out of the newly discovered neighborhoods into not-so-prime neighborhoods," says Harvard's Brown. "So just when the center city phenomenon began, gentrification and condo-conversion policies sensitive to the problem of the poor slowed it down." he says.

California trends: Housing groups invade capitol

Special to the Sun

The state's tight and expensive housing market is bad news for thousands of Californians who can't afford the high rents and outlandish home prices. But getting something done about the housing quagmire is full of political hurdles.

That explains why every conceivable interest group upset over the lack of affordable housing is converging on Sacramento this week to attend a battery of brainstorming sessions, strategy workshops and meetings with legislators and administrative leaders. In a five-day period, three consecutive conferences are being held, designed to elevate the importance of the housing issue among public officials.

The housing powwows are being sponsored by the California Coalition for Rural Housing, the California Homeless Coalition, and Old St. Mary's Housing Committee. Activists from every corner of the state representing the concerns of the homeless, the poor, the disabled, non-profit developers and farmworkers will travel to the capitol to participate in the events.

John Mealy of the Coachella Valley Housing Coalition in Riverside County will be one of those attending, and he plans to provide some input on how state housing programs can be improved. "We want people in Sacramento to know a little more about our problems down here."

Mealy's group is concerned about farmworker housing, and they are critical of how uneven state housing aid is dispersed. "There are 26 migrant farmworker camps and none of them are in Southern California."

He will also be drumming for the state to spend more money on housing assistance — a theme that will run throughout the conference. To illustrate the need, Mealy points to a recently completed development financed by the Farmers Home Administration where more than 800 people applied for 50 available units.

Another attendee, David Foster, director of the Santa Barbara Community Housing Corporation is nervous about how the cutbacks in federal and state aid will affect their work in housing development, cooperative housing conversions and housing rehabilitation.

"We used to be 80-90 percent funded by the state and federal government; now it is down to 10-15 percent," says Foster. The organization has had to rely more on local funding and "has had to become more professional and efficient in order to adjust to the shortage of resources," he says.

The money pinch has forced the Santa Barbara group to shift more of their attention from low-income housing problems to the problems of moderate-income families. "This will contribute to the homeless problem," says Foster.

Not surprisingly, a hot topic at the Sacramento confab will be the homeless problem — the ugliest side of the state's affordable housing squeeze. A recent Mervin D. Field California Poll found homelessness to be the fifth most frequently identified problem in the state.

But housing advocates are pessimistic about their ability to capitalize on the recent attention given to homelessness. "As I walk the halls of the legislature, I continue to hear that the time isn't right to do something about it," says California Rural Legal Assistance Foundation attorney Marcus Brown. "We are told to lower our expectations," he says.

Nevertheless, it hasn't slowed down their push to seek more assistance for the homeless. "We have a whole series of bills that could help solve the problem," says Brown.

No California housing symposium would be legitimate without some discussion of rent control. Consequently, the California Tenants Conference has a spot on their agenda for discussing "offensive strategies to fight anti-rent control bills."

No official announcement has been made about a housing industry bill aimed at curbing local rent control rules, but tenant advocates expect a rent control preemption bill to be introduced again this year. Attempts to limit local rent control rules have been averted in the last three sessions of the legislature.

"One of our major concerns is the anti-rent control measure — we know it will come up again," says Bruce Livingston, a San Francisco tenant and leader of the Old St. Mary's Housing Committee which is sponsoring the Tenants Conference.

Besieging state rent control hearings with busloads of angry tenants, Old St. Mary's has been a powerful organizer in previous campaigns to defeat the anti-rent control measures.

But Livingston says that rent control isn't the only purpose for organizing the conference. "We will also be looking for legislation that will support affordable housing subsidies, methods for handling illegal units, and ways for building more housing."

No one attending the low-income housing events in Sacramento this week expects to walk away with more money or policy commitments, but they plan to show why a dearth of affordable housing is worthy of more attention.

Industry searching for effective no-growth response

(Second of three parts.)

With the no-growth movement spreading to communities all over the state, the real estate industry has yet to come up with an effective response.

"On growth control, the industry is coming from behind in the political power curve," says Susan DeSantis, senior vice president of Nelson, Ralston, Robb Communications, a consulting firm that has handled a number of growth initiatives for developers in Southern California.

"When the real estate market got good, the industry became too engaged in the business of development and didn't look at the looming macro effects of growth control," says Gary Hambly, staff vice president of the Building Industry Association of Northern California.

As more and more communities take up the slow-growth cause, builders, real estate agents and other development groups are learning what doesn't work: espousing simplistic pro-growth rhetoric has no credibility when traffic levels reach near gridlock levels; blaming environmental extremists falls on deaf ears when the no-growth sentiment cuts across all political and economic lines; and hefty industry campaign war chests are useless when no one wants to listen to their campaign arguments.

"Today we are dealing with legitimate concerns about growth," says Ms. DeSantis. "Some of the recent defeats are starting to galvanize a keener understanding of that reality and the need for a pro-active developer response."

With a sharp crowd of suburbanites leading the charge, the slow-it-down movement of the '80s is sophisticated and organized. They understand planning and development issues, they grasp relevant land-use laws, and they don't preach with a tone of the lunatic-fringe. They talk about traffic congestion, infrastructure, levels of service, and environmental impacts with conviction and eloquence.

Developers are finding the conventional weapons for fighting growth control measures to be outdated. Mega-buck ballot box campaigns, proposals to have the state step in and override local decisions, and expensive lawsuits have been unsuccessful in holding back the tide of growth control.

In 1986, the industry's record at the ballot box was marginal. Of the 38 no-growth initiatives, 21 passed, according to a report by the California Association of Realtors. And it wasn't for lack of money.

More than $500,000 was spent last year on a single referendum in Newport Beach that was designed to stop the Irvine Co. from expanding its successful Newport Center; the bulk of the money was spent by Irvine to defeat the measure. Nevertheless, by a vote of 58-42 percent, the voters said no to the developer.

On the rent control front, industry groups have developed an invincible strategy for beating local initiatives — winning all but a handful in the last several years. But on growth control, every initiative is different, and as one industry lobbyist said, "the political consultants haven't found a cookie-cutter formula" for defeating them.

One gimmick being tried is to place an alternative and less restrictive initiative on the ballot at the same time a no-growth measure is being considered. The alternate initiative may slow down development but is not as draconian as the original measure. In 1986, this maneuver failed in San Mateo county but succeeded in Carlsbad. The Carlsbad victory has given real estate groups enough hope to try it in other parts of San Diego county.

Some builders want to see the state legislature tighten up on the local initiative process. But Building Industry Association (BIA) lobbyist Don Collins is not very optimistic: "No bill will pass that tries to circumvent the initiative process, and anything the legislature does the courts will undo."

Nevertheless, the BIA has a proposal that would require initiative ballot descriptions to include impartial titles and summaries. It is designed to discourage measures that exaggerate a growth problem or hype the effects of a proposed building plan. But Collins concedes the proposal has a major drawback: who would review the ballot measure to determine its objectivity?

The California Association of Realtors and the California Building Industry Association, leaders on this issue in the past, admit they have not developed a coordinated statewide plan for addressing the growth issue.

"We haven't turned our backs on the problem, but we haven't figured out exactly what to do about it," says Robert Rivinius, executive vice president of the California Building Industry Association. "It's a statewide problem, but it is happening at the local level where there is no simple statewide solution."

Bob Kaulick, chairman of the Realtors' Issue Mobilization Political Action Committee, thinks the upswing in no-growth measures can be blamed on a lack of education. "If people understand the consequences of their actions, then we say go ahead and enact growth control," he says. "But in the emotional moment of a no-growth vote, people don't realize what trade-offs they are making."

Kaulick says the Realtors will begin to discuss the idea of developing an education program on growth control. "But any successful plan will take at least five years," he says.

In the meantime, those determined to slow down growth have the upper hand.

Next week: Efforts to implement alternatives to strict no-growth measures are gaining favor in some communities.

Elmwood: Main Street with a twist

Special To the Examiner

LOOKING FOR Main Street, U.S.A., in the Bay Area? Try Berkeley's Elmwood district.

On the surface, it's as traditional as apple pie: tree-lined streets, a quaint little post office, a public library, a movie theater, a old-fashioned soda fountain, a couple of banks, and kids. Straddling College Avenue south of the university, it's a place where you would expect people to settle down and live happily ever after.

When you look closer at the neighborhood, however, you discover another side to this upper-middle-class community. In the tradition of Berkeley, Elmwood has been a rebel, a pacesetter and a laboratory for controversial—some would consider zany—ideas.

Since its days as an early warrior in the neighborhood movement of the 70s, Elmwood has been an incubator for such radical planning concepts as commercial rent control, permanent traffic barriers, and quotas on what types of businesses are allowed to locate in the area.

It's interesting, however, that all of these unorthodox proposals were advanced to retain traditional and conservative neighborhood qualities—an idealized small-town flavor with an insulated, peaceful and protected environment.

In practical terms, the planning schemes were intended to regulate out the glitzy intruders—the boutiques, the fern bars and the upscale restaurants. It was a way for the neighborhood to turn its back on the urban trends of the last decade and avoid becoming cuter than it already was.

When you visit Elmwood, you get the sense that the neighborhood activists have succeeded, though the jury is still out on the long-term impact of their policies.

Strategically located on the residential streets of Elmwood, traffic barriers purposely trip-up drivers when they attempt short cuts through the neighborhood.

When you try to beat the system, you wind up getting lost or totally confused and ultimately add to your drive time. I have been befuddled by the traffic maze more than once; it makes me feel like I'm up against a full-court press from Bobby Knight's Indiana Hoosiers—which is exactly the plan. I inevitably start mumbling nasty things about Berkeley.

By shunning certain types of businesses, the spot-zoning scheme also keeps the community provincial. The C1B (E) zoning district limits the number of women's clothing stores to seven, the number of full-service restaurants to seven and the number of banks to two.

With some exceptions, the 1982 commercial rent control ordinance rolled back rents on buildings along College and Ashby to 1981 levels and promised affordable rents for the existing merchants.

In combination, these policies have probably soured any market predilections for turnings Elmwood into a regional shopping hot spot.

Today, Elmwood has a weird blend of businesses. A few of the high-tech upscale shops, such as the Slater Marinoff furniture store, do business in Elmwood. You will also find a superb produce market, several cleaners, a hardware store, a drug store, and a shoe repair shop, along with dozens of other business establishments.

My favorite is Dream Fluff Donuts. Right out of the Midwest, they still serve traditional pig-out dough-nuts such as the colossal chocolate long john.

Another neighborhood gem is the Elmwood Post Office. Staffed by friendly postal employees and equipped with scales and visible facts on rates and zip codes, it is uniquely designed to expedite your visit. And if you get tired or want to read your P. O. Box mail, there are two couches in the lobby.

Don't let me mislead you about bliss in Elmwood: not everyone supports Elmwood's progressive public policies. When commercial rent control was proposed, red flags about property rights popped up all over. Some life-long residents concede that the traffic barriers can be a real irritant, and everyone agrees that parking is a big hassle in Elmwood.

While the land-use rules are busy preventing the commercial strip from being saturated with fashionable boutiques, the neighborhood itself is becoming increasingly affluent.

If you are looking to buy a home in Elmwood, expect to pay $200,000 to $400,000. And prices are on the upswing — eager buyers far outnumber the sellers.

For those who can afford to buy a home in Elmwood, there are some terrific traditional Berkeley brown-shingle homes. And up near the beautiful Claremont Hotel, expensive tudors and mediterraneans are occasionally on the market.

As for renters, residential rent controls keep rents down but vacancies are gobbled up in a flash.

Close to BART with ready access to the AC Transit express bus, Elmwood is an ideal mid-point for the San Francisco white-collar commuter.

Considering Elmwood lives in a big town with powerful urban pressures, my romanticized small-town impressions could dissolve quickly. Bordered by a booming university, socked with sky-high real estate values, loaded with hefty investments and heavyweight investors, Elmwood's foundation of neighborhood control is subject to wear and tear.

On my sensible and livable scale: There is nothing spectacular about Elmwood; and, for now, that's what Elmwood residents seem to like about it.

Low-income housing tax credit pushed

Making the 1986 Tax Reform Act work for affordable housing is easier said than done. Five months after the revolutionary federal tax reform law took effect, housing groups are scrambling to take advantage of an obscure element of tax reform: credits for investment in low-income housing.

The credits were intended to be a bright spot in the morass of bad news that tax reform created for real estate; the radical tax law change levies a stiffer capital gains tax, lengthens the depreciable life of property and restricts the benefits for passive losses.

And while low-income housing is one of the only tax-shelter games in town, the jury is still out on how well the idea of tax benefits for investment in housing will perform in the market place.

"Eight out of every 10 real estate deals you look at for potential tax credit use will not work," says property owner and real estate investor John Stewart.

Offering an attractive tax windfall to investors in low-income housing, the new law is designed to give a financial boost to new and rehabilitated apartment projects. In return, it requires that the rents on a share of the apartments be maintained at below-market levels.

"The trade-off in lost rents can create a penalty that is greater than the benefit of the tax credits," says Stewart. These concerns have delayed making the tax scheme an attractive investment reality.

"The sub-title to a story on tax credits is 'What if they gave a tax credit party and nobody came?'" says Paul Grogan, president of the New York-based Local Initiatives Support Corporation (LISC). "People are starting to ask if it is just off to a slow start or is it basically a flawed concept," he says.

"Nevertheless, we are trying to show that low-income housing tax credits can work in particular circumstances," says Grogan. LISC has launched a national campaign to attract corporate investors to their National Equity Fund.

Using the low-income tax credit as a hook, LISC is successfully luring corporations to fund a $20-$30 million pool for low-income housing. It's a laudable and attainable goal according to Grogan: LISC has commitments from Continental Insurance Company of New York, Connecticut's Stanley Tool Company, and Hallmark Corporation of Kansas City, and they are busy selling one million dollar shares to other corporations. According to Grogan, LISC has raised 50 percent of its goal.

The business community is being targeted for the investment because the full benefit of the tax credit is not as attractive to the traditional real estate investor — which explains why big stock brokerage firms and syndicators are cautiously moving into the tax credit game. Individual investors can only take $7,000 in credits in any one year, and eligibility for tax reductions phase out for those earning more than $200,000.

The LISC program is modeled after an equity fund that was successfully launched in Chicago in 1985 — before tax considerations made the idea more attractive. The Chicago Equity Fund raised more than $11 million from twenty major Chicago companies; their efforts generated $45 million in affordable housing investment in the Chicago area.

Created by East Coast developer and philanthropist James Rouse, the Enterprise Foundation has also become a leader in attracting business investment to affordable housing. A socially-motivated non-profit organization, Enterprise has convinced the largest corporations in Cleveland to take advantage of the tax credit by investing $2.1 million in low-income housing projects.

In San Francisco, the International Hotel site is slated to be financed by low-income housing tax credit investors. In the heart of Chinatown, the 126-unit elderly project hopes to attract $7.5 million in equity financing from local corporations.

The San Francisco development does, however, depend on other government subsidies. To make the deal possible, the City of San Francisco is throwing in a $3 million grant and additional public support will be necessary.

Experts agree that the tax credit alone will not make affordable housing possible. "For every dollar of tax credit, another $1.25 to $2.50 in public funds will be required," says Gary Squier, Vice President of the Corporate Fund for Housing in Los Angeles.

For this reason, housing experts predict that California will be slow to take full advantage of the tax credit. Compared to other states with major affordable housing problems such as New York and Massachusetts, California has retreated from spending more government funds for housing.

Housing expert Dan Pearlman of the National Housing Law Project said, "The state allocation for tax credits is $32 million . . . and I think it will be oversubscribed."

In the final analysis, it will be "neither a bonanza nor a bust in the real estate investment market place," says Steve Roulac, head of the Roulac Real Estate Consulting Group at Deloitte, Haskins and Sells.

Special to the Examiner: San Rafael: the hub of Marin County

WHEN YOU DRIVE through San Rafael on 101, you can't miss seeing the ugly sound walls that line both sides of the highway. And if you didn't know that these atrocious 12-foot-high brick bulwarks were designed to deaden the automobile noise, you might conclude that you are passing through an exclusionary Marin County community.

It's not true, however. Dubbed the Hub, the 22-squaremile community of San Rafael is a heterogeneous and vibrant mini-city that straddles the center of the county but defies Marin stereotyping.

With its unique suburban/urban/small town identity, San Rafael should never feel the need to emulate its more celebrated neighbors to the south, Sausalito et al, or Novato, its boom-town neighbor to the north. San Rafael is a self-reliant little city of 45,000 people — many of whom live and work in the town.

With the only major commercial, light-industrial and office uses north of San Francisco, San Rafael is the job center for the county, as well as its retail mecca and county seat. Add that to a wide range of housing choices near the water, in the hills and on the flats, and it becomes a formula for a livable community.

Giving San Rafael a rich metro flavor is a trend towards ethnic diversity. Nearly one third of the students in the San Rafael public schools belong to a minority group — predominately Asian and Hispanic — and twenty-six different languages are spoken as a second language.

On any housing non-affordarbility scale from 1-10, Marin County always earns a ten. In the context of Marin's outrageous home prices, however, San Rafael has some values.

For example, along the densely developed parts of the canal which runs from the Bay to the freeway, there are hundreds of relatively inexpensive condominiums and apartments. Small condos on the canal can be snatched up for as low as $70,000, and rents begin at about $550 to $600 a month.

For determined single-family home buyers, the best values are in Sun Valley and Gerstle Park where prices begin at around $170,000. In well-maintained flatland neighborhoods, older homes sit on tree-lined streets.

The vast majority of the new development is occuring on the east side around Peacock Gap Country Club. You'll pay a premium, but you'll get a prestigious address in a well planned part of town.

For those who prefer historic older homes, San Rafael has plenty of choices on the west side in the Dominican College area. In this neighborhood you can buy a small starter home that needs work for under $200,000, and at the other extreme, you can pay more than one million dollars for homes in this area.

In Culloden Park, across town from the college, grand old estates and converted carriage houses are occasionally on the market — some with spectacular views of Mt. Tamalpais.

For individuals with special housing needs. San Rafael has several opportunities. Built with a terrific view of the civic center, the valley and the bay, the Villa Marin life-care facility is a very livable senior development.

For seniors who need affordable housing, the Rotary Manor development is an alternative. It was built by the local Rotarians in partnership with the county.

San Rafael had a scare a couple of years ago when the Village shopping center opened in Corte Madera and threatened to kill the vibrant San Rafael downtown. But the competition hasn't been all that bad. Today, downtown vacancies are rare, and the space that was left vacant when the Village opened has been gobbled back up.

A more serious dilemma is the 101 traffic mess which has forced the political leaders in all of Marin County to engage in some intense collective civic introspection. Located in the middle of the notorious 101 traffic snarl, San Rafael is at the center of the debate.

The scramble to find solutions to traffic has spilled over to deliberations on the city's proposed general plan—a blueprint for San Rafael's future growth and development. To mitigate future traffic congestion, the futuristic document hopes to achieve a greater equilibrium between employment and residences.

"The city will still be a jobs center in the county, but less so than under the existing plan," states the plan. It doesn't necessarily call for a radical slow-down in the pace of job growth, though it does recommend a shift in policy.

Released late last year, the plan is now facing a barrage of criticism from those who would like to see economic development accelerate rather than creep along. "The proposed plans are long on preservation of the status quo and short on alternatives . . . that accept growth and support an innovative plan to meet its challenges," says Lloyd LeBlanc, a land-use consultant hired by a disgruntled group of landowners and developers.

In the simplest terms, the citizens of San Rafael and their elected officials must decide if they want their community to be a village or a city. It is a decision that was made, in part, a long time ago. On the other hand, it's a choice that must always be re-examined in a place as livable as Marin County.

On My Sensible and Livable Scale: For now, San Rafael is a community that appears to work very well.

California trends: Builders, cities listen when this group is talking

Troubled by the high-cost California housing market, the senior-citizen community is flexing its grass-roots political muscle.

To demonstrate their support for more affordable housing, elderly activists are popping up at city council, planning commission and board of supervisor meetings pushing elected officials to adopt pro-housing plans and approve affordable housing developments.

Organized support for housing is rare in an environment where the opponents get the most attention. Builders have learned the hard way that community resistance can be a powerful force which results in their projects being scaled back or denied altogether. But a large senior citizen contingent, rallying behind a housing development, can tip the scales in favor of the builder.

In Contra Costa County, 150 members of the Gray Panthers showed up to support the 118-unit Alamo Villa project. Armed with senior allies, the developers won approval for their development despite a storm of protest from residents in the community of Alamo.

"The Gray Panthers are very well organized and they have the ability to counter opposition with pure numbers," says Contra Costa County planner Eric Parfrey. "There is no question that they contributed to (the project) being approved."

In Santa Clara County, the local chapter of the Gray Panthers worked for five years defending a proposed 28-unit project that provided needed housing for the disabled. Gray Panther spokesman Richard Gregory of Santa Clara, points out that his organization doesn't exclusively support senior developments. "We push for inter-generational projects," he says. "One of the stereotypes is that we are only for seniors," says 50-year-old Gregory who heads up the Housing Task Force for the National Gray Panther organization.

Senior citizen support for housing isn't always welcomed, however. Referring to the multi-family project in Alamo, community leader Larry Regan says, "it was too big and too close to a busy commercial intersection."

"We may have been able to support senior congregate care housing at this location but not at the density the developer proposed," says Eve Auch, president of the Alamo Improvement Association.

In some cities, the resistance to new housing is so overpowering that senior activists don't bother trying to convince elected officials to approve affordable developments. "We have to concentrate on communities that are somewhat willing," says Gregory.

And senior advocates warn that their support shouldn't be taken for granted by developers. In Santa Barbara, the Gray Panther chapter opposed a controversial life-care development proposed along the coast. "It will only help a very few affluent people," says Sarah Shoresman, a member of the steering committee of the Santa Barbara Gray Panther chapter. "Poor people won't be able to afford the housing."

In Sacramento, the Gray Panthers supported the conversion of the top two floors of a local YWCA for housing low-income women, but they are wary about lending their influence to market-rate senior developments according to Sacramento Gray Panther member Mildred Becker. 'They are too expensive," she says.

Not limiting themselves to development proposals, seniors have turned their political clout on other housing issues as well. In Sacramento, they lobbied for regulations that preserve single-occupancy hotels, and in Santa Barbara, the Gray Panthers have advocated anti-demolition controls that prevent affordable housing from being replaced with market-rate housing and office buildings.

Activists in Contra Costa supported a proposal which designates specific sites in the community's general plan for congregate-care senior housing. "We were concerned that someone might get approval for senior citizen housing and then build another type of housing," says county planner Jim Cutler who conceived the innovative land-use plan.

The state legislature has also responded to mounting political pressure from the senior community. For example, Assemblyman Mike Roos of Los Angeles introduced legislation which would reallocate the renters tax credit — giving a greater advantage to poor seniors.

Assembly Bill 888 would take the current $80 renter tax credit away from single persons who have an adjusted gross income exceeding $40,000 and from married couples who file separate income tax returns and earn more than $50,000.

According to the bill, the tax savings to the state will go to individuals who are 65 years and older, whose monthly income doesn't exceed the average social security income (approximately $560), and who pay at least 60 percent of their monthly income on rent.

The bill is currently before the Assembly Ways and Means Committee. "We expect to face some opposition from renters who are cut out of the program, but we hope they understand the plight of those who are rent poor," says Lynn Montgomery, consultant to Assemblyman Roos.

As their numbers increase, seniors will exercise greater political clout. And housing is sure to be at the top of their agenda.

California trends: Fewer housing discrimination charges

THE NUMBER of Californians reporting incidents of housing discrimination fell to its lowest level since the 1983-1984 period, according to year-end statistics obtained from the California Department of Fair Employment and Housing.

For the 12-month period ending June 1987, 732 cases of housing discrimination were filed with the DFEH, the chief enforcer of the state's fair housing laws — a 16 percent decline from the previous year.

Fair housing experts and state officials are quick to point out, however, that a one-year downturn isn't sufficient evidence to show that episodes of housing discrimination are on the wane.

They believe that the decline can be attributed to more subtle forms of discrimination, which are just as threatening but are more difficult to detect. Others argue that higher apartment vacancies may be helping to temporarily curb discrimination in some markets.

The new state report lists those groups most frequently discriminated against as well as industry groups most often accused of bias.

Racial discrimination represents 36.4 percent of all cases with blacks filing 28.2 percent of the complaints and Caucasians and Mexican/ Americans filing 4.8 percent and 3.7 percent respectively.

Child discrimination represented 35 percent of all cases and age bias was reported in 3 percent of the complaints.

Fifteen percent of the cases were filed by those who were discriminated against because of marital status, with single persons representing 12 percent of the complaints filed.

According to the DFEH the vast majority of the discrimination occurrences took place in the rental market — 82 percent of those accused were apartment owners or managers. Real estate companies were singled out in 5.5 percent of the cases, individual homeowners in 3.5 percent and trailer park owners in 4 percent.

More than 30 percent of the complaints were filed in Los Angeles, 16 percent in the Bay Area (San Francisco, San Jose and Oakland), 12 percent in San Diego and 8 percent in Fresno.

Most experts believe that the one-year drop in housing discrimination data doesn't necessarily prove that there is less bias in the housing market place. Instead, they argue that the injustice is becoming less blatant.

"Nobody puts signs on their doors that say we don't want these types of people," says Earl Sullaway, Deputy Director of the DFEH. "But more subtle forms of discrimination continue to occur with the same frequency."

For example, some landlords use occupancy standards to discriminate against children according to DFEH Director Talmadge Jones. "When a landlord strictly dictates how many people can live in a unit, doesn't that affect large families?" asks Jones.

Acts of discrimination are also perpetuated by landlords who tell prospective tenants that an advertised apartment has already been rented or that there is a waiting list. In the 80s, racial and sexual slurs may be carefully avoided, but the result is the same if people are denied access to housing.

By using "checkers" to identify the offenders, nonprofit fair housing groups are attempting to grapple with this more complicated form of discrimination. They send a white and then later a minority couple to seek an apartment in the same building. If the "checkers" are treated differently, there may be evidence that the manager or owner is engaging in a pattern of discrimination.

For example, the Westside Fair Housing Council in Los Angeles used this technique to build a court case against a Westside apartment complex where their checkers experienced differential treatment on three different occasions according to WFHC Executive Director Blanche Rosloff.

Fair housing investigators also look for landlords who alter the terms of the rent or increase the size of the security deposit for those who the landlord or owner doesn't want to rent to. "The rent might be $200 higher or the security deposit might be much larger," says Rosloff.

According to some experts, a statewide rental construction boom that has bumped up the number of vacancies may, in the short term, be helping to reduce housing discrimination. When landlords have more competition in the rental market, they are less likely to discriminate, according to Ann Marquart, Director of Operation Sentinel, a nonprofit fair housing group located on the Stanford campus.

Marquart believes that the overall atmosphere may be changing. "There is still racism and child discrimination, but I think the environment is improving; our population is getting better educated."

Nevertheless, Marquart and other fair housing leaders worry about the people who don't realize that they have been discriminated against as well as those who don't report it when they know they have been victimized.

"Like any crime, 80 percent go unreported," says Marquart.

California Trends: High technology in real estate marketing

WHEN PROSPECTIVE home buyers visit Morningside in Rancho Mirage, Calif., not only do they get the standard marketing brochure that touts the benefits of buying a home in this expensive resort subdivision, but they also get a soft-sell VHS video that highlights the merits of the development and the surrounding area.

Viewing tranquil desert images set to music, potential buyers can get a home-cinematic look at this upscale country-club lifestyle.

Increasingly, new technologies—from on-line data services to million-dollar multi-media marketing centers—are being used to sell both residential and commercial projects. The personalized real estate hustle, that begins and ends with a handshake, hasn't been replaced with the high-tech approach. But realty brokers, buyers and developers are discovering ways to use the latest video, computer and slide show technology to improve their sale's pitch.

For example, on-line data services are a recent technological innovation that list properties in a computerized data base. Like an electronic multiple-listing service, they give business- and home-computer users ready access to available properties around the country. The listings can be called up on the terminal screen with a few simple commands.

The Robnor Group, Coudersport, PA, produces the computerized Real Estate Sellers Directory which lists properties that sell for more than $500,000. Sellers list their property on the Directory for as little as $25 and pay a nominal fee to update it each month.

To obtain access to the listings, computer users must have a telecommunications modem and subscribe to one of the major on-line data services such as Dow Jones, NewsNet, Easy Net or CompuServe. They pay an up-front fee to subscribe to these services, and they are billed for their on-line time.

A spokesman for Conway Data, Norcross, Ga., says its SiteNet service offers 4,000 property listings. Individuals and companies pay $750-$1,500 to list a property with Conway, but computer users can reach the system at no charge by dialing an 800 number that eliminates long-distance costs.

Real estate market research has also been improved by data bases that include demographic information, vacancy statistics and construction trends. Tapping into a computerized data base, a market researcher can avoid a tedious and expensive library search. Large development firms and real estate consultants use the data to make projections about overbuilt markets and the economic feasibility of developments.

To help market residential projects, videos "have arrived," according to Tom Merle, project manager for Chevron Land and Development Co. in San Francisco. For house hunters seeking a condominium in San Francisco, a six-minute video is available on the Daniel Burnham condo project, developed by Chevron along San Francisco's Van Ness Avenue.

These "animated brochures" are perfect for high-end resort communities where potential buyers don't live near the development, according to Merle. "More and more real estate brokers have VCRs," he says, "and the videos are also used at the sales office where they help set the mood."

Though the master tapes are expensive to produce, the per-unit costs for duplicating videos have come down. That explains why the marketing tool has become increasingly popular.

For business parks and office towers, marketing centers help developers pre-lease space. For example, more than 7,000 people have passed through the 20,000-square-foot Irvine Exhibit in Orange

County. Like a high-tech museum, the two-story display takes a futuristic look at the development of the Irvine Company's real estate holdings.

Two years in the making, the Irvine Exhibit is equipped with a scale model of Orange County and planned office buildings, inter-reactive video shows, laser tricks and a multi-projector slide show.

"You try to capture a glimpse of a development that hasn't been built yet—you are selling a vision," says Lawrence Marshall, who owns a Canadian-based multi-media production firm that produces slide shows for marketing centers.

The Irvine Exhibit isn't designed just to sell land to developers and lease building space to tenants: it is part of Irvine's community-relations strategy that helps market the development to area residents who are becoming increasingly upset with growth and traffic problems in Orange County.

The City Center marketing show in Oakland is another example of an exhibit that goes beyond traditional marketing goals. Aimed to overcome negative Oakland images, the slide show "is more about the Oakland community than about City Center," says Marshall.

The razzle-dazzle City Center tour starts off with a slide show that tries to shore up the Oakland reputation and ends with a look at a scale model of the Bramalea Pacific Company's five-million-square-foot mixed-use development in downtown Oakland.

California Trends: Reagan's modest property tax

SANTA BARBARA — How modest is President Ronald Reagan's Santa Barbara vacation getaway? Tucked away in the Santa Ynez Mountains on 688 acres, the ranch house at Rancho del Cielo has only two bedrooms and two baths.

But according to Jim Groessl, President of the Santa Ynez Valley Board of Realtors, land in the surrounding area sells for $1,500 to $2,000 an acre, which would give the Reagan property a market value of more than $1 million dollars.

Nearby, a 70-acre ranch owned by tennis ace Jimmy Connors is on the market for $6 million, Groessl says.

However, property taxes on the rugged Reagan estate aren't as steep as might be expected. The President pays only $3,100 in property taxes a year, according to Santa Barbara County Assistant Assessor Walter Alves. The relatively modest tax bite comes because the land is granted an agricultural exemption and has a taxable value of only $69,000. Buildings on the site have a taxable value of $227,000.

In order to be eligible for this special tax treatment, a property owner must file an annual declaration of agricultural income and an inventory of livestock and farm equipment.

Top housing

Any list of the nation's most expensive housing markets includes hot spots such as San Francisco, Orange County and New York City. Conspicuously absent from the list, however, is the high-cost Santa Barbara market.

There's an explanation: Home price statistics on Santa Barbara include data collected from the entire county, which includes home sales from the more moderately priced northern cities of Santa Maria and Lompoc.

The median home price for the entire county is $145,383 — an average that gives Santa Barbara a lower ranking compared with other parts of the country. For the City of Santa Barbara and other southern county areas, however, the median price exceeds $200,000 — making Santa Barbara proper the most expensive housing market in the country.

Improvement in the affordability picture may be on the way, however. An economic downturn has driven up the number of vacant homes, condos and apartments in the Santa Barbara South Coast area. The overall vacancy rate has risen from 1.7 percent to 2.8 percent in the last year, according to the Federal Home Loan Bank of San Francisco.

Motels into housing

Thanks to the handiwork of the Santa Barbara Community Housing Corp., small steps are being taken to help residents cope with the housing crunch.

In the last 12 years, this non-profit group has built, converted or rehabilitated more than 500 affordable housing units.

For example, it recently acquired the bankrupt Cypress Tree Motel in Carpinteria from La Cumbre Savings Bank. Eighty percent complete when it went belly up, the motel was purchased by CHC and converted to 27 studio apartments with rents pegged at 10 percent below market.

This innovative arrangement was made possible through a loan from the Savings Association Mortgage Corp., a statewide non-profit organization that places high risk housing loans with participating California savings and loans.

After securing a second trust deed from La Cumbre Savings Bank, the county government kicked in a $40,000 grant from a special housing fund from fees paid by developers who build market-rate housing (nonsubsidized housing) in the county.

Oil on troubled waters

Housing advocates had hoped that an off-shore oil drilling boom would help solve local housing ills, but a plan to have major oil companies pay into the housing fund has not panned out.

Their anticipated contribution to affordable housing was predicated on the theory that increased work in oil industry would increase housing demand and aggravate the housing situation along the south coast area of Santa Barbara.

The formula for oil-company donations was pegged to the number of vacant housing units and overall housing demand in the south coast. Because workers are choosing to live in the more affordable north county, demand has diminished in the south, and consequently, an oil-industry financial commitment to low-cost housing has not been required.

The program is similar to a City of San Francisco program that requires office developers to fund housing programs.

California Trends: Cities move to aid mobile home owners

WORRIED ABOUT losing a last bastion of affordable housing, a number of California cities are passing laws which make it more expensive for mobilehome park owners to sell or convert their parks to a more lucrative use.

More than fifty cities have passed or have considered laws that would ease the burden for displaced mobilehome owners and discourage park owners who wish to sell or convert their parks.

"If we don't come up with local legislation, (mobilehome owners) will be put out on the street," says Dave Hennessy, a regional director with the Golden State Mobilehome Owner's Association, San Jose. In most cases, the mobilehome owners are elderly on fixed incomes with very' few other housing alternatives, according to Hennessy.

Avoiding the high costs of a conventional home, more than a million Californians live in 439,000 mobilehomes in 3500 parks. The average monthly park fee of $200 combined with an inexpensive mortgage payment on the coach adds up to average housing costs of $400 to $600 per month, according to a 1986 study conducted by the State Department of housing and Community Development.

Many parks are located in areas where land values have appreciated dramatically — prompting some eager park owners to sell to developers who want sites for new apartments, single-family homes, shop-ping centers or office buildings.

"In urbanized areas, there is market pressure to convert mobilehome parks — developable land is scarce and the parks have been around for years," says Linda Lauzze, associate planner with the City of Sunnyvale.

When park owners decide to sell their land for an entirely different use, the mobilehome owners are frequently left in a quandary: they have very little equity, they face the expense of moving their coach to another location, and they must try to find a space in a real estate market that has a dearth of desirable spaces.

The predicament has aroused the interest of local officials.

In Sunnyvale, for instance, the city passed a law which provides relocation benefits to mobilehome owners who have been displaced by a conversion. The city requires that the park owner (or developer) pay for the cost to move the mobilehome to another park; and if the mobilehome owner cannot find a suitable space in a neighboring park, then the park owner is obligated to purchase the mobilehome, at 85 percent of its fair market value—which includes both the coach and the land.

In Northern California, San Jose has also passed a conversion ordinance, and the cities of Concord and Fremont are considering similar proposals.

In Southern California, the cities of Carson, Westminister and Los Angeles regulate conversions and Santa Barbara will soon act on such a proposal.

Not surprisingly, park owners are upset about this latest trend in mobilehome regulation.

"It is becoming a runaway problem," says Chuck Hughes, Director for Local Government and Community Relations, Western Mobilehome Association (WMA), Sacramento. "It forces the park owners to pay market value for their own property.... so in effect, they have to buy back their own park," he says.

Park owners claim that asking them to pay for the coach and the land may be in conflict with a state law that says local mitigation damages may not exceed the "reasonable cost of relocation."

WMA officials are using this state law to argue against restrictive local conversion ordinances and have not ruled out the possibility of lawsuits in certain communities.

The latest regulatory push on conversions has further aggravated the rift between park owners and mobilehome owners who have been battling over rent increases and rent control for more than five years.

Mobilehome owners argue that rent control protects them from exorbitant rent increases.

Park owners claim that the motivation to sell a park is heightened by the presence of a local mobile-home rent control ordinance. Currently, seventy-five California jurisdictions have regulations that control rents in mobilehome parks.

"Where rent control is very restrictive, the frustrations are very high, and it can precipitate the sale of parks," says WMA Executive Director Dennis Amundson.

Until a more equitable approach to dealing with displaced mobile-home owners is found, however, tougher regulations are inevitable.

California Trends: Many woes of state's planned developments

(First of three parts)

MANAGEMENT, LEGAL, and construction problems are plaguing a substantial number of the 15,000-16,000 California condominium and other planned-development homeowner associations, according to a new study prepared for the Department of Real Estate (DRE) by researchers at Berkeley's Institute of Urban and Regional Development.

"There are some serious problems with CIDs (common interest developments); and they could become much worse in the future," says U.C. Berkeley sociologist Carol J, Silverman, Ph.D., who collaborated with urban planning specialist Stephen Barton, Ph.D., to conduct the study.

The first of its kind, the analysis surveys 579 presidents of both condominium and other planned-development associations — the volunteer organizations that make decisions regarding common ground maintenance, association rules and dues, and all other legal and business matters affecting the management of condo developments.

Homeowners, association leaders, attorneys and consultants interviewed for this column say the study findings, which point to pervasive problems in many CIDs, are consistent with their experiences.

Thirty-seven percent of all common interest developments report major construction defects, with roof leaks being the most common type of problem identified by association officials in the DRE study. The construction problems can be subtle: "Our 28-unit project is 13 years old and needs painting. The developer said the stucco would never need painting, and now we have an expensive problem on our hands," says Trina Woods, an association president from Northern California.

Fifty-eight percent of those surveyed indicated that the homeowners' dues were set too low initially by the developer. In many cases, monthly fees are made more affordable by the developers so that they can better market the units — but this practice often contributes to association fiscal problems later on. The Berkeley researchers point out, however, that industry education and regulations are helping to curb this practice in newer developments — forty-eight percent of the developments occupied after 1984 have fees that were set too low.

"Legal conflicts between homeowners' associations and developers is widespread," says the report — more than 24 percent of those surveyed reported the incidence of a lawsuit or the threat of one. Moreover, "44 percent of the voluntary boards have been harassed or threatened with lawsuits by members of their own association." The report concludes that many board members are not knowledgeable about their role and that member support is weak.

One third of those surveyed do not have a preventative maintenance program which includes regular building inspections and timely replacement of roofs, electrical systems and plumbing. Thirty-three percent have not done a reserve study, an assessment of building needs and a financial plan that helps the association decide how much money to set aside for future repairs. The reserve study is mandated by a four-year-old state law.

The median size of associations surveyed is 43 units, and the researchers concluded that management problems are more prevalent in smaller projects where they can't afford professional assistance and board members are unclear about their legal and professional obligations.

Financial and legal issues aren't the only problems that haunt many CIDs; minor infractions with association rules are even more frequent. Late dues payments, noise or disorderly conduct, complaints about pets and parking violations are some of the problems that frequently arise. "Many are densely populated structures and so you need to have rules—sometimes they are broken," says Marlene Fong, an Oakland attorney who specializes in association legal issues.

Many buyers make the decision to live in a condo because they want to avoid the hassles of maintenance and want somebody else to take care of it for them.

"On the one hand, many residents feel they are homeowners, but on the other hand, they aren't just owners; they also bought into an association and expect it to deliver services," says Silverman.

Each year, 40,000 homeowners are elected to the board of directors of CIDs, according to Barton. Consequently, a small group of residents who volunteer to run the association must shoulder the burden for everyone, according to Silverman and Barton.

"My original intention in purchasing a condominium was not to be concerned with maintenance; I now have that concern for 125 units," said one association president who responded to the survey.

The state agency that regulates new condo and planned-unit developments, the Department of Real Estate, commissioned the study after it received frequent calls from disgruntled homeowners, according to DRE Commissioner James Edmonds, Jr.

"We have one group that says legislate and another that says don't — so we are looking for direction," says Edmonds.

Associations must involve the tenants

Soon after Sue moved into her new San Francisco condominium, she learned from the minutes of a board of directors meeting that her condo association was upset about some rules she had purportedly broken.

Feeling compelled to vindicate herself, she attended her first board meeting and realized that living in a condominium development isn't free of responsibilities and hassles. There are some restrictions on her freedom that she didn't expect.

Second of three parts

In common-interest developments, several small mistakes and minor infractions can lead to other more serious problems, such as lawsuits, harassment and fiscal mismanagement, according to a new report published by the state Department of Real Estate, which surveyed association presidents throughout the state.

But when associations make homeowner education a priority, many conflicts can be avoided, according to Berkeley researchers Stephen Barton and Carol Silver-man, who conducted the study for the department.

Responsible for maintaining common property, collecting dues and enforcing rules, the homeowners association is a "community organization that has the power to foreclose on members" homes if they don't pay their dues, is a management company that can tell its owners what they can do with their homes, and is a local government where absentee owners can vote but renters cannot," say Barton.

Despite the dire condition of some condo associations, many are well-managed with very few problems Moreover, preventative steps can be taken to keep these communities more livable and out of litigation, according to the UC Berkeley team.

Beyond urging associations to follow legal requirements and generally accepted accounting practices, the researchers recommend that associations help homeowners better understand their development and its rules.

"The first concern of an association should be to ensure that homebuyers are informed of the responsibilities they are taking on and of the resources available to them," says Barton and Silverman.

State law requires all sellers to give buyers copies of the association's legal documents and a current financial statement — a seller can be assessed a $500 fine for violating this law. The Department of Real Estate study recommends that associations notify their membership of this requirement and offer legal assistance to improve enforcement of the law.

Because the percentage of renters is increasing in many condo developments and because tenants are often blamed for problems in common interest developments, Barton and Silverman recommend that associations take special steps to reach out to renters.

Problems with renters, such as late dues payments and rule violations, can in part be overcome with greater tenant understanding and their involvement in association activities.

"As residents, they need to be contacted, kept informed and persuaded of the value of the association," says the report.

There are several ways associations can involve renters in the affairs of the common-interest developments: permitting them to serve on association committees, including their names on the mailing list to receive board newsletters, and designing a welcome program to establish a positive relationship between the tenant and the association.

"The more you make renters a part of the association the better," says Oliver Burford, president of the Executive Council of Home-owners, San Jose, a non-profit organization representing owners who live in common-interest developments in California. Speaking of his own homeowners' association, Burford says, "35 percent of our units are rentals; we send them the newsletter and let them serve on committees."

He concedes that tenants do not get a personal welcome but agrees that it is a good idea.

Finding either owners or renters who are willing to give up some of their time for volunteer association activities can be difficult, however. And when successful with getting more people involved, it can prevent a quick consensus.

"Participation in governance is all well and good, but dispersion of the authority can be a problem — such that no one makes a decision," says property manager Doug Christison.

Another challenge is learning to "balance efficient business management with effective governance and neighborliness," says the report. In some cases, too much emphasis is placed on management and not enough on the dynamics of collective decision making.

The majority of all associations have professional managers who handle the business affairs of common-interest developments. Silverman warns, however, that professional managers should serve in more of an advisory capacity and not try to do all of the work for the volunteers."

"Managers are often portrayed as the bad guys, but we would prefer to be a consultant to the board and not the boss," says Kristen Bergman, client service manager with Property Management Network, San Jose.

Next Week: Are Stiffer Regulations Necessary?

Special to the Examiner: Artists hope to preserve live-work spaces

POUNDING AWAY at my computer only ten feet from my kitchen and 15 feet above my bedroom has its advantages: cheap office rent, no lines for the bathroom, and no mindless home-to-job commute.

And whenever I fret that it's not very professional to work in my house, I remind myself that, among others, Ronald Reagan, Jack Anderson and Gay Talese bring home the bacon without leaving home.

Working at home is becoming more popular. But before an estimated nine million Americans figured out that homeworking had merit, there were artists — the pioneers of the live/work experience.

"Live/work is the salt marsh of the urban ecology; it's the first link in the chain that nourishes cultural life in the community," said San Francisco sculptor and artist activist Richard Mayer in 1979.

New York's SoHo district popularized the notion of artist live/work space. But long before SoHo got its reputation, working at home has been an alternative for struggling artists who couldn't afford to pay rent in two locations.

In the expensive Bay Area real estate market where artists abound, the predicament is the same: studio spaces are difficult to find, rents are high, and elected officials and property owners sometimes ignore or misunderstand the needs of artists.

Faced with these obstacles, San Francisco artists and their patrons banned together to help create new live/work space and salvage that which already exists. Organized by the California Lawyers for the Arts and the San Francisco Arts Commission, the ArtHouse project was formed last year and acts as an information clearinghouse for Bay Area artists who need or have problems with their living environment.

Last Saturday at a conference organized by ArtHouse, artists, developers and architects gathered at the Theatre Artaud, an old warehouse that was converted to 69 live/work units, two theaters, a gallery and two dance studios.

They spent the entire day mulling over solutions to the various problems that haunt the live/work artist crowd.

UNIQUE SPACE NEEDS. *For me, a 250-square-foot room packed with a computer, a fax machine, a copier, and a telephone is a functional in-home work environment, but for the typical artist, an extra bedroom or den won't do. While generally content with nominal space for their personal residence, artists need at least 400 or 500 square feet of high ceiling studio space.*

FINDING SUITABLE SPACE AND AVOIDING EMOTIONS. *Artists tend to congregate in industrial wastelands such as South of Market in San Francisco, and parts of Emeryville and West Oakland. But as these neighborhoods become more popular, rents go up and artists are forced to look elsewhere.*

BUILDING CODE VIOLATIONS. *Working at home raises red flags for city building inspectors— many go crazy when they see how artists blend their two settings.*

Many artists, on the other hand, ignore the dangers of working and living in space that has code violations—they argue that the codes are out of touch and impractical for live work situations.

State law requires cities to be flexible when regulating live/work space. While the cities of San Francisco and Emeryville are sensitive to artists, most communities have been slow to follow their progressive lead.

Helping the art community overcome these problems, Art House offers a 24-hour telephone hotline and a housing referral service. At their conference, experts addressed issues of design, architecture, legal requirements, and finance gimmicks. And a handbook was distributed which Includes the latest word on city codes, leases and tenant protection.

Tuning Into this latest trend in real estate consumption are a handful of architects and developers who have come forward with new schemes to meet the demand for this odd-ball space.

In Oakland, for Instance, sculptor Bruce Beasley is developing his second new live/work building. While most spaces are carved out of older industrial buildings, Beasleyand his architect Thomas Dolan are blazing new ground by building from the ground up.

Across the street from Beasley's first project. South Prescott Village is under construction and will span two blocks between Henry and Lewis Streets in West Oakland. Ranging in size from 600 to 2300 square feet, the units have a kitchen and small living area on the main floor and a mezzanine above with a bedroom and bath. Having plenty of light, the units will rent for $300 to $1500 per month.

In San Francisco, the renovation of the old Sears building at Army and Valencia was one of the first live/work conversions in the city. Rents in the fifty-two unit landmark range from $650 to $1100 a month for the 1,000-square-foot units.

One of the oldest live/work organizations in the region is the Emeryville Artists Cooperative (EAC), a non-profit group which has successfully converted three old warehouses into home/studio combinations for 100 painters, sculptors, photographers, and other artists. One building is a cooperative where the residents have a limited-equity position in the property.

On My Sensible and Livable Scale: It's not surprising that people are figuring out ways to solve housing problems for Bay Area artists: there is too much at stake to do otherwise.

o discuss possible solutions to the problems that were raised in the study.

Special to the Examiner: Home industry slams interest deduction limit

HONOLULU — A U.S. House of Representatives vote to place a $1 million cap on the amount of mortgage debt homeowners can deduct from their federal income tax has the real estate industry up in arms.

Under current law, homeowners are permitted to deduct the interest on their home loan payments when they file their income tax returns — reducing their annual tax bite.

Part of an overall budget reduction measure, the plan approved by the House limits the mortgage debt that can be deducted on a first and second home for wealthy taxpayers who have a combined outstanding loan balance of $1 million.

"It (the congressional proposal) strikes at the core and sanctity of the home mortgage interest deduction and should strongly be opposed," says a background paper, distributed by the California Association of Realtors to California's U.S. congressional delegation.

For example, an affluent homeowner in the 33 percent tax bracket with a mortgage of $1.5 million at an 11 percent interest rate could have, $165,000 deducted under the current law and only $110,000 under the new proposal. Consequently, the amount that could be deducted would decrease by $55,000, and the homeowner's tax liability would increase by $18,000.

The National Association of Realtors who are convening their annual convention in Hawaii this week, is encouraging its 750,000 members to lobby their congressional representatives on this issue, according to Jeffrey Lubar, NAR vice president.

The proposal must still be approved by the Senate and signed by President Reagan.

Proponents of the measure argue the change will only affect a small group of homeowners and help reduce the federal deficit.

The measure originated in the U.S. House Ways and Means Committee and was approved last week by the full House.

White only a tiny percentage of the home-buying public would be affected by the change, objecting members view it as "the proverbial foot in "the door," said William ness. Moore, NAR president.

Moore called the proposal "an orchestrated plan of the tax staffs to repeal the mortgage interest deduction for homeowners at all income levels."

Incoming president of the National Association of Homebuilders, Dale Stuard, agreed, calling the tax change "the camel's nose under the tent."

Industry officials concede their position is going to be difficult to defend, however.

"Who's going to get upset about people rich enough to have million-dollar mortgages not being able to deduct as much on their federal tax forms?" Realtor News, a weekly magazine published by NAR, said in a recent editorial.

Some industry leaders are embarrassed to fight the congressional proposal. "We are all going to look like idiots again. We complain about the budget deficit but we aren't willing to give up anything — even a few deductions for the richest people in the country," said a Northern California building industry official who didn't want to be identified.

Special to the Examiner: Realtors cautious about future

HONOLULU — The moment the real-estate forecast session was scheduled to begin at the National Association of Realtors convention, the power went out at the Halekulani Hotel.

Despite the darkness, the economists attending were somewhat optimistic about the performance of the real-estate industry in the coming months.

However, they warned that interest rate swings are likely and predicted an upward trend. They also said uncertainty in the financial markets will slow the economy, causing a slight reduction in the number of home sales and housing starts.

In the aftermath of the stock crash, "we are going to have to live with volatility," said John Tuccillo, NAR's chief economist.

Tuccillo's view was shared by three other economists on the panel, which included Don Straszheim, chief economist at Merrill Lynch; Charles Wurtz-bach, vice president at Prudential Realty; and Larry White, a new member of the Federal Home Loan Bank Board.

The association predicted that interest rates on 30-year, fixed-rate mortgages will average 10.7 percent in 1988, up slightly from 10.1 percent in 1987. Home sales in 1988 should fall 3.2 percent from 1987 figures and new home construction fall by 8.3 percent, NAR said.

Despite higher interest rates and fewer sales, which often indicate stable prices, NAR predicts that the nation's medium home price will rise 4.7 percent: from $84,600 to $88,600.

Underlying the relatively upbeat forecast was the prediction that the disarray in the financial markets would not cause the economy to go into a deep recession.

"The stock crash was damaging but not fatal," said Don Straszheim.

However, the panelists agreed that consumer spending would slow. They said that the economy is capable of a major fall if action isn't taken on the budget deficit.

"If the resolution of this recent budget summit is just art acrimonious statement by the president and Congress ... then hold onto your wallet," Straszheim Said.

Concern about the federal deficit has prompted the Realtors association to consider a strong policy position in support of across the board budget cuts, which could reduce spending on all federal programs, including housing.

California trends: Big brokerage firms begin to dominate

Bill Patterson runs a family-owned real estate business in Gilmer, Texas, and isn't worried about the corporate real estate giants such as Coldwell Banker, RE/MAX, Century 21, or ERA who are gobbling up a larger and larger share of the home sale market place.

But as the national companies expand and new Fortune 500 firms such as Prudential jump into the real estate brokerage market, the question is yet unanswered as to whether homebuyers and sellers are being better served.

Patterson doesn't believe so, nor does he believe that the name and the backing of a major national firm is necessary to successfully sell real estate in Gilmer.

"In a small town, you know everybody and they know you," says Patterson. "I hope my name is worth something in my own community."

But in the last five years — particularly in many of the large urban markets — the national firms are playing a bigger role in representing homesellers. Throughout the country, local firms are being bought up or are choosing to affiliate as a franchise with a national company.

"Real estate is still a mom-and-pop business, an entre-preneuring opportunity where people can get in and out of the business very quickly; but the trend is that the big guys are getting bigger," says Lon Carlston, senior editor of Roulac Strategic Real Estate newsletter in San Francisco.

The medium-sized firms will feel the squeeze most dramatically, according to John Tuccillo, senior vice president and chief economist of the National Association of Realtors. "The very small firm — the boutiques who specialize — satisfy a market niche that big firms don't do as well with," he says.

In the large franchise companies such as Century 21, RE/MAX, ERA, and Better Homes and Gardens, the real estate brokers pay a franchise fee to the company and percentage of their gross revenue.

In exchange, the company offers its independently owned and operated offices name recognition, national advertising and a sophisticated network that stimulates referrals from homebuyers and homesellers moving in and out of areas throughout the country.

Choosing to shun the franchise model, some major companies, such as Merrill Lynch Realty, own and manage all of their local sales offices.

Newport Beach-based Coldwell Banker has combined both strategies — they own 1,000 local offices and also have 1,000 affiliate franchises.

The franchised-owned companies account for 30 percent of all home sales, according to the National Association of Realtors; and the five largest national real estate companies accounted for $2.3 billion in total home sales last year, according to a survey published in the Roulac newsletter.

The competition among national companies will become keener as Prudential Insurance Company enters the field. This past week in Hawaii at the annual convention of the National Association of Realtors, the company announced plans to sell 3,000 Prudential real estate franchises throughout the country.

Dubbed Prudential Realty Associates, the company is investing $20 million into the new subsidiary, according to company representatives. They expect Prudential's name identification to be the most important selling feature for both the public and prospective agents who wish to affiliate with a national company.

Whether the consumer will benefit from these changes in the real estate industry is an open question.

With the promise that big is better, the large company-owned and operated firms brag about their national network which purportedly brings more buyers and sellers together.

The small independents, on the other hand, claim to be closer to the needs of the buyers and sellers and, therefore, better equipped to make transactions smoother.

"The public sees those big franchises, and it's so impersonal," says Carm Corazolo, a small real estate broker from Norwalk, Conn.

The large franchise companies brag about offering the best of both worlds. Their offices are independently owned and they have the backing of a large national company.

Competition among the big national companies has prompted some of the firms to offer new services — which Tera Boltz of Coldwell Banker, Newport Beach, says is good news for the consumer.

Last month, for instance, Coldwell Banker announced a new program that offers homesellers a guarantee regarding the marketing of their property. When Coldwell Banker fails to meet this specific standard, the company promises to rectify the problem in 24 hours or lose the agreement to list the property.

Promenade now in second phase

RANCHO CUCAMONGA — The Warmington Homes enclave of Promenade is well into its second phase due to strong sales of its two and three bedroom homes in the master-planned community of Victoria.

Promenade homes are priced from $91,900 and the most popular plan to date has been the single-story three-bedroom Plan 2..

Legislators poised to pass bills on asbestos

CONCERNED ABOUT mounting public fears associated with asbestos in homes and apartments, the California legislature is poised to pass a number of asbestos-related bills when they reconvene in January.

But while legislators already have specific ideas on consumer-oriented legislation, they are also concerned that the asbestos scare may depress property values where asbestos is considered a risk.

"While the debate over health dangers is far from complete, there is no doubting that asbestos in buildings is truly an economic hazard in California," says a statement from the Assembly Committee on Housing and Community Development.

To begin the discussion, both the health risks and implications for property sales will be probed at a state Assembly hearing scheduled for December 9th in Sacramento.

"We are trying to get an honest, overview of the problem and take some action without further alarming buyers and sellers of property," says Michael Krisman, Principal Consultant to the Housing Committee which is conducting the hearing.

Used in furnace insulation and surfacing materials such as tile, asbestos products were common to homes and rental units built in the 1950s, 1960s and early 1970s. But it is only considered dangerous when the asbestos is friable (easely crumbled by hand pressure) and released into the air—and even then, the medical experts don't agree on how great the risk is.

"Current medical research indicates that the health risks posed by low-level exposure to asbestos in buildings are minimal," states an Assembly memorandum on the subject.

The legislature's interest in asbestos isn't confined to the health risks, however. State assembly leaders are also worried about how the escalating fears could lower real estate values.

Buildings with asbestos are being devalued, according to Michael J. Krisman, Principal Consultant to the Committee. When buyers are aware of an asbestos problem, they use the problem as a "bargaining chip" to obtain a lower selling price, he says.

Moreover, financial institutions are hesitating to lend on commercial buildings with asbestos, according to the Committee memo. There is no evidence, however, that mortgage lenders have refused to make home loans because of the presence of asbestos.

Not surprisingly, real estate firms share in this concern. Worried that the hearings would aggravate citizen fears and depress sales, two industry groups discouraged the Assembly from holding the December 9th hearing.

An unregulated, enterprising, and sometimes unscrupulous asbestos-abatement industry is also part of the problem, according to legislative consultant Richard Steffen. He points to a potential conflict of interest when "homeowners call in a contractor who does both the inspection and the removal."

Troubled by this practice, the legislature will consider tighter regulations on inspectors and contractors who specialize in asbestos removal, according to Steffen.

Currently, federal laws do nothing to address asbestos problems in residential buildings. A 1982 federal law regulates the asbestos hazard in schools, and the Asbestos Hazard Emergency Response Act of 1986 requires the Environmental protection Agency to conduct a study on the problem in other public and commercial buildings (including apartment houses exceeding 10 units). Due to have been released on October 15, the study has not yet been published.

To help alert the public to the threat of an asbestos hazard, one state proposal calls for the creation of a special category for asbestos on the mandatory home sellers disclosure form. This would require a home seller to specifically explain an asbestos problem to the buyer.

Another proposal would establish a toll free phone number for consumers to call when they believe they have an asbestos hazard.

But if this year's legislative record is any indication, modest improvements such as these will not be approved without a fight.

This year, controversy erupted when the legislature considered a measure which would have defined an asbestos hazard. Still on the table, Assembly Bill 1348 (Floyd) and Senate Bill 894 (Marks) would add a definition of asbestos hazard to the state health and safety code. By so doing, a building could be declared substandard by building inspectors when an unsafe asbestos level is identified.

With opposition from the California Association of Realtors and the California Apartment Association, the bills are stalled in committee.

Holding on to affordable housing

Special to the Examiner

JUST WHEN I thought that I had written enough about the dire need for more affordable housing, a reader writes: "Low-cost housing attracts low-cost people and low-cost environments, which turn into don't-give-a-damn slums."

The tone of this letter, with its pick-yourself-up-by-the-bootstraps philosophy, convinced me that much more needs to be said about affordable housing.

With that as my motivation, I want your input on an affordable housing puzzle that has no easy answers; it's the kind of predicament that policymakers too often are destined to bungle. If you take the time to fill out and return the coupon on page F-2, I will publish a summary of your sentiments and the most creative solutions recommended.

Here's the problem.

During the benevolent mood of the, 1960s, the federal government began pumping billions of dollars into building low-cost housing projects. In most cases, it was accomplished by dangling the carrot of low-interest-rate loans in front of eager developers who agreed to build and keep the housing affordable for poor people, senior citizens and middle-in-come families for a specified time (usually 15 to 20 years).

It was an expensive experiment but, for a while, everything was hunky-dory; a select group of developers made money and thousands of affordable housing units were built.

But the scheme started to fall apart when the allotted time for keeping the rents low began to run out. When that happens, the property owners have the legal right to prepay the low-cost loans, sell the developments to new investors and kick up the rents in order to earn a higher return.

If the rents are increased to market levels, they can go up 200 or 300 percent — not the kind of rent hikes that poor people and senior citizens on fixed incomes can stomach.

Under the least desirable scenario, people are put out on the streets and the pathetic homeless quandary gets worse.

Unfortunately, the problem isn't isolated to a few small developments. In the next 20 years, up to 20,000 Bay Area households who live in this type of housing could face eviction notices or unmanageable rent boosts.

Just this month, hundreds of families in Alameda, Vallejo and Fremont have had to grip themselves for this situation.

But before you pass judgment on who's the bad guy in this public policy fiasco, consider what it might take for elected officials and building owners to back out of this dilemma gracefully.

Throwing money at the problem is probably the fairest approach, but it's the solution the taxpayers can least afford.

For example, politicians point to the Victoria Gardens apartment project in Fremont as an example of how the problem can be licked. But they also concede that it was an expensive piece of bureaucratic and political handiwork.

Victoria Gardens is supported by five-year federal subsidies, which keep the rents low for 55 low-income elderly tenants. The subsidies will cost the federal treasury an estimated $1.3 million over the five-year period, which just began recently.

It would require an estimated $100 million annually to pay rent subsidies for the close to 20,000 Bay Area apartments that are scheduled to be converted to market-rate housing. Unfortunately, very little thought was given to this problem when the plan went into effect in the 1960s.

The least expensive alternative would be to force the private owners to carry the financial burden of renting to poor people for a longer period of time. Slapping moratoriums on rent increases and making tenant evictions illegal would insure affordability, and doesn't cost the taxpayers a dime.

But as you can imagine, apartment owners would go berserk. In many cases, the projects are owned by limited partners or investors who were promised deep tax shelters as well as an opportunity to reap an attractive return when the buildings were sold.

Some people argue that the owners have a moral obligation to sacrifice these profits for the larger social good. But that seems incredibly unfair. The owners, for good or naught, entered into a written agreement with the federal government that gave them the right to bow out at a specified time. Would you have the government saying, "thanks for holding up your end of the bargain, but sorry we can't hold up ours?"

I, for one, would like to see the Federal National Mortgage Association get into the act. The federally chartered organization, known as Fannie Mae, is a profitable and sophisticated private company that buys home loans from lenders. The government endorsement gives it a unique advantage in the national mortgage market.

When the U.S. Congress privatized Fannie Mae in the late '60s, it did so with a caveat that the company never forget its responsibility to solve low-income housing problems. Here's a chance for Fannie Mae to put its profits and expertise to work on a problem of national importance. I'm not talking about token gifts, but big bucks and entrepreneuring leadership.

Obviously, none of the solutions are easy. They all require gutsy political will, delicate negotiations and a keen sense of fairness.

In fact, this week, state legislative leaders are planning to announce a major state-wide ballot initiative to address the conversion and other housing problems.

In the meantime, what's your suggestion?

California Trends: Real Estate deals that save the enviroment

TO BE SUCCESSFUL, a real estate company must have access to capital, a track record, a willingness to assume risk, and a sophisticated team of attorneys and real estate experts.

With an unusual twist, the Trust for Public Land (TPL) fits that profile well. In the last fifteen years, this innovative nonprofit organization has arranged $300 million worth of property transactions in 34 states. But along with acquiring and selling more than 400 parcels of land, TPL has protected 381,471 acres of scenic, recreational, park, and wilderness land.

"We do deals, but we are not value neutral," says Martin Rosen, President of the Trust. "We are involved in public-benefit real estate transactions."

With offices in Boston, New York, Cleveland, Tallahassee, Santa Fe, and Seattle, the San Francisco based conservation group relies on the tried and tested rules of real estate deal making to preserve some of the country's most valuable land.

For example, the organization turns to federal tax laws to help in its land acquisitions. Because donations of "land value" to nonprofit groups are tax-deductible, companies and individuals who sell property at a discount to the trust can realize substantial tax benefits.

But risk is involved. TPL purchases environmentally-sensitive land at below-market prices, holds the property and resells it to government agencies who maintain the land for parks and recreational areas—keeping the sites permanently of limits to development.

In a recent transaction, for instance, TPL purchased 80,000 acres of Wisconsin timber and recreational land from the Primerica Corporation, formerly the American Can Company, which is divesting itself of major landholdings.

Vast amounts of the acreage will be sold to the U.S. Forest Service and the Wisconsin Department of Natural Resources who will place the land into a fish and wildlife preserve. The land that is inappropriate for public ownership will be sold to private buyers.

The same successful formula was applied to the three-thousand-acre Cascade Ranch located along San Mateo's coastal Route 1 just east of a popular breeding ground for the elephant seal. TPL arranged for the California state park system to acquire 2400 acres of the Ranch and then obtained approval for development on another 400 acres of the site.

In this instance, benevolence wasn't the developer's only motivation for doing business with a conservation organization. Originally planned for residential development, Cascade Ranch faced a barrage of environmental lawsuits. When the prospects of obtaining the necessary approvals to build turned sour, TPL got involved and negotiated the land sale to the state.

"We offer an attractive alternative to a developer spending years in court," says Rosen. "We elevate self-interest to mutual-interest."

Often unbending defenders of private property rights, some landowners and developers must overcome their hesitation to deal with an organization whose primary goal is to preserve not — develop — open space.

Property owners become more comfortable with the relationship, however, when "they discover we are more interested in innovation than ideology," says Rosen.

Pristine open spaces aren't the only candidates for a land gift to the Trust. Properties having no park or recreational value have been donated including urban railroad right-of-way in Winter Haven,

Florida, a vacant steel fabrication plant in Clinton, Iowa, and a collection of fast food restaurant sites. Utilizing its real estate expertise to acquire properties that can later be sold, leased or exchanged, TPL raises its operating funds in the process.

Property owners can explore making a gift to the Trust by providing information on their land. TPL will then conduct an analysis which itemizes the benefits to making a donation. One of their publications points out that "the donation value (the amount deductible for tax purposes) is the full appraised value, but the actual cost to the donor is only the difference between the market value and their tax savings. These can be remarkably close."

Not all property and/or building donations are welcomed, however. Cleaning up an asbestos or a hazardous waste problem, for example, can be more costly than the donation is worth, according to Rosen.

To avoid getting themselves in a bind, TPL hires skilled real estate specialists who thoroughly examine each property being donated or purchased.

"Competence is essential in this type of work," says Rosen.

Scramble for day-care facilities

With the rise in the number of two-in-come households and a baby boom, the demand for day-care facilities has outstripped supply.

In response to the problem, political leaders are scrambling to find ways to expand day-care services. At the local level, real estate developers have become a popular mark for picking up the slack.

Viewing it as a marketing technique, some developers are eager to make accommodations for day-care facilities in their developments. Others are disgruntled with the trend.

We don't think it is the responsibility of the new homeowner to subsidize childcare," says Gary Hambly, Vice President, Building Association, San Ramon, who argues that building fees and land grants for day care increase the cost of the home.

No one will deny that there is a shortage of day-care centers, however. In California, three times as many children need day care as there are services available, according to National Organization for Women spokesperson Pat Griffith, Los Angeles.

"There will never be enough day-care centers until the government steps in to solve the problem," says Griffith. "And affordable day care is impossible without public aid."

Originating in San Francisco and Concord in 1985, cities began to turn to commercial developers for assistance in providing money, land, and facilities for day-care services.

More recently, cities such as Irvine, Clayton, San Ramon and Los Angeles are considering proposals that look to residential developers for support.

An ordinance approved last week in San Ramon, for instance, will require housing developers to pay $210 per unit for childcare.

"As long as local government isn't very well funded, someone has to pay for it," says Victoria Clark, a spokesperson for the California League of Cities, Sacramento. "Though some developers may not like it, they may be the only source officials can turn to," she says.

Southern California developer Barratt American Corporation argues that including plans for day-care facilities in large master planned communities is good business.

"It makes economic and political sense," says Barratt President Mark Frazer. Moreover, including two day-care centers in their 2500-unit Creekside Community in Ontario helped the developer market the homes.

"I don't think developers should wait to be told to do it; they should be doing it on their own," says Frazer. "You can make just as much money selling a small part of your land to a day-care operator as you can building five more houses."

He concedes, however, that what works for large-scale developers may not be as feasible for smaller builders.

Concerned about the trend, the Building Industry Association of Orange County would like to see "some incentives go along with these new day-care policies," says John Withers, Director of Governmental Affairs, Building Industry Association, Santa Ana.

Last year, a proposal for a fee system was considered but turned back by the Irvine city council when they adopted a comprehensive day-care policy. It did include the creation of a task force, however, that will devise incentives to encourage developers to fund or donate land for centers.

Los Angeles Mayor Tom Bradley introduced a proposal last month that would allow builders to put up larger buildings if they include space in their projects for day-care centers.

According to experts, inducing developers to fund centers is only half of the battle, however. Finding sites acceptable to the surrounding neighborhoods is the other challenge.

"People don't want a playground next to their home, and parking is a real problem," says Sheri VanderDussen, senior planner, the City of Irvine.

The city council there is considering a proposal in which the city would lease city-owned park land to day-care providers.

Other communities have designated special childcare zones where neighborhood opposition to them wouldn't be as severe.

The least amount of opposition occurs when the centers are located in the workplace.

But "many people prefer to have day care close to home so it is convenient for both parents," says Griffith.

In the final analysis, more facilities are needed wherever they are located, and developers should expect to be part of the solution.

California Trends: To make money in real estate, know local politics

Reflecting on the 1929 stock market crash, Will Rogers once said, "I guess I will just have to give thanks that we had invested in land, instead of Wall Sttreet, even if we can't sell the land and have to pay taxes on it, we can at least walk out on it."

Particularly enamored with buying property in California, Rogers' investment advice would, on surface, appear to be very sound.

In the last 60 years the assessed value of all taxable land in California has risen from $10 billion to $410 billion. Since the 1970s alone the value of privately owned land has jumped up 388 percent. During the same period the Consumer Price Index rose 193 percent.

But while property ownership is a symbol of wealth and power, buying land with the expectation that rapid dividends are forthcoming is naive. Big returns on California land holdings require a sophisticated understanding of local politics and a major investment of time and resources.

Merely sitting on a land investment doesn't guarantee big financial rewards. "If you ony get 10 percent a year inflation and you borrowed 10 percent to purchase it, then you aren't earning much," says Jerry Bernau, executive vice president, Center Financial Group, Houston.

Aside from any agricultural value, vacant land doesn't produce income.

The largest leaps in value occur through converting the land to a higher and more profitable use — from agriculture and large lot zoning to residential or commercial use, for example.

When a 10-acre site owned by Bridge Housing Corp. was rezoned by the city of Livermore from low-density residential to high-density residential, for instance, the appraised value went from $800,000 to $1.67 million.

In many parts of the state, "buildable lots with all of the proper government permits and approvals have substantial value," says Georgia Dutro, accounting vice president at Conam, a San Diego-based development firm.

Will Rogers' real estate holdings are another example. With the proper zoning, his 186-acre ranch in Pacific Palisades — now an historic state park — could be sold for as much as $1 million an acre on the private market, according to Pacific Palisades real estate broker Dolly Niemann, who is office manager with the John Douglas Co.

As a park, the land has no value in the private market.

The decisions that create land value aren't made in corporate board rooms; they are made in city council and board of supervisor chambers.

In California cities, large and small, hundreds of high-stakes zoning decisions are made each week. Influenced by well-paid consultants and sophisticated political strategy, these decisions not only affect the size and location of specific developments but they also create billions of dollars worth of real estate values.

Moreover, some local zoning changes that cause some private property ownners to scream "foul" work favorably for other land owners.

"Limiting land supply (through environmental regulations) can have a substantial affect on surrounding land costs," says Washington University Law School professor Daniel R. Mandelker, St. Louis, who has written extensively on this subject.

The fact that the Will Rogers State Park is off limits to development, for instance, has boosted the value of surrounding property owners.

Pointing to flood plain rules, postal zone regulations, wetlands restrictions and open space and parklands zoning as examples, Mandelker argues that government laws which are designed to protect the environment have caused the price of California land to soar.

For new home buyers, the government regulation and regulation-avoidance game explains why California housing costs are 50 percent higher than the national average. Nationwide, the median price of a home is $85,000; in California, it exceeds $145,000.

For the typical house, the cost of labor, materials, land, overhead, profit and financing make up the price of a home. Nationally, labor and materials represent 47 percent of the cost and land represents 25 percent, according to the National Association of Home Builders, Washington, D.C.

In California, land represents 35 to as high as 75 percent of the average house price.

This explains why many Californians cannot afford to act on Will Rogers' investment advice.

Ideas on how to save affordable housing

Special to the Examiner

HOMELESSNESS has seized the front pages, captured the fancy of presidential candidates, received top billing in back-to-back airings of T.V.'s 60 Minutes, and ignited passions in millions of American citizens.

Has the mega-trend of the year been enough, however, to convince the general public and policy makers that every citizen is entitled to decent housing?

In 1949, the U.S. Congress decided it was the law of the land. But today, as California State University Professor Darril Hudson pointed out in a letter he wrote me, "This seems not to be a point of consensus in our society."

Hudson's letter was one of two hundred I received in reaction to my December 20th column about the loss of low-cost government-financed housing in the Bay Area. With loaded disagreements on what should be done to house the poor, there was also a surprising dearth of enthusiasm among many readers about doing anything at all.

In my diatribe about this housing quandary, I described a set of freakish policy blunders and market odysseys that in the next ten to fifteen years could make 20,000 Bay Area low-cost residences unaffordable.

It the Sixties and Seventies, developers, received inexpensive government loans in exchange for building low-cost housing and keeping it affordable for a specified period of time. When the clock runs out on the affordability commitment, however, investors are permitted to evict the tenants, raise the rents and reap a financial windfall.

I offered up three policy options for getting us out of this jumble:

*Force landlords to keep the rents low when their contract
with the federal government to do so has expired.*

Put more public money into the developments to guarantee affordability in the future.

*When their contract with the feds has elapsed, allow
landlords to raise rents and/or evict tenants.*

The voluntary survey raised more questions than it provided answers. Sixty-six percent said property owners should not be forced to keep the rents down.

Tod Spieker of Palo Alto wrote, "Why should the government be allowed to unilaterally go back on a contract."

On the other hand, sixty-five percent said apartment owners should not be allowed to raise rents or evict their tenants.

"It is a simple question of whether private affluence is to take preference over the basic needs of the most vulnerable members of our society," wrote Jack Hillis of Capitola-by-the-Sea.

The mail shows compassion for the rights of tenants, but the altruism is mixed with an eagerness to defend private property rights and the sanctity of a government contract.

It wasn't until I finished reading the letters that I realized this housing puzzle was nothing more than a modern version of the centuries-old rift between renter and landlord.

Defenders of the tenant's plight characterize it as "greed vs. need." The property owner standard-bearers call it "free market vs. screwed-up market."

And because the public respects both ideologies to a point, an arbiter must be found that will balance the rights of the two sides.

Enter the federal government.

The majority seem to accept the same filled-with-hope policy framework that spawned the Great Society programs and created thousands of housing opportuntites. Fifty-eight percent said more government money should be spent to fix the problem.

It's an expensive remedy that feeds the self-interests of both sides: subsicies to investors and relief for the disadvantaged.

Not everyone goes along with this strategy, however. Forty-two percent of those sending along their comments, argued that the government messed it up the first time around and should not be trusted to avoid the same mistakes twice.

As one reader wrote, "With friends like the government, I don't need any more enemies."

Nevertheless, it's timely for this debate to sharpen. The homeless problem is festering in cities everywhere, and it will become more infected if our political caretakers fail to hold onto what little affordable housing we currently have.

On the other hand, for the first time in twenty years housing is becoming a vogue issue, and proposals for big buck quick fixes are pouring out from the nation's capital like water from a broken fire hydrant. The new enlightenment about our country's housing problems is welcomed, but there is a danger that solutions will be hastily conceived and too expensive to defend.

In the past, the politicalization of a problem — however necessary for funding the solution — is often contrary to fiscal wisdom, practicality and rationality.

Fortunately, a cadre of housing pros are devising ways to keep everyone happy within the bounds of good real estate judgement.

One local group that has become outspoken on the issue is the Northern California Association for Non Profit Housing (see **letter below**). Making the problem its number one priority, the organization should be complimented for its civic diligence.

Note: In my column last week, I wrote about another Brad Inman who lives and works in the Bay Area — same name but two different people. After the article appeared, I was informed by the other Mr. Inman's public relations firm that he is not a developer, as I mentioned in my column. He is a building contractor.

Author says builders were once heroes

In 1986 the voters of Newport Beach overwhelmingly rejected a plan by the highly-regarded Irvine Company to expand its Newport Center development.

It wasn't the first time that a powerful California development firm had sand kicked in its face; in this period of no-growth hysteria, developers are frequently belittled, scorned and taunted.

This wasn't always the case, however. "Until the 60's, developers were often considered heroes," says Marc A. Weiss, author of a new book "The Rise of the Community Builders," which provides unique insight into the history of California real estate.

Weiss points to a 1947 Time Magazine cover which was graced with a picture of William Levitt, the famous tract-home sub divider who built New York's Levittown and became a popular symbol of the new suburban concept.

"There may have been differences about how to go about it, but everyone involved shared the common goal of facilitating more housing development," says Weiss.

"Now you have incompatible goals — some groups see land-use rules as an opportunity to promote building and others use them as a way to kill it."

Through the first half of this century, policy makers, developers, and real estate trade associations teamed up to spawn the legal framework for the modern residential subdivision which opened up housing opportunities for millions of American families.

Prior to the explosion in tract-home subdividing, "land was carved into building lots and sold for whatever use the new owners intended," writes Weiss.

"What made the Levittown story of the late 1940s so important was not just that the Levitts had found a way to mass produce affordable housing, but that the housing was an attractive investment for young families precisely because of the planning and construction of a complete community," according to the book.

Pushed by the real estate industry, a complicated set of federal, state and local development regulations created greater efficiency in the homebuilding business, helped spark an unparalleled housing production boom, and boosted the homeownership rate.

Subdivision regulations approved by the California legislature in 1929, for instance, were designed to make new housing sites accessible to parks, highways, and other public facilities.

And while the new rules were intended to increase the quality of community design, they were also a way to minimize competition. By increasing developer start-up costs, the laws were barriers to those who were considering entering the development business.

"One group of subdividers, referred to as curbstoners, fly-by-nighters, land butchers, and lot sellers were a source of scandal and market instability that community builders hoped to eliminate as competitors through government regulation. . ." writes Weiss.

Today, the housing industry is incensed with some of the same building regulations and frequently berates urban planners who wish to impose unreasonable rules on homebuilders.

In California in the 1920s it was a different story. Though private property rights was an issue then as now, the state's largest homebuilders and real estate brokers provided the political muscle behind California's subdivision map and planning acts. These state laws set the stage for today's stiffer development guidelines which are constantly under attack by the industry.

"California was widely regarded. . .as the state in which Realtors as an organized force were strongly involved in promoting urban land-use planning legislation," writes Weiss. At the time, brokers and developers believed "there was too much at stake to leave private land-use to the vicissitudes of a free market."

In this session of the legislature, for instance, the California Building Industry Association and the California Association of Realtors are pushing legislation which would spread around the costs for providing schools, highways and other public facilities — taking financial pressure off the developer.

Sixty years ago, real estate groups "wanted the public sector to socialize more of the costs of urban land development, whether it be roads, schools, parks or water. . .they wanted public officials to better coordinate. . .so that the cost burden could be reduced. . .," according to Weiss.

Community losing image as a funky neighborhood

Special to the Examiner

AFTER I wrote about the ANIMBYs ("Not-In-My-Backyard" neighborhood activists) last year, I promptly heard from Glen Park neighborhood leader Joan Seiwald who said she was a "card-carrying NIMBY and proud of it."

From fighting BART and halting the freeway expansion to spawning a neighborhood home rehabilitation program, she and her husband have spent nearly 30 years improving and preserving the quality of life in Glen Park in San Francisco.

Often overshadowed by Bernal Heights and Noe Valley, Glen Park is just now getting the recognition it deserves. In response to my recent article on neighborhoods destined to become trendy, it was the overwhelming reader choice.

Last week, after sniffing around for more than hour along the crooked residential pathways that weave through Glen Park, I couldn't figure out what the local boosters were cooing about. They had used words like "charming "and "quaint."

Then I drove along Diamond where it intersects with Chenery, and I discovered the Glen Park secret. I parked next to the Glen Park hardware store, spotted a Bank of America, a shoe repair shop, the Glen Park cleaners that offers 10 percent prepaid discounts and the Glen Park Station bar that sells carry-out liquor.

Because of its distinctive flavor, it reminded me of a mountain village.

It also has favorable weather. The climate "isn't as good as the Mission but it's better than the Sunset," says Seiwald.

I sat on the bench in the middle of the commercial hub at Chenery and Diamond and watched the automobiles go by — a reliable way to measure a community's character.

A rather typical array of middle-class domestic and foreign sedans and wagons passed by along with a couple of jeeps and one of those new 4x4 Monteros. I thought I saw two Jaguars within minutes of each other, but then I realized it was the same car. It was probably owned by a realty agent or someone lost trying to find their way to Noe Valley.

Nonetheless, there is evidence that this place is no longer a backwater. The neighborhood already has a tanning salon, at least one gourmet 'sandwich shop and a proliferation of sky lights on residential roof tops — a sign that the neighborhood is going upscale.

Folks mustn't worry about Glen Park ever looking like Union Street, however, but funky may no longer be an appropriate adjective either.

"It's still a little rough around the edges, but new development, for one, is a sign that change is in the winds," says neighborhood resident Carol Gamble.

The role of BART in this transformation can't be underestimated. When the plan to build a BART stop was first proposed, residents argued that their neighborhood was a working-class community that didn't need BART because it was designed for downtown office workers who wouldn't live in Glen Park.

That's no longer true today.

The neighborhood's proximity to rapid transit gives the community an exalted ranking on the accessible commute scale and helps make it a prime spot for the urban home buyers who work downtown. Here's the scenario: white and pink collar semi-upscale homeowners exit BART, walk one block to pick up their cleaning, walk across the street to purchase a Koala four pack, grab copies of the Glen Park News and go home.

"I feel safe walking home at night (from BART), and frankly you can't say that about all places in the city," says Gamble who is active in the neighborhood association.

Finding a home priced under $200,000 today is almost impossible in Glen Park. If you can find one, it's probably going to take a lot of work and it won't have more than two bedrooms. Expect to pay about $250,000. For a three bedroom, the price is in excess of $300,000.

Though determined to protect the community from too much change, long-time residents such as Seiwald believe there are benefits with a more affluent crowd moving in. "They spend more to buy their house, and so are more concerned about the neighborhood and want to get involved," she says.

Because of the vigilance of local neighborhood leaders, change here will never be too dramatic. Not as ideological as the activists in Bernal Heights or as slick as the Noe Valley crowd, the Glen Park Association is organized into a variety of committees that monitor neighborhood issues.

Last month, the public safety committee hosted Sgt. David Robinson of the Police Narcotics Division who gave residents a presentation on drug sales. A tree planting program is in the works and the Association continues to sponsor Cub and Boy Scout packs.

On My Livable and Sensible Scale:

In 1982, I nearly bought my first house in Glen Park. After visiting the neighborhood last week, I regret that I hadn't made this cute little community my home.

Congress eyes mortgage break

There are rumblings in the nation's capital that the sacred housing tax break — the deductibility of mortgage interest — may come under attack, as the U.S. Congress scrambles to reduce the deficit.

Under current law, homeowners can only deduct interest on home mortgages valued at less than $1 million on their federal income tax returns, giving them a generous tax break but costing the federal Treasury billions of dollars a year.

'We may not want to touch it, but reducing the deficit may take precedent over everything else,' says Congressman Robert Matsui, Committee. Matsui doesn't believe Congress will act this year but says that it may be "on the table in 1989 or 1990."

The door was opened last year for chipping away at the homeownership tax break when the Congress placed the $1 million cap on mortgage deduction.

Congressmen, lobbyists, analysts and industry representatives interviewed for this column all agree that the Congress isn't finished tampering with the 75-year-old mortgage interest deduction. Last week, presidential candidate Jesse Jackson stirred up the debate further with his budget proposal that called for tightening up the mortgage deduction.

Not surprisingly, real estate groups are gripping for a fight.

"Homeowners should be fully aware that there are some people in the bowels of Congress who will threaten it (the deduction)," says Kent Colton, executive vice president of the National Association of Home Builders, Washington, D.C.

Last year, while conceding that the new ceiling would only pinch a handful of very affluent home owners, the builders unsuccessfully argued that putting a cap on the home mortgage deduction was the "camel's nose under the tent" and that the congress would come along later and lower it some more.

With a budget conscious Congress, however, it isn't easy to defend moneyed home buyers who benefit from the mortgage interest tax deduction when buying million dollar homes.

"The mortgage interest deduction is as American as motherhood and apple pie but the million dollar cap was saying that there were excesses," says Matsui.

And despite the new ceiling, the distribution of the mortgage interest tax benefit still makes it vulnerable. More than 65 percent of the total amount of home loan interest deducted is claimed by the most affluent American households, or those who earn in excess of $50,000.

For the average homeowner, the deduction provides a significant boost, however. For example, a family making $30,000 a year with a $80,000 home loan at today's interest rates would pay approximately $10,000 in mortgage interest. With the home loan interest deduction, their tax bite is reduced by more than $2,000 a year.

And by increasing the number of exemptions on their W-2 form, homeowners can realize the tax savings in their pay check right away.

Though deficit concerns prevail, no one expects the Congress to take away the mortgage deduction for the average homeowner. 'The outcry from the middle class would be too great,' says Matsui.

But the very rich are an easier target. One way is to reduce the $1 million cap. At $300,000 for instance, still only a small fraction of homeowners would be affected.

The Congress could also decide to limit the deductibility of mortgage interest to primary residences, which would cut out the tax benefit for vacation homes. Tax writers proposed this change several years ago but were beaten back by real estate groups who are unwilling to compromise on any changes to the mortgage interest deduction.

Nevertheless, the Congress is likely to ignore their hard line. "Since the 1986 tax reform act took away the deductibility of other consumer interest, it (the mortgage deduction) stands out there all by itself," says Barry Zigas, executive director of the National Low-Income Housing Coalition.

Home buyer tax credit is catching on

After four years of bureaucratic and legislative entanglements, hundreds of California first-time home buyers are availing themselves of a federal income tax credit that substantially reduces the cost of owning a home.

Dubbed Mortgage Credit Certificates (MCCs), the program has helped more than 1,700 first-time home buyers in Sacramento and 800 in Santa Clara County. Similar efforts are underway in the cities of Compton and Fairfield and in Sutter and Marin counties.

Despite the success in a handful of California communities, however, most cities are reluctant to carry out the MCC program. As a consequence, more than 25,000 middle-income California home buyers are missing out on a lucrative tax break each year.

Unlike many complicated government programs, MCCs are simple to administer. They are a direct federal income tax credit that is granted to home buyers who obtain a market-rate mortgage.

The credit reduces the home buyer's federal tax liability by an amount tied to how much is paid in annual mortgage interest.

For example, a home buyer in Sacramento who borrows $75,000 receives an annual tax credit of approximately $1,500. The benefit is realized when taxpayers file their year end income tax returns.

Experiences from cities that are using MCCs debunk several myths about the program. Marin and Santa Clara counties, for instance, are proof that the innovative tax scheme can work in a high cost housing market. Critics claimed it was only doable in modestly-priced areas.

A statistical profile of home buyers who have used MCCs disproves the notion that they are an expensive government program that only aids affluent home buyers. Sixty percent of the MCC recipients in Sacramento have incomes of less than $30,000. Serving a group with an average age below 35, MCCs are most helpful for younger families.

To prevent abuse, federal rules restrict how much a borrower can earn and place a ceiling on the price of homes that can be purchased with a MCC.

In Sacramento, the average mortgage amount is $72,998 and 70 percent of the homes sold involving a credit certificate sell for less than $80,000.

MCCs are proving to a be a cost-effective government subsidy as well. In one study prepared by the California Association of Realtors, a MCC program provided assistance to 743 home buyers compared to 550 for another popular housing subsidy program, mortgage revenue bonds.

But if MCCs make so much sense, why has local government been hesitant to get behind them?

"Tax reform put a ton of uncertainty into the program," says analyst Mark Thompson of the California Association of Realtors. In fact, MCCs were in limbo at least twice in the last few years when Congress worked on changes to the tax code.

In the most recent twist, the program was halted altogether because of a sunset provision in the 1986 tax reform law. Technically, only those cities already issuing certificates can offer them in the future, though a bill currently working its way through the legislature would open them up to other communities.

There may be a more fundamental reason for the lack of enthusiasm for MCCs. Unlike other government subsidy programs that have industry constituencies who directly benefit from fees and low interest rate loans, MCCs have no constituency to lobby elected officials. In the absence of an organized group of home buyers pushing them, local officials have ignored the opportunity.

Because cities and counties have been reluctant to implement the MCC program, state Senator John Seymour of Orange County asked the state to get involved. He specifically requested the California Housing Finance Agency (CHFA) to take up the cause of issuing credit certificates to qualified first-time home buyers.

But Housing Finance Agency Executive Director Karney Hodge argues that the program is more suited for local government.

Without local or state leadership, Seymour is considering legislation that would force the state's involvement.

"In a state with out-of-control housing costs, it's disgraceful we can't make this thing work," says Seymour.

State heading for real estate crisis

Last week, it was reported that the median price for a used home in California jumped more than 4.6 percent in one month (June). It's news which is certain to feed the suspicion that higher California home prices equal fatter real estate commissions and a rosy picture for the housing industry.

Shortsighted, say the experts.

There's a new theory: Skyrocketing home prices have worsened the state's affordability problem which will reduce the number of home sales and, in the long term, will hurt the real estate brokerage business and other segments of the housing industry, which are temporarily enjoying prosperity.

"With first-time buyers effectively shut out of many markets, housing in California may face the danger of becoming a zero-sum game," argues California Association of Realtors (CAR) economist Joel Singer, Los Angeles.

The new worry explains why—despite a dynamic housing market—CAR is speaking out on the affordability squeeze that many new home buyers face. Moreover, the state-wide trade association is promoting new policies at the national level which will aid first-time buyers. This isn't altruism, it's in the self-interest of an industry already worried about fewer home sales.

"Right now, business is good for the average real estate broker and they may not be worrying about such things, but they must realize that if we don't have affordable housing we won't have sales," says Ira Gribin, President-Elect, National Association of Realtors (NAR), Encino.

Housing policy gurus believe the real estate market depends on trickle up. Over the long term, without an adequate number of new home buyers getting into homeownership the entire housing market — and the volume of home sales — slows down. Because of the price squeeze on thousands of entry-level buyers, the now-robust trade-up market will eventually evaporate, say experts.

"If you can't get on the bottom rung of homeownership and begin to develop equity then you never have the opportunity to move up the housing market ladder," says Ken Rosen, chairman of the U.C. Berkeley Center for Real Estate and Urban Economics, Berkeley.

Statistics on home prices and house sales support the notion. In the last ten years, the median home price in California has jumped more than 127 percent. Today, less than 30 percent of all households can afford a home in California.

And as affordability diminished, the volume of home sales shrank. According to CAR, single-family sales in California peaked in 1978 at 605,000 units and have continued at an average annual pace of 579,000 in the late seventies, but have fallen to an average of around 500,000 in the last four years.

"It doesn't hurt just brokers; it also hurts builders, lenders and others involved in delivering housing," says Rosen.

If the trend doesn't reverse itself, it means hard times for the home building industry, says Dale Stuard, President of the National Association of Home Builders, Newport Beach.

The vast majority of builders today are responding to the monied move-up buyers but Stuard warns that the market has limits. 'My advice is don't ignore the lower end of the market, and keep in mind that today's first-time buyers are the trade-up buyers of tomorrow,' says Stuard.

Solving the problem takes more than marketing savvy and good will, however. It requires resources because one of the biggest obstacles to buying a home is the sizable down payments that are often required.

"The housing affordability crisis isn't a monthly payment crisis, it's a down payment crisis; with the median price of a home exceeding $170,000, the downpayment is as high as $35,000," says Rosen. Even with two members of a household working, many young new home buyers have trouble accumulating the necessary downpayment.

Rosen advocates the creation of a federal housing retirement account similar to an IRA which would protect savings from income taxes and spawn greater savings for downpayments.

But such a tax break may not be enough in high-cost states such as California. "It may require a direct federal subsidy," says Rosen.

In the meantime, the bleak affordability picture for new home buyers is expected to get worse. And everyone involved in housing will be worse off for it.

Road to yuppies' pockets is through their stomachs

Special to the Examiner

OAKLAND — "We know who grows our peaches," brags produce man Bill Gentner as he carves up a Brentwood Farms peach, shares a slice and plops another into his mouth. Then he closes his eyes, smiles and says, "These things give me a rush everytime."

In the Del Tomaso produce store in the new open-air fresh food Rockridge Market Hall, Gentner is stocking five varieties of beans, including dragon tongue and purple french. With more than 40 percent of his products organically grown, he also proudly carries nine varieties of tomatoes.

The 2,000-square-foot produce store in North Oakland is one of eight upscale, independent food vendors who occupy space in the latest East Bay retail success story.

Real estate experts believe that the demand exists for public food markets because they have cachet among the young with money. The on-the-move yuppie of the early '80s is evolving into the "new traditionalist" who — often with kids — spends more time at home, and in the kitchen.

Therefore, the once thankless and hurried task of grocery shopping has taken on new meaning. And to meet this demand, food merchants are trying to make the experience more exciting.

Developing a successful neighborhood or a regional public food market, however, is fraught with difficulties, including unusual property management problems. There's also the financial risk. Last week, the highly touted Farmer's Ranch Market in affluent Irvine went belly up.

With its 16,000 square feet fully leased, the $4 million Rockridge Market Hall has sailed the rocky waters well. With no chains or franchises, other vendors include Grace's Bakery, the Pasta Shop, Sam's Meat and Poultry, the Rockridge Fish Market, Paul Marcus Wine and E.G. Kroeger, which sells coffee, tea and chocolate.

Contributing to the European atmosphere and guaranteeing a morning-to-midnight stream of shoppers is Oliveto's Cafe, which occupies the first and second floors of the year-old development.

An example of the hottest trend in retail development, Market Hall is in the center of one of the strongest East Bay neighborhood commercial strips.

Because of its ideal location at Shatter and College avenues, commercial brokers dub it a prized "100 percent corner." Thousands of professionals pour out of the adjacent BART station each weekday evening eager to spend a few dollars before heading home.

"A lot of what we did was in response to the site," says Tony Wilson, who developed Market Hall with his sister, Sarah, and brother, Peter. "The only way to make it work was to have a single-use building so people would enter and shop throughout the space. In this case, we decided on food."

Emphasizing personal service, unusual items and high-grade priducts, the project embraces the "wholesale concept and the idea of getting the customer closer to the product."

"We'll cut open any product in the market upon request for the customer to inspect," says Gentner, who offers sample trays for many of his produce items.

Wilson estimates that 600 to 1,000 people pass through daily. And their tastes are extravagant.

For example, one of the house beers at Oliveto's is Portmunden Union, a German pilsner. In the stores, shoppers can find blue corn tortilla chips, seven grain pretzels and fudge made by the Briggantine Monks.

"Whenever we put the inexpensive fish out, it doesn't sell; (consumers) want the boneless, the highest quality," Bays Daniel Lambert, who with partner Allen Kuehn owns the fish market.

Typical of other operators in Market Hall, Lambert and Kuehn have a combined 30 years' experience in the fish business.

Wilson developed Market Hall amid protests from the Rockridge neighborhood. Now complete, with the last vendor space just rented, it has made regular, opponents of many opponents.

Being in the heart of a lively and dense neighborhood is crucial to Market Hall's success.

But heavy demand doesn't solve other problems. Developing a food market has tenant-improvement and property-management challenges uncommon in a conventional retail development.

Because of the food, Wilson says: "public health regulations present all sorts of barriers. We constructed elaborate door systems and retrofitted the building with special air curtains because some of the food uses must be sealed.

"Most grocery stores work with an air-conditioning system so when they get changes in the weather there aren't any problems. It may be difficult trying this in Contra Costa because of the hot climate."

Putting the tenant mix together was another obstacle. While the independent operators are experienced, they aren't always well capitalized. 'They're hard to find," he says.

And it involves intense management. "We are in the business of managing a market; it's not like renting space to 10 store fronts where you just collect the rent."

Nevertheless, city officials and realty developers all over the country are clamoring to copy Market Hall. Just completed is a 47,000-square-foot public market in Mountain View. And under construction in Emeryville is a 55,000-square-foot food market. Both are being developed by California Public Markets Inc. and are modeled after Granville Island food market in Vancouver, B.C.

In planning the original scheme for redeveloping San Francisco's Pier 45, a group of local officials visited Pike's public market in Seattle.

The next time they want advice on how a public food market operates, they need travel no farther than Oakland.

Bragging rights

Editor's note: Hume ownership is often referred to as part of the American dream. It also can be an obsession in a home-buying market as difficult as the Bay Area's. Here's one writer's view of how crazy home ownership can be.

THE WACKY Bay Area real estate market is making people crazy. The only thing homeowners want to talk about these days is how their home values have skyrocketed. In fact, the "my-house-is-worth" chit chat that infects cocktail parties, over-the-fence scuttlebutt and lunchtime shmoozing is crowding out the important issues of the day.

Ask intelligent people what the greenhouse effect is and they are apt to tell you it's the green stuff they are earning through the equity built up in their house. Instead of poring over the positions of the presidential candidates, equity-fat homeowners are fishing around for the latest tidbits on how much their home has inflated.

I'm not talking about your average greedy moron; these are people who ordinarily discuss such weighty issues as our public schools, the Persian Gulf or the war on drugs. Now, they are figuring out ways to turn the discussion politely to how much their neighbor's house sold for.

Salty debates about religion, literature and politics have given way to conversations that are peppered with "$225,000? Wow"; "Six offers over asking price, can you believe it?" and "To think we only bought it four years ago, incredible."

Why silence is golden

Well it's time to stop all of this nonsense. Here are eight reasons why it is rude and unwise to go around talking to people about how the value of your home tripled in only five years.

When you brag about your home price appreciation, remember you sound like a money-driven goof. One of the first rules of etiquette is never to boast about how much you earn or how much you own. Crowing about your house inflation is downright uncivil.

Be aware that when talking about appreciation in a room full of people the odds are good that you are making half of the people there feel bad — 50 percent of the households in the Bay Area are renters.

Moreover, never bring it up in front of your secretary, the local police officer or firefighter. On their salaries, most of them can't afford to buy a home in the Bay Area and don't need to be reminded of that scary fact.

Talking about the price spiral may lead you to believe that you are smarter than you are. Because your house appreciated 100 percent, you conclude you must be bright; at least that's what your dad from Peoria tells you. Of course he lives in a place where prices are headed south and he doesn't understand that every Bay Area homeowner — dumb or brilliant — is raking it in.

Don't forget, there is a way to lose your job in this scenario. If prices continue to climb, young skilled workers won't be able to afford to live here; companies will move out; and the economy will go to hell. You'll be out of a job with nobody left here to buy your over-priced house.

These are only paper profits. Much like the stock market, they aren't worth much until you sell. But unlike Wall Street, there is a hefty charge for cashing out, like the interest and points you will pay to refinance the debt.

Don't forget that all of this chatter is great fodder for political "redistributionists." When a whole bunch of people begin boasting about their obscene profits, the progressive crowd will figure out ways to take some of it away from you. For example, watch the mortgage interest deduction go out the window when the deficit worsens and windfall real estate profits begin to look gluttonous. Just ask a big oil exec what happened in the 1970s.

There are some economic costs that you should consider. When your home prices go up, the entire social strata of your neighborhood is elevated. Even if you can't afford it, this trend puts pressure on you to buy new furniture, hire a gardener, put in better landscaping and purchase a new car.

Then there's the higher car and house insurance premiums, and shops start moving into the neighborhood with merchandise you can't afford.

Finally, some more sobering news. While real estate types are determined to persuade you otherwise, there is bound to be a market correction. The last surge in home prices in the late 1970s was followed by a change that saw some properties lose value. In fact, the last ones in during that boom were condominium buyers and they are still shell-shocked.

If despite this advice you still can't contain yourself, then talk about your equity gains with a little tact. Don't exaggerate by more than 10 percent. Don't mention it more than once a week to the same person.

Never bring it up in front of your children; they will assume you are worth more than you are and use it against you someday.

And lastly, don't forget to enjoy your home. Pipe down and have some quiet time with your gold mine.

Legislation will ban discrimination against children

Special to the Examiner

HUNDREDS OF California mobile park owners, faced with federal legislation requiring them to open up adult-only parks to children, are converting to either senior-only or family parks.

Adult parks, which limit occupancy to residents over age 18, represent a majority of the estimated 500,000 mobile home spaces in California.

The conversion has alarmed some housing advocates who are worried about the number of parks that switch to senior-only status to get around the anti-discrimination measure. That's because senior-only parks will be allowed to keep out children and teen-agers; but they also won't be able to rent to young couples without children.

"Opportunity for first-time home buyers are difficult already in the Bay Area," said Thomas Cook, director of housing and land use for the Bay Area Council. "Anything that reduces the stock of affordable housing will bid up the cost of the few starter homes we do have."

The rush to convert to senior park status is due to HR 1158, a landmark fair housing bill sponsored by U. S. Rep. Don Edwards, D-San Jose. President Reagan is expected to sign the bill into law, possibly as early as next week.

The bill is designed to wipe out the remaining vestiges of housing discrimination and outlaw adult-only parks or discrimination based on "familial" status.

However, mobile home parks throughout the state are taking steps to prevent occupancy by tenants younger than age 55 because .of fears about the new ban.

Santa Clara County a hotbed

In Santa Clara County alone, as many as 13,500 mobile home tenants could be notified that their parks may be converted to senior-only or family parks, according to Jorj Tilson, executive director of the Santa Clara Manufactured Housing Educational Trust. The trust is an industry lobbying group.

Santa Clara County has a large concentration of mobile homes, 75 percent of them adult only.

A senior park is one of three different categories with specific rules that govern who and who cannot live in a mobile home park.

Senior parks only permit people over the age of 55 or 62, depending on the make-up of the household.

Generally, anyone is permitted to live in a family park. An adult-only park is restricted to tenants over the age of 18 and therefore exclude children and most teen-agers.

As originally drafted, Edwards' bill would have superceded current California law which permits mobile home parks designated as senior parks to bar those under age 18. But because of an intense lobbying campaign on the part of the Western Mobile Home Association, the bill was amended.

As finally approved by Congress earlier this month, it provides owners with a way around the ban against children.

By converting their adult-only park.to senior-only, adults can continue to exclude children. The new bill exempts housing occupied solely by persons 62 years and older from the new rules.

The other exemption is if a park has less than 80 percent of its coaches occupied by at least one person who is 55 or older and all new occupancies are restricted to only older persons.

Michael Walters, president of the San Diego Chapter .Mobile Home Association and an attorney, estimates that as many as 50 percent of the 250 parks he advises will convert to family parks.

Many others are expected to go the senior route. "Park owners who have promised their residents that they will be adult-only parks may have no other choice," says Michael McGuire of the association. "Senior citizens don't want to trip over tricycles, and there are certain amenities (in adult-only parks) that kids will ruin."

Current residents under the age of 55 will not be affected by the changeover if the bill becomes law. The new law only affects leasing practices when a vacancy arises.

Some experts say the conversions to senior-only could contribute to a glut in mobile homes, which may lower the value of mobile homes throughout the state.

"Converting to a senior park kills the resale market," says Thomas Kerr, a mobile home park owner and publisher of the Mobile-home Parks Report, a monthly newsletter for the industry.

Calling it an overreaction by some park owners, Kerr says he sees it as "a window of opportunity." He says, "I am thinking of going the other way and (converting) to a family park. There will be a lot of demand (from existing coach owners who are younger) who don't want to live in a geriatric ghetto."

Low-cost housing's red flag

In 1985, against a storm of protest from residents in the surrounding area, a proposed 60-unit afford-able housing development in Corta Madera was vetoed by the voters at the ballot box. Disgruntled homeowners were convinced the housing project would drive down their property values, which is a common reaction to controversial low-cost developments.

But such fears are unfounded, according to a new report just released by the California Department of Housing and Community Development (HCD), Sacramento.

"This paper is offered in the hope that planners, city officials, housing developers and affordable housing advocates will find it useful in countering or defusing the argument of damaged property val-ues (that is used) in opposition to the development of affordable housing," reads the executive sum-mary of the report, "The Effects of Subsidized and Affordable Housing on Property Values."

A compendium of fifteen different studies examining housing projects in cities throughout the country, the analysis offers convincing evidence that "subsidized or affordable housing will not lower property values," says William Murphy, Assistant Chief, HCD.

The study looks at government-owned and privately developed subsidized projects including housing for the handicapped, group homes for the mentally disabled and mixed-income developments in which both affordable and market-rate units are integrated into the same project. In no case, did the presence of these developments cause property values in the area to decline.

In the worst case scenario, the proximity to a low-cost development in Fairfax, Va., was a factor in slowing down the rate of inflation on adjacent homes. While still appreciating in value, those closest to the subsidized units didn't increase as fast in value as those farther away.

But in 14 of the 15 studies even this modest difference was absent when affordable housing was built next door.

For housing advocates, the study affirms what they have been saying for a long time.

"Property values have not declined near our projects," argues Donald Terner who heads up the San Francisco-based non-profit corporation BRIDGE that builds affordable housing in the Bay Area. "In fact, we have seen a spate of upgrading and higher values around our recently completed units."

Not only true of subsidized housing, the reduced-property-value red flag is thrown up to oppose market-rate multi-family housing developments.

"Even though it is irrational, people develop anxiety quickly about renters moving in nearby," says Lynn Sedway, urban real estate economist and consultant, San Francisco.

The presence of condominiums in some instances can bring new buyers into the market and actu-ally lift property values, says real estate consultant Michael Meyers, Kenneth Leventhal & Company, Newport Beach. "(Home buyers) come into an area looking at condos but they will also look at nearby single-family homes. Even if they are slightly higher, they will often choose the single-family because that is really what they want, which puts more pressure on single-family home values," says Meyers.

Many times the people who move in earn more than the people who already live there, according to Sedway but, "opponents often don't take the time to look at those facts."

If the evidence is so persuasive, why do these myths linger? Some housing advocates believe the property value argument is a red herring that is used to cover up fears about economic or racial integration that an affordable development might bring on. Other opponents worry about the loss of open space or increased traffic.

More often, the apprehension is a hangover from an earlier period, says Terner. "People have the stereoptypical image of burned out public housing with drugs and crime, which did decrease property values."

Murphy says that it would "take a psychologist" to figure out the motives of those who oppose housing and that what's needed is better education. He is hopeful that affordable housing proponents will use the new report as "ammunition against the fears and get across the overwhelming conclusions that affordable housing is not something people need to fret about."

Flexibility allows Hacienda to thrive in changing market

Special to the Examiner

DURING A meeting several years ago about the approval of the mammoth Hacienda Business Park in Pleasanton, a disgruntled resident of the bedroom community compared the development to a "whale in a small pond."

In the early 1980s, plans for the Bay Area's two colossal campus-style business parks —585-acre Bishop Ranch in San Ramon and 876-acre Hacienda — had plenty of skeptics. Would companies move to the suburbs? Would employees want to work there? Would the no-growth movement stall their progress? Would they be a good long-term investment? Would they change suburban life forever?

The answers to these questions are starting to come in. Only eight miles apart, Bishop Ranch and Hacienda provide ample evidence to evaluate the long-term outlook for suburban business parks in the Bay Area.

"It's no longer a new or pioneering idea," says Angelo J. Siracusa, president of the business-sponsored Bay Area Council. "Industry moving to the suburbs is a national trend of suburbanizing economic activity."

Business parks are good economic policy, he argues, because they offer an alternative to Bay Area companies that might otherwise move out of the region, and they are good public policy because "firms are closer to affordable housing."

"You don't have to squint very hard or get very philosophical to see where the growth is going to in the Bay Area," says Steve Chamberlin of Rouse and Associates, which has built two office buildings i at Hacienda. "Where else can you go with room to expand and satisfy the desires of your work force?"

UC-Berkeley professor David Dowall coined the phrase "suburban industrialization." He says it's a trend that has picked up momentum in the last couple of years. "The drive to get higher quality labor has intensified and the suburbs provide direct access to the secondary labor force."

Studies point to "incredible absorption levels of (office) space in the suburbs," Dowall says. For instance, Hacienda and Bishop Ranch absorb as much office space annually as the entire San Francis co office market.

Environmentalist are contemptuous of the conversion of prime open space into neatly groomed plots for dozens of large commercial buildings.

"It would be a big mistake to produce more of these large-scale cookie-cutter business parks," says Larry Orman, head of of People for Open Space of San Francisco. "They worsen traffic congestion and pause the region to expand further and further out to places like the Central Valley. Some day we will wake up and wonder what happened to our economy in the Bay Area."

Nevertheless, developers like Alex Mehran, who built Bishop Ranch with his father, Masud, are looking for new locations that may set off the second wave of these mega-parks.

Hacienda Business Park

A co-venture of Prudential Property Co. and maverick developer Joe Callahan, Hacienda is Northern California's largest business park. With a scheduled build out by the year 2000, it is planned to contain more than 11.75 million square feet of mixed-used space at a total price tag of $1.86 billion. The development will boost Pleasanton's work force by 36,000 people.

The project is proof that a large i business park plan must be adapt able to changing market conditions and the scrutinizing Bay Area political environment.

An example of that flexibility was the decision to open the park to more than 2,000 units of housing — a land use that wasn't even conceived of less than four years ago. It was one of several adjustments made in response to rising vacancy rates and falling rents in the region's commercial real estate market.

"If you're going to get through a project the scale of Hacienda, then you have to be opportunistic," says Prudential Vice President Robert Shallenberger. "There has been an evolution in specialization — some firms get used to doing just residential or just commercial or only shopping centers — but when you're dealing with a park of this size, you can't take that approach."

When Callahan and Prudential began to tie up land in the late 1970s, Hacienda was to be perfectly poised for capturing the overflow from Silicon Valley's high-tech boom.

"If you look at our older buildings you can still see the truck-loading docks built for (research and development) space," says park spokesman David Williams. "Now we don't have zilch of that (high tech).

"When the Silicon Valley went bust, they had to scramble to shift gears," says Charles Wiser of Corn-core Commercial Real Estate Services in Pleasanton. "The fact they went from nothing in 1983 to more than more than 3 million square feet leased space today is remarkable."

Still, depressed office market conditions have dramatically slowed the pace of Hacienda's build out "Prudential is carrying a little more land than they would have liked," Williams says.

At an economic conference last year Callahan said, "It has taken me a while to learn that you had to take tenants without them paying rent. This isn't a business you make money in every year. You have got be in it for the long term."

Prudential understands the long-term view. When Shallenberger was asked whether the project was a winner he said, "We have every reason to believe that we are on target but you are going to have to come back in five years and ask me that question."

Rough beginnings

Creating problems for the development in the early days were the expensive steps Callahan and Prudential took to defuse community resistance, which included two ballot initiatives and several lawsuit. The park's $260 million infrastructure was an important factor in winning over community sentiment Williams says, and will create long-term value.

But the political problems also delayed the project at a key juncture in its development

"We had 200 acres of third-party transactions (sales to tenants or developers) when we were sued under California land use and environmental law," Callahan says. "We lost about half of the transactions" because legally the deals couldn't be consummated until the lawsuits were settled.

With the external battles complete, the internal leadership at Hacienda has also changed. Prudential, the institution, is taking over 'the reins from Joe Callahan, the personality. Callahan's vision, his outspoken, sometimes brash style, were closely identified with the park.

While admitting that Hacienda has taken a heavy financial toll on him, Callahan is philosophical about the outcome. "Most guys that go after a 1,000 acres and try to subdivide it aren't around to talk about it. I am still here and I'm still kicking."

It's an eccentric little town — but that's its charm

Special to the Examiner

LAST WEEK, when I drove along El Camino Real in the San Mateo County community of Colma, I quickly realized this town was a little bizarre. There's something about a million dead people buried in an assortment of cemeteries lying next door to hundreds of brand new spick-and-span cars lined up at the many car dealers that form the gateway to Colma.

No doubt about it, the small town of Colma is an odd place, a perfect setting for an off-beat movie like the new award-winning documentary created by student filmmaker Barry Brann.

His 26-minute flick is dubbed the "King of Colma." It profiles Raymond Ottoboni Jr. whose family ran Colma for nearly 30 years. With a reputation as a notorious, gambler, he was mayor, councilman, policeman amd chief of police. For decades his family was one of the town's largest property owner.

Although he was indicted for voter fraud in 1976, Ottoboni gave the place some style. He pleaded no contest — the equivalent of a guilty plea — to the charge. He moved to Rono in 1987 and he still proclaims his innocence.

The town's earlier history was quieter. Because of fears about annexation by San Francisco, the owners of the cemeteries in Colma incorporated the city in 1921. But they had a tricky time finding a name that would stick.

Sari Mateo County rejected the town's first name, Memorial Park, and the post office said no to their use of Lawndale because of confusion with the Southern California town with the same name.

Some locals say the term Colma was derived from a young boy's expression about the weather there: it's "cold, Ma."

With a cemetery for every conceivable religion and only a handful of living residents, the city has been best known as a place to rest after death. It wasn't until 1982 that the city incorporated a tract of county land called Sterling Park, which tripled the town's population. Today, 717 people live there in 250 homes. There are few apartments.

Built in the 1950s, Sterling Park is perched on a hill. The architectural styles are your plain vanilla variety and have "always been starter homes," says City Manager Frances Liston. Still, "finding a place for less than $200,000 is getting tough."

Hal Donahue, realty salesman, travel agent and city councilman, has a duplex on the market for $419,000. He thinks he'll have no problem Belling it. "Prices are going up here like everywhere."

Some of the small bungalows have views of the vast open spaces created by the cemeteries. The day I was there, the fog that regularly' visits the town created a blur over the grave stones. For a few minutes, I forgot what was out there.

The cemeteries offer another tangible benefit. Cypress Lawn will bury local residents at no charge. The unique city perk may not be enough of an incentive to move there but it's a nice touch.

The bad news is that the cemeteries, like public parks, don't contribute a dime in taxes to the city. Due to a quirk in Proposition 13, none of the property taxes collected in Colma go to city government. Only 20 cities in the state are in this bind in which the county tax collector keeps all of the revenue.

The dilemma explains why the city has been eager to attract new retail facilities. "We depend on the sales tax revenue," Liston says. "Without it we couldn't run the city."

The car dealers are the fattest contributor to the sales tax rolls. The new Metro Center shopping mall off Interstate 280, which includes the Nordstrom's Rack (a discount outlet for the department store), also generates sizable revenue.

But the auto dealers and the retail center are expensive to police, according to Donahue, which explains why a town of only 717 people needs 15 policemen.

And the city is figuring out how to prepare for the costs for the new BART line, scheduled for completion in 1994. While many suburban cities would give anything to get BART connection, officials in Colma are less eager.

"BART is going to w a major problem," Liston says. "Just imagine the traffic — our streets won't be able to handle it. And then there is the crime that will come."

BART's presence created another rift around town when some county officials complained to the Legislature that the Colma Volunteer Fire Department wasn't prepared to handle BART. That burned up some hard-working volunteer firefighters.

When I heard this story I realized why I liked Colma. I come from a weird small Southern Illinois town — a little like Colma — where people are unpretentious and where you don't insult or even joke about the volunteer fire department.

On My Livable and Sensible Scale:

Colma is eccentric, but I wouldn't have it any other way.

Bishop Ranch attracted PG&E, Chevron

Special to the Examiner

BATTERED with record-high vacancy rates, tumbling rents and costly tenant give-aways, many commercial real estate developers are scrambling to retrench, reduce debt and fend off creditors.

Adorned with teak and brass, the plush corporate office of Sunset Development Co. in San Ramon has an altogether different mood. Owned and operated by the father and son team of Masud and Alex Mehran, this closely held private firm is an anamoly in the sick commercial real estate market.

The firm's success is due to the massive Bishop Ranch business park, its only major development. With more than 6.5 million-square-feet of leased space, the near-completed $2 billion, 585-acre development has a 9 percent vacancy rate. In nearby Walnut Creek vacancies in commercial office buildings are running as high as 25 percent.

Sunset's fortunes have motivated Alex, who is 37 to scout around the Bay Area for another large site that can accommodate a business park the scale of Bishop Ranch. He says he has narrowed the search to three locations, which he will not disclose. All three are at least "750 acres, arc within an hour of San Francisco and could easily become another business hub of the region," he says.

Because of the guarded political mood about growth in the Bay Area, Alex says he is "surprised with the number of cities wanting us to develop in their communities."

"The workplace is no longer defined by downtown," he says. "There is respectability in the sub urban park."

Replicating the Bishop Ranch story will not be easy.

"Perfect size, perfect location and perfect timing," is how residential developer Daniel Van Voorhis describes Bishop Ranch. He is president of nearby Blackhawk, the upscale residential development which has benefited handsomely from the number of executives who work at Bishop Ranch and bought homes at Blackhawk.

While competitors, tenants and real estate experts credit the Mehrans' savvy and personalized approach to development, the changing Bay Area business climate was on their side in making Bishop Ranch a real estate triumph. In the early 1980s, industrializing the suburbs was the trend as companies scrambled to get closer to the skilled labor force.

"Forty percent of the employees that were to be assigned to that facility (Bishop Ranch) were already living in Contra Costa," says Steve Maita, manager of media relations at Pacific Bell, which has a 2 million-square-foot building for 7,000 employees in Bishop Ranch.

Other large companies that packed up and relocated major facilities to Bishop Ranch were Chevron Pacific Bell, Toyota, Beckman Instruments, and Westinghouse Electric.

The story of Bishop Ranch begins almost 10 years ago when the Contra Costa County Board of Supervisors rejected the Mehrans' proposal for a housing development on the site.

Iranian immigrant Masud, now 62, had made his first fortune by building more than 4,000 homes in Livermore in Alameda County, and he believed housing would also work on the Contra Costa site that he had purchased from Western Electric Co.

Residential home builders in the area were the most resolute opponents of the Mehrans' first proposal At the time, a group of home builders packed a public hearing wearing black hats. When the Board rejected Mehrans' proposal, they slipped off their black hats and put on white ones.

Undeterred, the Mehrans came back with plans for a massive business park that the county supervisors embraced with very little scrutiny of the project's environmental impact.

"In the early 1980s, the county was strongly committed to jobs to help ease the out-commute and expand economic growth in the county," says Contra Costa County Supervisor Sunne McPeak.

A strong supporter of Bishop Ranch, McPeak says Sunset has been responsive to the community. She points to its child care program, employee shuttles to BART, and involvement in local charities.

While Van Voorhis credits Alex Mehran's style and determination, he says Pacific Bell and Chevron set the tone for Bishop Ranch. "When they walked in, the county listened," he says.

The Mehrans hooked up with Chevron on a tip. In 1980, Marin land planner Dan Coleman told Alex that a Chevron search committee was secretly looking for a major suburban location for a sizable share of its San Francisco work force.

That phone call set in motion a decision that affected the lives of thousands of Chevron workers and cost the company millions of dollars in corporate relocation costs. The oil company ultimately purchased 143 acres of the park and constructed more than li million square feet of space.

Soon after, Pacific Bell and several other Fortune 500 companies announced plans to move to San Ramon.

Coleman's message to Mehran was also a signal that development patterns in the Bay Area were changing. It was the first sign that tranquil bedroom communities would become homes for industry; that the region's traffic system would be turned upside down; that the growth control debate would take on new fervor in the suburbs; and that San Francisco could no longer take home-based Fortune 500 companies for granted.

But at the time "the Chevron announcement wasn't perceived as that big of a deal," says Angelo J. Siracusa, president of the business-sponsored Bay Area Council.

Masud Mehran made his fortune building homes in Livermore

"It wasn't until much later that political leaders, the press and even the business community recognized the importance of these business relocations."

Chevron's decision to relocate a substantial portion of its facilities to Bishop Ranch from San Francisco gave the park a headstart that set it apart from competitors. For example, while the 876-acre Hacienda Business Park in Pleasanton was fighting no-growth ballot measures and shifting gears to revise it's original plan to attract high-tech research and development firms, Bishop Ranch was cutting land deals with Pacific Bell and Chevron.

Nevertheless, "the market is (still) fiercely competitive because all of the big players have their line in the pond," Alex says.

Successful commercial development companies that are owned and managed by individuals like the Mehrans are becoming rare. And some experts believe the quality of development may suffer as a result.

"There is old Chinese proverb that says that the best fertilizer is the shadow of the owner "Alex Mehran says.

More and more, the development of commercial real estate is being dominated by large institutions such as Prudential Life Insurance Co. of America, Metropolitan Life Insurance Co., Aetna Life & Casualty Co., and New England Mutual Insurance Co., which have the deep pockets necessary to survive the downturn in the office market.

"I would never say never, but the entrepreneur or the individual finds it more difficult to get into the (large-scale development) business today," says Dale Walker, executive vice president, Wells Fargo Bank, which has provided financing for Mehran since Masud began building homes 37 years ago.

"In this market, it takes a level of financial strength and (the developer) must have something special like track record and location," Walker says.

Some new flats seem to meld into the neighborhood

Second of two parts

Special to the Examiner

Henry James in the American in 1877 described an apartment in Paris as a "series of rooms gilded from floor to ceiling a foot thick, draped in various light shades of satin, and chiefly furnished with mirrors and clocks."

His words aptly describe a scene and a period in which apartment living enjoyed respectability. In the United States where home ownership is supreme, however, renters haven't always fared as well.

"Living close together has never appealed to most Americans, except temporarily ... apartment houses — their chief virtue for most has been necessity," writes Vassar Professor Richard Pommer in a report about high-rise living.

Adding to the poor image of renters are the special tax breaks that only homeowners are entitled to, such as the deduction of mortgage interest It's an example of a "macho deed-of-trust attitude" in which renters get no respect That attitude has been around for decades.

In 1922, a government manual said, "The man who owns his own home is the least susceptible to the so-called Bolshevist doctrines and (least likely) to join in civic disturbances."

Today, the National Association of Realtors publishes statistics that try to show how discontent renters are with their lives compared to home owners.

This stuff would be OK if people had a choice about being homeowners. But today, for thousands of renters, home ownership is out of reach. Like it or not, they're stuck.

There's good news. An overbuilt apartment market has temporarily created an unusual assortment of choices for Bay Area renters. In San Francisco alone, more than 3,000 new apartments are being added to the market this year and next.

They aren't all being built in unfriendly or way-out parts of town. Two of the nicer projects -Potrero Court and Post Street Towers - have popped up in neighborhoods that most folks would be proud to write home to mom about.

Potrero Court

Although it's hard for me to admit this, the 132-unit Potrero Court apartments is proof that neighborhood involvement in an affordable housing project doesn't confirm the death of that development. In this case, active community participation in the design review process helped insure that the project fits neatly into the established Potrero Hill neighborhood.

Mayor Agnos facilitated the process of approval. At the time he was a resident of Potrero and a state legislator. He worked to balance the economic interests of the developer, Cal Fed Enterprises, with neighborhood concerns about the scale and aesthetics of the development.

Thanks to Berkeley architect Edmund Burger, the outcome was a project that has ample — but out-of-sight — parking (underground) and a building that blends well into the neighborhood.

"The other places we looked at were a little too corporate," says Potrero Court tenant Marty Becker. He rents a three-bedroom unit with two roommates for $1,175 a month.

Becker was the first tenant to move into Potrero Court. He says the place has "a neighborhood feeling, plus I wanted to stay in the sunny side of town."

Twelve three-bedroom flats opened for occupancy late this summer. In four-unit clusters, the flats are elongated and go from the front to the back of the building. The remaining units are apartments with more of a dormitory feeling.

Unlike other new apartment projects in the City, Potrero Court has attracted families with children as well as singles. Most are moving from other San Francisco locations, and many work in the South of Market area, adjacent to Potrero Hill.

The bedrooms seem small, but the units are stocked with amenities such as track lighting, garbage disposals and Levolor blinds. Because the project sits next to Highway 101 I expected traffic noise, but double-pane windows lower the decibel level.

The complex has no swimming pool, but it has two spas and a comfortable club house. Unfortunately, Cal Fed's plan to install one of those nifty swim-in-place jet pools was nixed by the city Health Department.

Post Street Tower

On-site property manager Betty Reddington adds an unexpected in gredient to the 248-unit Post Street Towers apartment project. This friendly and unpretentious matron reminded me of the rooming house owners I rented rooms from in Boston and New York. They had a certain pride of ownership that gave their buildings a special quality.

During my tour, Reddington referred to "our" deck, "our" security system, "our" courtyard, etc.

She gives a warm and down-to-earth feeling to Post Street Towers, which sits above Union Square in the middle of the theater district below Nob Hill. The Post Street marketing brochure calls this part of town "mid-town."

I had heard a lot of stories about Post Street Towers: It was a corporate dumping ground, the units were too small, the rents were high, there were no amenities, it was in the wrong part of town.

The truth is kinder. Yes, the units are small — the studios use fold-down Murphy beds. And while the rents are little higher than the competition, the location is hard to beat. These are urban apartments in an urban location.

A variety of mom-and-pop markets, ethnic restaurants and service shops such as cleaners are found throughout the area. It's near the most pricey shops in the Bay Area, so residents can spend oodles more on unnecessary and expensive items.

Not surprisingly, companies such as ATT have rented units there. So have actors and actresses.

I'm not sure they need it, but such social events as wine tastings and clothing outlet shopping sprees have been planned for the tenants.

On My Livable and Sensible Scale:

Not the typical apartment experience, Potrero Court and Post Street Towers offer renters an interesting alternative.

Special to the Examiner: Jerry Brown's Urban Strategy needs a close second look

Did Jerry Brown's Urban Strategy Have It Right? If today's government officials who are concerned about growth and development were to dust off former Gov. Jerry Brown's 10-year-old Urban Strategy, the refrain "I told you so" might scream from the pages.

In 1978, the 36-page "Urban Development Strategy for California" boldly challenged political leaders to face the pressures caused by the state's growth explosion. But because the scheme included controversial elements that the real estate industry couldn't stomach, most of the plan was shelved.

Some experts believe the absence of a meaningful statewide plan for growth has contributed to California's burgeoning traffic mess and has spawned a surge in local slow-growth ballot measures.

"People are beginning to understand the need for a state role; the lack of state level policies on growth and development are becoming obvious to people of all points of view," says Peter Detwiler, senior consultant for the Senate Local Government Committee in Sacramento. All zoning and land-use decisions are now made at the local level.

Designed to prepare the state for growth problems, the Urban Strategy report was the work of Bill Press. Now a southern California TV commentator, he was director of the Governor's Office of Planning and Research during the Brown administration.

At the time, the action plan was considered pro-environment and anti-growth, which explains why it drove the real estate industry batty But the report also included severa proposals that builders and realty agents unwittingly hail as solution to today's traffic and growth-control mess.

For example, the report called for legislation requiring local government to adopt a five-year capital improvement plain Such a plan should "indicate the size, timing and means of financing all new capital improvements" such as roads, sewers and schools. Today, the housing industry is pushing local government to do a better job of planning for similar infrastructure improvements.

This year Orange County Republican Marion Bergeson proposed legislation that would force better regional cooperation among cities on such issues as affordable housing, transportation and infrastructure: A central theme of the Urban Strategy was promoting reigionalism as a way of overcoming problems among neighboring jurisdictions.

But despite the apparent wisdom of some of the proposals, Brown's scheme became an easy mark for criticism.

At the time, Citizens for Responsible Government in Rancho Cordova called it a blueprint for "state dictatorship." And Orange County Assemblyman Gil Ferguson criticized the scheme as a "radical plan for a peaceful revolution through land reform, economic planning and social engineering." At the lime, he directed a pro-development advocacy group from Orange County.

On one occasion, the California Association of Realtors (CAR) held a meeting where Press was attacked by "highly charged" real estate agents,' according to an association press release from 1978. For one, the Realtors were upset with the report's recommendation to enact an anti-speculation tax on real estate transactions.

Today, CAR is still fiercely opposed to such taxes, but the organization has changed its stance on other issues included in the report. In some cases, they are closely in line with those in the Urban report.

Real estate interests weren't the only ones upset with Jerry Brown's plan. In 1978, environmentalist and regional planner Samuel E Wood said the report "was seriously flawed." He argued that it didn't go far enough with ideas to carry out regional government.

While California fought over dogma, other high-growth states such as Florida and Massachusetts were busy with plans for local capital improvement financing, regional government and a program of carrots and sticks for steering development.

The fate of the California plan can be blamed in part on Brown, Detwiler says. "There was no political will to implement (it)."

This year, the Legislature passed a bill that earmarks money for studying the growth problem. Study consultants might begin by doing a thorough review of the Urban Strategy report. This is one study that may have been sitting on the shelf toe long.

Classical units part of experiment in senior living

Special to the Examiner

BILL AND Penny Hughes are newlyweds. Just back from a cruise, they are looking forward to many good times together. They have a vacation home at Sea Ranch and they love to jump on the keyboard and play jazz piano duets. Penny has her tennis; Bill swims and hikes.

Last month, the Hughes spent most of their spare time moving into their new luxury condominium in San Mateo. There was just one snag: squeezing all of their things into a condo was tough.

"When I saw the rooms empty, my heart sank because I didn't think they could handle all of our stuff," Penny Hughes says.

Over the years, they have collected a lot of belongings. You see, while this is the Hughes' first condominium, it isn't their first home. Penny is 68 and Bill is 76. Both have lived long and separate lives, tending to the duties of domestic life in single-family homes: Penny in Minnesota and Bill on the Peninsula.

It's a similar story for Whit McFarland. The 79-year-old retired attorney and tax man lived for 30 years in a single-family home on Gramercy Drive in San Mateo. Now he is a neighbor of the Hughes.

Tired of 'rattling around'

"It's a lot smaller than my house but it relieves me of trimming the hedges and mowing the lawn," McFarland says. "I was tired of rattling around that big place."

McFarland and the Hughes are part of an experiment in senior living. They are charter members in the Peninsula Regent, a 207-unit life-care development created by the seasoned Bay Area development team of Gerson Bakar, Tom Callinan and Peter Applegate.

Designed by architect Richard Beard of Backen, Arrigoni & Ross Inc. in San Francisco, the 11-story Peninsula Regent has an upscale institution look, but it's more like a hotel than a hospital.

When I was kid, I remember traveling to the Chase Park Plaza Hotel in St. Louis with my father and watching the permanent residents of the hotel stroll through the lobby. It always seemed like a dignified way to live out the final phase of a successful life. The Pen insula Regent brought back those memories.

Upscale company

"It's a hybrid in the sense that it integrates the best qualities of an elegant residential complex with those of a fine resort," Beard says.

Its interiors, in fact, were designed by Glenn Texeira, who specializes in hotels such as the Mayfair Regent in New York, the Turtle Creek Mansion in Dallas and the Beverly Wilshire Hotel in Beverly Hills.

"We have had to overcome the myth of the old folks home," Peninsula Regent marketing whiz Peter J. Palmisano says.

Packed with amenities, the scheme seems to work. The structure is a Mediterranean-style midrise with grand entrances, a stately lobby and terra cotta roof tiles. It has a library, private dining room, exercise room, art studio, swimming pool and a croquet lawn. This place is a far cry from a stale nursing home.

Palmisano brags that this new upscale retirement spot is a "proud housing choice" for the elderly. "They rented an apartment at 20, bought their first home at 30 and bought a nicer home at 40; they always had housing choices that they could be proud of. This is another one," he says.

Retirement facility opens in San Mateo

Its tenants are from places such as Hillsborough, San Mateo, Burlingame and San Francisco. "These are people who have successfully planned what they want and can afford to get what they want," Palmisano says. "They aren't here by default."

The price tag certainly does screen out the beggars. Costs are higher than the traditional life-care retirement development. Regent members pay a lump sump payment of $200,000 to $475,000, depending on the size of the unit. They also pay a monthly stipend ($1,500 on average) which covers meals, medical care and all other amenities such as maid service and security.

Services provided to Peninsula Regent residents are managed by Bay Area Senior Services, a non-profit organization. With 30-member team of health care and senior care professionals, BASS works under the umbrella of the San Francisco-based nonprofit group BRIDGE Housing, which is known for its affordable housing developments.

The Peninsula Regent offers its residents three levels of care: independent living, home health and personal care. When residents are in need of skilled nursing or acute care, they are moved to a neighboring facility, but the Regent membership pays all of the bills. When they improve, they can return home.

One wing of the building is devoted to personal care. The clinic includes a medical director, a nurse practitioner and a certified nurse assistant. For residents under this type of medical treatment the wing also includes living units, a lounge and a dining room.

To maintain the mood of healthy independent living, patients occupying the personal care wing cannot enter other wings of the Peninsula Regent.

Eighty percent of the units in the Peninsula Regent have been sold, and residents just began moving in two weeks ago.

With construction and landscape crews putting on the finishing touches and only a fraction of the residents moved in, it's difficult to get a real feel for the lifestyle at the Peninsula Regent.

Those already here, however, are very excited. 'There just aren't any files on it," Bill Hughes says.

On My Livable And Sensible Scale:

If you got mounds of equity and are willing to give up that single-family home, the Peninsula Regent is probably one of the best senior alternatives available in the Bay Area.

California trends: Private groups, politicians jump on bandwagon to help homeless

In the past, housing advocates became cynical during the holidays about the temporary outpouring of good will aimed at aiding the homeless. After Jan. 1, they watched the philanthropic spirit wear off, while a handful of non-profit church groups continued to patch together programs that housed and served the homeless. All year, they were long on goodwill but short on resources and political support for helping the homeless.

Today, the mood of indifference towards this burgeoning population — estimated at 100,000 people in California — has changed dramatically. In the last 24 months, helping the homeless has become a year-round political crusade. Heightened public concern about their plight has prompted national, state and local politicians and private organizations to jump on the homeless bandwagon.

With mixed results, hundreds of millions of dollars in new government aid has been appropriated and a horde of pioneering policies and programs have been, adopted. To date, however, there is little evidence that the homeless population is better cared for or is shrinking in size.

"It (government support) is going from nothing to all an uncoordinated flood of activity," says Robert Tobin, Executive Director, Hospitality House, San Francisco. "It's totally unstructured and unorganized with people who know nothing about the history of the problem, and it's too little too late."

Nine different agencies and 20 departments of the state government are working on the homeless problem. They include the Department of Military, which provides state armories as temporary homeless shelters, and the Department of Social Services, which spends more than $20 million annually for helping homeless individuals who are mentally disabled.

As an example, she points to the California Conservation Corps. The Corps already provides room, board and minimum wage to its recruits which creates a perfect alternative for homeless youth. After a change in policy, the Corps now makes a special effort to recruit homeless teen-agers.

"We asked the various departments to figure out how they could help; simply tinkering with what they currently do makes a big difference," says DeBow.

Changing the rules at the national Guard is another example. The Guard already has responsibility for housing people who are victims of a state emergency. By altering the definition of emergency to include weather conditions of 40 degrees or below, the Guard can now turn their emergency facilities into temporary homeless shelters.

But synchronizing these efforts is becoming more and more complicated as a greater number of federal and state political leaders advance new initiatives to solve this problem. In California, the Governor, the Republican Assembly Caucus and the Democratic leadership have all crafted various state schemes to help the homeless.

This year, even the voters got into the act when they approved two statewide ballot measures, Prop 77 and 84. The propositions earmark more than $25 million for homeless shelters and another $200,000 for low-income housing, which will provide apartments for low-income families who are threatened with homelessness.

The fedral government is also heavily involved in funding such programs. The Department of Housing and Urban Development make more than 200 grants — amounting to $82.6 million — to local homeless programs in California, according to the Interagency Council on the Homeless, Washington D.C.

Because of the sense of emergency that shrouds the homeless quagmire, some of the federl programs were "put together very piecemeal and much too quickly." says John Sidor, Executive Director, Council of State Community Affairs Agencies, Washington D.C.

With political support in hand, now the most pressing challenge for individuals and groups working to solve the homeless problem is showing results. And no one predicts that to be easy.

Oh, hills are hills, and flats are flats, and never the twain shall meet

Special to the Examiner

Take your soaring heights and windy views

I don 't want them anymore

I'm shielded in the flatlands

The hills at my backdoor

Amidst babbling brook and towering trees

I'm cozy as can be.

And the folks around here, we're good friends!

In our garden greenery.

— Jeannine Tellerman, Novate

TELLERMAN'S PROFLATS poem was one of nearly a hundred letters I received in response to my column on the flats vs. the hills ("The low-down on rising expectations and middle classes," Oct. 16, 1988). I asked you to tell me why you chose to live on a hilltop or in a denser flatland community.

My premise .was that your choice of topography might say something about neighborhood or personal values. I once believed that living in the flatlands was a sign of economic failure. But as I begin to explore neighborhoods more closely, I found that where you lived merely reflected different attitudes about life.

Hills and flatlands: Two views of life

The number of responses was almost evenly split between hill dwellers and flatlanders.

The hills are alive ...

Not surprisingly, peace and solitude is a frequent refrain from hill dwellers.

Though the "everyday conveniences one takes for granted (in the flats) don't exist when you live if the mountain, I'm here for the duration," says Cindy Rizzo who lives atop Mount Tamalpais. "No one comes to your door to borrow an egg, and you respect that same privacy for others."

Diane Miller shares that philosophy. She used to live in the flats but now makes her home in the hills. Miller, who didn't identify which Bay Area hills she lives in, says she enjoys getting away from the "madding crowd."

"There are more birds, trees and plenty of quiet here, but the best (comes) after being gridlocked on some freeway — I'm away from people.

Seeking solitude is understandable. But racism isn't. One bigoted writer says he prefers the hills because he would hate to have a "poor black destitute family" as a neighbor. "We may have the drug dealers in our neighborhood but not his users."

He signed his letter "NIMN," which I assume means "Not In My Neighborhood." I'm glad he's not in mine.

Myra Alvarado is a San Francisco Mission District flatlander who desires the hills. "I prefer to sit or position myself where I can observe and watch everything around me." Presumably that's easier in the hills than the flats.

It's the same for Brisbane resident Paul Baffico. After moving to the hills, "I could see the world... and watch the cycles of nature and the seasons unfold before me. Flatlands never again."

Letter writer "Nob Hill Nellie" offered this historic perspective. "A colleague advised me (in 1956) if buying property in San Francisco to buy on a hillside. She remembered the floods when Market Street was navigable only by boat with water gushing down California, Mason and Taylor Streets."

A level-headed group

The Rev. Robbie Cranch from Berkeley feels the flats are safer than the hills. If he lived in the hills, "come the earthquake, my house would tumble down the hillside and mash me like a bug," he writes. Moreover, life in the flats allows him to "smell the sea air, hear the foghorns," and "I can bicycle without risking a heart attack and my brakes last longer."

If hill dwellers prefer to get away from folks, the flatlanders I heard from enjoy contact with people. One booster for the flats writes, "I don't like all of my neighbors, but I like most of them and some is always better than none."

And there's the weather. Robert Befonte likes his new house in San Francisco's Inner Mission more than his old place in the Noe Valley hills because of the warmer temperatures.

"What an amazing seven-minute drive," says Befonte, referring to the distance between his old and new neighborhood. In Noe Valley, "the neighbors were bundled and scarved lumps rushing from warm car to warm house." Now, in the flats of the Inner Mission, "my favorite view in San Francisco is from my back porch where I look up at the fog swirling around my old house on the hill, Then I take off my shirt and sit down to pick up a few more degrees on my tan."

Berkeley resident Ira Serkes cites practical reasons for preferring the flats. "A decade ago, I'd rented a lovely one-bedroom apartment on Buena Vista Way in the Berkeley Hills. The view — especially when we were above the fog and loomed over an early morning sea of white — was spectacular. But shopping? None."

Several readers accused me of being, an effete snob for my once held belief that "you may buy a starter home close to sea level, but if you don't move to the top of a lush green hill then something has gone awry with your upward mobility plan.

"You're article was so snobbish," chides Marinwood resident Diana. "We choose to live in the less expensive flats where I can afford to stay home and raise our children. It's obvious you do not have any children and still look to a view to fulfill your needs."

Maybe the best place to live is somewhere between the hills and the flats. In looking for sites for his buildings, architect Frank Lloyd Wright often preferred the brow or the edge of a steep place.

Katherine Moberg says she found an example of this middle ground in the Loma Vista area in the hills of Burlingame.

"No fantastic view but above the congested traffic and polluted air, this flat street never floods but is a perfect place for children to roller skate," she writes.

"We've got the best of the flats together with the best of the hills.

It's a lot more than a connector to Marin County and points north

Special to the Examiner

FOR YEARS, I thought of Van Ness Avenue just as a big blur where Henry Africa's cocktail lounge was located. I remember visiting California 10 years ago and having a Sunday brunch at the now erstwhile fern bar after a long night of partying. The meal included fresh-squeezed orange juice and eggs benedict, and I told dozens of people back in Illinois about it. It was reason enough to come back to the Bay Area and stay a lifetime.

For many people, San Francisco's Van Ness Avenue is merely a connector — a high-speed, multilane link to another location. As a throughway, it's an artery some Marin commuters use to travel home and one route for the rest of us to get to the Palace of Fine Arts, Perry's, Stinson Beach, Ukiah and Fort Mason.

This prominent spine is also a divider, splitting the bustle of commerce and residential life. Van Ness Avenue stretches through a valley shadowed by Pacific Heights and one side, and Russian Hill and Nob Hill on the other.

Van Ness Avenue's reputation as the great divide began 83 years ago when it accidentally served as a fire break after the 1906 earthquake.

Pacific Heights should be forever grateful because the street's awesome width saved it from the flames of destruction. Today, 93-foot-wide roads and 16-foot-wide sidewalks give it the distinction of being the widest boulevard in The City.

If you consider it as a place at all, Van Ness is a temporary stopping-off point for many of us. It's where your in-laws might stay when visiting from out of town, a place to rent or buy furniture, a stretch where you can buy or lease a new or used car or a spot to see a movie or dine out.

But there's more. Several thousand people live on Van Ness Avenue.

This 63-block (12,000-foot) urban roadway is a mixed-use adventure. As Van Ness has been transforming itself for decades, several generations of urban life co-exist on the Avenue.

Since the 1920s the auto dealers have occupied several magnificent historic buildings. While the number of dealers has declined, there are still cars for sale here. (I had always been nervous about buying a car in one of these places because

I figured they deserved to charge more just to pay for the upkeep on their buildings.)

The night life on Van Ness has blossomed since I hung out at Henry Africa's, which has been closed for two years. For one thing, there are more movie theaters, clustered around California Street. And now Harry's Bar, the Hard Rock Cafe, Max's Opera Cafe, Rosalie's and the Mesquite Bar & Grill are all on Van Ness.

For the traditionalist, there's still Tommy's Joynt, where a draft beer costs a buck, and Zims, where a cup of coffee runs you 85 cents with refills at no charge.

But new housing is the biggest change along Van Ness Avenue. Eight years ago there were 1,500 multifamily units along the corridor. Since then, more than 1,000 new housing units have been built.

To this day I regret not buying a condominium in Opera Plaza, a 450-unit project close to City Hall and built in 1981. It's a nifty little development with an attractive courtyard and underground parking. Condos sell for $155,000 to $290,000. I remember when they were $99,000 with 9 percent fixed-rate mortgages. While inflation there hasn't been wild, in the long run this area will be a good investment and the idea of $100,000 condos laughable.

For a more expensive choice, eight condos are still available at Daniel Burnham Court farther north on Van Ness at Post Street. They sell for $260,000 to $350,000.

Thirty percent of the 245 units are occupied by people who bought them as second and third homes — some from as far away as Japan and Hong Kong, others as close in as Hillsborough. It seems a bit extravagant, but suburban buyers want a place close to the Opera House on Van Ness and Grove.

New luxury apartments are available at a new 42-unit mixed-used development on Van Ness at California Street. Built as condos, 1700 California includes a 24-hour doorman, underground parking, a fitness room and marble bathrooms.

Housing isn't new to Van Ness. In the 1880s, the street was a spectacular residential strip with grand estates owned by the Spreckles, the Crockers and the Gianninis.

The force behind reviving housing on Van Ness is Dean Macris, San Francisco planning director. Last year The City adopted his Van Ness Plan expecting to turn the street into a grand boulevard or promenade. Third Avenue on New York's Upper East Side would be a good role model.

I have always been a fan of Macris' vision for Van Ness. His plan rightfully promotes housing and reflects a certain fondness for the Avenue.

Even without the plan, Van Ness has much going for it The street hasn't been engulfed by high rises, but neither has it sank into urban shame. And it's full of good memories.

On My Livable and Sensible Scale

Changes to an already interesting place are making Van Ness an appealing place to live and always a fun place to hang out.

Realtors want extensive aid to help buyers get first house

CONCERNED THAT the housing affordability problem is threatening home sales and bruising the state's economy, the California Association of Realtors is preparing a sweeping proposal that could substantially aid cash-strapped new home buyers.

If the Legislature acts on it, the state would become much more active in providing mortgages with lower down payments. In addition, a new program of state-insured, low-interest-rate loans would be available to first-time buyers.

The Realtors' track record in Sacramento on other real estate issues is impressive, but this is the first time in the association's 83-year history that it has advanced a comprehensive plan to revamp state housing policy.

The 33-page policy document is being pushed by a special Housing Policy Task Force of the association, which represents more than 120,000 real estate agents.

A picture of gloom and doom

The document paints a picture of gloom and doom unless solutions to the housing crunch are found. "California is entering the 1990s with a housing crisis in the making," it says. "Numerous forces are adversely impacting the housing market including soaring housing prices and rents increasing far faster than the growth in incomes."

The task force offers a "blue print to help ensure that California is well-positioned to address the housing needs of a new decade."

The group calls for creating a special investment market for California mortgages. Modeled after the Federal National Mortgage Association, known as Fannie Mae, it would guarantee an ample supply of mortgage money.

The association calls for a state-funded loan insurance program, similar to the federal FHA program, that would reduce down payments on state-insured mortgages.

To further overcome down-payment problems, the association suggests "a state-sponsored shared-appreciation program to increase the amount of investment capital for first-time home buyers while reducing the risks." It would allow them to buy a house in partnership with an investor, permitting a smaller down payment. Buyers would be obligated to share the appreciation with the investor.

A review of Proposition 13

The Realtors also say the consequences of Proposition 13 "need to be reviewed . . . given the growing disparity between residential property tax payments." Prop. 13 rules now favor long-time owners and punishes new home buyers, who are required to pay higher property tax bills.

The Realtors also are supporting a rental program that would help low-income tenants with their security deposits. The association advocates expanding current state tax incentives to build privately financed low-income housing.

The association also wants a statewide constitutional amendment that would "exempt new housing production from rent control." It's less controversial than it appears — the proposal has been endorsed by major tenant organizations. In fact, some industry groups are likely to criticize the association for not taking a harder line on rent control.

The new Realtor policy also takes aim at local communities that adopt zoning and growth-control policies that threaten housing opportunities. The proposal says these cities may face legal challenges supported by the Realtors.

Once its 1,500-member board of directors approves the proposal, the association is expected to pressure the Legislature to adopt many of the concepts.

The plan isn't expected to find its way into legislation until later this year at the earliest, legislators and their consultants say the ideas are expected to stir a rousing debate in Sacramento.

Why it's unwise to talk about your home's value

Special to the Sun

The 1988 wacky California real estate market has made people crazy. The only thing homeowners want to talk about is how their home values skyrocketed. In fact, the "my-house-is-worth" chit-chat that infects cocktail parties, over-the-fence scuttlebutt and lunchtime shmoozing is crowding out real issues of the day.

With home prices somewhere beyond the ozone, ask intelligent people what the greenhouse effect is, and they are apt to tell you it's the green stuff they are earning through the equity built up in their house. Instead of poring over the appointments of the new-Bush Administration, equity-fat homeowners are fishing around for the latest tidbits on how much their home has inflated.

I'm not talking about your average greedy moron; these are people who ordinarily discuss such weighty issues as our public school system, the Persian Gulf or the war on drugs. Now, they are figuring out ways to politely turn the discussion to how much their neighbor's house sold for.

Salty debates about religion, literature, and politics have given way to conversations that are peppered with "$225,000? Wow!", "Six offers over asking price...can you believe it?", and "To think we only bought it four years ago. Incredible!"

Well it's time to stop all of this nonsense. Let's all make a New Year's resolution not to talk too much about our house prices in 1989. And here are eight reasons why it is rude and unwise to go around talking to people about how the value of your home tripled in only five years.

When you brag about your home price appreciation, remember you sound like a money-driven goof. One of the first rules of etiquette is never to boast about how much you earn or how much you own. Crowing about your house inflation is the same thing and is downright uncivil.

Be aware that when talking about your home price appreciation in a room full of people, the odds are good that you are making half of the people there feel bad — 50 percent of the households in California are renters.

Moreover, never bring it up in front of your secretary, the local policeman or the local fireman. On their salaries, most of them can't afford to buy a home in California and don't need to be reminded of that scary fact.

Talking about the price spiral may lead you to believe that you are smarter than you are. Because your house appreciated 100 percent, you conclude you must be bright; at least that's what your dad from Peoria tells you. Of course he lives in a place where prices are headed south, and he doesn't understand that every California homeowner — dumb or brilliant — is raking it in.

Don't forget, there is a way to lose your job in this scenario. If prices continue to climb, young skilled workers won't be able to afford to live here; companies will move out; and the economy will go to hell. You'll be out of a job with nobody left here to buy your overpriced house.

Remember these are only paper profits. Much like the stock market, they aren't worth much until you sell. But unlike Wall Street, there is a hefty charge for cashing out, like the capital gains tax when selling or the interest and points you will pay to refinance the debt.

Don't forget that all of this chatter is great fodder for political redistributionists. When a whole bunch of people begin boasting about their obscene profits, the progressive crowd will figure out ways to take some of it away from you. For example, watch the mortgage interest deduction go out the window when the deficit worsens and windfall real estate profits begin to look gluttonous.

There are some economic costs that you should consider. When your home prices go up, the entire social strata of your neighborhood is elevated. Even if you can't afford it, this trend puts pressure on you to buy new furniture, hire a gardener, put in better landscaping and purchase a new car. Then there's the higher car and house insurance premiums, and shops start moving into the neighborhood with merchandise you can't afford.

And for more sobering news. While some real estate types are determined to convince you otherwise, there is bound to be a market correction. The last surge in home prices in the late 1970's was followed by a downturn that saw some properties lose value. In fact, the last ones in during that boom were condo buyers and they are still shell-shocked from the experience.

If despite this advice you still can't contain yourself, then talk about your equity gains with a little tact. Don't exaggerate by more than 10 percent. Don't mention it more than once a week to the same person. And never bring it up in front of your children. They will assume you are worth more than you are and use it against you someday.

And lastly, don't forget to enjoy your home; pipe down and have some quiet time with your goldmine.

Cities rethink low-income housing

Stung by a state Supreme Court decision that makes it much more difficult to build low-cost housing, local government officials and housing advocates are scrambling to get the high court to modify its ruling and convince the legislature to enact a bill that will soften the blow of the court edict.

Because of the high court's ruling in the case of Davis v. City of Berkeley last month, thousands of units of affordable housing in the state have been put on hold. Moreover, millions of dollars in federal housing aid could be turned back to Washington, according to housing experts.

The fallout from the decision was immediate.

"City attorneys are halting planned housing projects because of the decision, because they are worried about the consequences of the court's action," says Marjorie Gelb, Deputy City Attorney, City of Berkeley.

"It's disastrous," says Santa Clara County housing official Matt Steinle. More than 3,000 units of voter-approved affordable housing are in jeopardy in Santa Clara County alone, according to Steinle.

Aimed at toppling a Berkeley ballot measure which authorized the construction of 75 low-cost housing units, the controversial case was launched by a group of disgruntled citizens who did not want to see the subsidized units built in their neighborhoods.

Failing to convince the city council to reverse its decision, they sued the city.

The court ruled that communities must be much more specific when seeking voter approval for the construction of low-cost subsidized housing. In Los Angeles, San Mateo, Oakland, Fresno, Sacramento, San Diego, San Jose and several other communities, voters approved measures in the last several years which gave 'blanket' approval to build a fixed number of low-cost housing units.

Berkeley voters gave permission in 1977 and 1981 for the construction of 500 units without specifying their location.

The court did not require the city to tear down the 75 units, which are nearing completion, but it faulted Berkeley and other communities for failing to describe where the units would be built and how much they would cost the city.

The real damage is to units 'stockpiled' by blanket ballot measures. They will now face voter scrutiny one project at a time.

As an example, Steinle points to four housing ballot measures approved just last November by more than 70 percent of the voters in Santa Clara County. Wiped out by the court decision, the four measures authorized funding for purchasing and building thousands of low-cost units in the expensive Silicon Valley housing market.

While housing advocates and city attorneys sort out the ruling, the city of Berkeley has already asked the court to modify one aspect of the decision that could foul up the construction of all federally funded public housing projects in the state.

Because the U.S. Department of Housing and Urban Development (HUD) requires a community to have local approval before funding local public housing developments, Gelb is worried that "if the court doesn't change this one aspect (of its decision) then one obvious ramification will be no more HUD money in California for new public housing."

Though federal aid to public housing has shrunk substantially in the last few years, several projects on the drawing boards would be in trouble.

Cities interested in building low-cost housing are now looking to the Legislature for clarification on the ruling. The Supreme Court put the burden on the legislature to adopt specific guidelines on what a community must say in an affordable housing ballot measure.

While housing advocates predict a tussle over the legislation, they expect state lawmakers to give them some flexibility in seeking voter approval of subsidized housing.

The court's decision has aroused feelings among some housing advocates that it is time to consider challenging Article 34, the part of the Constitution that requires all subsidized housing projects to receive voter approval. But overturning an article of the Constitution requires a statewide ballot measure, and even the most optimistic housing supporter isn't completely confident that the voters are ready for that.

Soon the 'theys' will outnumber the town 'wes'

Special to the Examiner

IN WORLD War II, a German POW camp was located in the community of Windsor, off Windsor River Road in an abandoned farmworker labor camp on the west side of town.

While the presence of German troops in this southern Sonoma County hamlet might seem frightening, locals today say they don't recall a sense of danger.

Theirs is a kinder and more common recollection: stories of unthreatening, young and innocent German soldiers singing as they hiked through central Windsor. People remember seeing a 16-year-old German prisoner gently caressing a kitten as he marched with his fellow POWs through the streets.

Today, the folks in this unincorporated community are showing a different sort of tolerance: They've accepted, and even welcomed, an explosion in new residential development.

"It's exciting to see young new families move into the community," says Barbara Ray, the unofficial town historian and a freelance writer.

A fellow resident, Blaine Hunt, agrees. "I don't think you can stop growth and there will be some good families moving in and my son will make some new friends."

Windsor, the fastest-growing town in Sonoma County, is a Bay Area boom town. Upon entering the village off Old Redwood Road 15 miles north of Santa Rosa, I noticed a sign saying the population is 5,600.

Then I learned that 4,000 new homes have been built, are on the drawing boards or have been approved. That's a growth rate no community in the Bay Area can begin to match.

More of 'them' than 'us'

"We are reaching a point when we will have more new people than long-time residents," says Tim Souza, a Windsor resident since 1958.

Coming from a small town, I can understand how odd this rate of growth must be. We used to make a big deal about just a single new family moving into my home town of Carlinville, Ill. (which also had a population of. 5,600). Even a stranger passing through might .raise eyebrows. Having a town filled with more of "them" than us would have seemed down right bizarre.

Indeed, the changes in Windsor present an odd sight.

Next to patches of raw land cluttered with broken farm equipment and black and white cows, blond wooden housing frames have shot up everywhere.

When I passed the parking lot at Guadalupe Parish after the noon Mass and saw churchgoers lingering and chatting, I felt I was in the middle of a rural heartland. But when I visited the new nearby sub-division tracts, the town was no different from any other look-alike burb.

Once Marin County was the only bedroom community north of San Francisco. Then Santa Rosa became a bedroom community to San Rafael and Novato. Then Rohnert Park became a bedroom community to Santa Rosa. Now it's Windsor turn to become a bedroom community. Ukiah is probably next.

A rural poverty pocket

The ingredients for a blast of growth in Windsor were perfect: lots of inexpensive raw land close to an emerging suburban job belt, and unlike Santa Rosa plenty of sewer capacity.

Moreover, Windsor historically has been a rural poverty pocket, which makes it a more acceptable target for development. Since the days when its fields were flush with hops and it was home for seasonal migrant workers, the community has been fighting an image of blight.

Windsor resident Tim Souza: *'We are reaching a point when we will have more new people than long-time residents'*

Even today its main downtown area on the west side looks sickly. A long-awaited county redevelopment plan has never been executed, and it's sorely missed.

The blight has softened misgivings about growth. "Development brings improvement," says Souza, who is a real estate agent.

Yet a number of disgruntled citizens fret over the pace of development, and everybody wants to make sure it's managed properly.

"We don't want this place to become another Santa Clara Valley packed full of houses," Ray says. "There are horse ranches and open spaces we want to protect; most people would like this area to mix a little urban with the rural."

In fact, a free-for-all county land-use philosophy has prompted some locals to consider cityhood, and it's probably in the cards. Fiscal fears have delayed action — the cost for police services range from $600,000 to more than a $1 million.

In the end, it will be interesting to see whether the newcomers are as amiable as the old-timers I met.

Not unlike the POW with the kitten, they behaved gently. But that may be characteristic of a rural way of life. If so, it too may be a memory before long.

Windsor is an eccentric rural village immersed in a tide of regional change. How well it turns out is an open question.

You might pay $500,000, but it's ever so nice

Special to the Examiner

AFTER THEY were married in 1983, Los Angelenos Rob and Kenis Dunne bought a map of California and began doing where-do-we-want-to-live research.

Their criteria: The setting had to be low on crime, have good weather, be close to the ocean, have a sense of community, be near a professional sports team, be scenic and have ample job opportunities in the vicinity.

Oh, and "anywhere but L.A.," recalls Kenis Dunne.

They narrowed the field to San Diego, Sacramento, Sonoma, Newport Beach and Los Gatos. After a couple of weekend jaunts to the Bay Area, they started their new life in the Santa Clara County community of Los Gatos.

Los Gatos on the one hand is a yuppie dreamland. Not Beverly Hills but not too funky, it has suburban stability with urban charm and resort vitality. It reminds me of Palo Alto or San Francisco's Marina District.

Los Gatos gets its name from a Mexican land grant. It's a bedroom community with history and is proud of its heritage; the town's Forbes Mill Museum is devoted exclusively to community history. Incorporated in 1887, Los Gatos is one of the oldest communities in Silicon Valley.

Tradition dies slowly

Spanish for "the Cats," Los Gatos is a town where tradition dies slowly. This week, for instance, the police will switch uniforms from light blue to navy blue.

"Los Gatos is the last municipal police agency in the Bay Area to change to navy blue shirts and navy blue pants with a gold stripe," according to an article in the Los Gatos Weekly.

Los Gatos defies the stereotypical San Jose image of suburban sameness. "This is a community with boundaries and definition," Dunne says. "You know you are here; it's not a blur."

With a vibrant commercial strip located near a quaint civic center and the classic old Los Gatos High School, the town's urban geography is simple and functional. Developed long before the rat-a-tat Santa Clara subdivisions of the 1950s and 1960s, Los Gatos lacks monotonous suburban symmetry.

The town stands just a few miles west of San Jose on the edge of the Santa Cruz mountains. It has its own newspaper, radio station and a couple of vineyards.

Los Gatos was once home to author John Steinbeck. Today it boasts of such contemporary legends as computer wizard Steve Wozinak, who recently donated $3,000 to the Los Gatos police department for a new mobile communications center.

Uncharacteristic of the Silicon Valley burb scene, Los Gatos has a center, Santa Cruz Avenue, which is packed with shoppers and cars. Complaining about the traffic, one old-timer said, "You can walk it faster than you can drive it."

A great place to spend a day

Nevertheless, it's a great place to spend an entire day. Along Santa Cruz Avenue you can find an obscure book, an eccentric gift, a hearty sandwich, a $1,000 dress, an antique Mission-style chair and, if you insist, a Mrs. Field's chocolate pecan cookie or a loaf of bread from a franchise bakery.

The strength of the retail sector puts the community in a strong financial position.

Like all nice places in the Bay Area, Los Gatos has one big drawback for outsiders who want in: "The one thing we didn't check out in our investigation was the price of housing," says Kenis Dunne, an editor. After renting for two years, she and her husband, a lawyer, finally bought a house on the edge of Los Gatos. Today, small homes located near the downtown area bring $400,000 to $500,000.

Los Gatos has one of the toughest rent control laws in the state, which has kept rents down for current renters. The community is packed with apartments and the odd thing is that they are located throughout the community. For example, you may find a small apartment project wedged between two half-million-dollar homes.

Some of our intolerant Bay Area single-family homeowners should take notice: This development pattern is proof that renters and homeowners can live together without too much trouble. Also, it's evidence that apartments don't kill property values.

Los Gatos has few problems. Some folks worry about the loss of a food market and a drug store along Santa Cruz. Others fret about the tourist bustle that invades the avenue by day and the teen-age cruisers who come out at night. Almost everyone is nervous about the new Highway 85, which will soon cut a swathe through the community.

But generally this is a community that's been around long enough to find its cadence. There are no menacing threats here.

On My Livable and Sensible Scale:

With scads of rental opportunities and expensive single-family homes, Los Gatos is a town with history and charm.

New rules inflame rural folks

Recent calamitous fires in the wildlands of California have prompted the State Department of Forestry to propose tough new fire prevention regulations for rural areas. Released late last year, the draft rules have sparked controversy among rural homeowners, who are worried about the cost of implementing the new rules. More generally, they are concerned that the state is unnecessarily meddling in their rustic way of life.

Required under Senate Bill 1075 which passed in 1987, the proposed regulations would impose stiff requirements on current property owners. For example, the rules call for improving access to wooded areas where homes are located. In some cases, this would require clearing vegetation and increasing the turning radius on roads so that fire equipment can traverse narrow and winding country lanes.

In addition, the rules would increase the water supply for secluded areas by requiring new water tanks and better access to ponds and lakes. Under unusual conditions or hardship cases, state officials say that a homeowner could be exempt from these requirements.

Nevertheless, rural homeowners are irate. They argue that the proposed rules will be very costly for individual residents. For example, they estimate the cost of building a new water tank to be as high as $5,000.

"Rural communities tend to be retirement communities, and these folks can afford nonsense the least. Especially when it is nonsense that really will not do much good," says Fresno County rural property owner Sandra Brock.

They also fear that fire safety won't be substantially improved by enacting the rules. "Nothing can stop a Santa Ana wind," claims Brock. "We aren't stupid, we don't want to burn."

The state argues that the regulations are necessary to prevent the growing number of property losses that are caused by wildfires. "Since 1923, 4,500 structures have been destroyed by wildfires," says Rich Schell, Division Chief, Department of Forestry, Sacramento. "But 85 percent of those structures were destroyed since 1959 and 69 percent since 1970 — the problem is getting much worse."

Last September, 148 homes were destroyed by the "Off-49" wildfire alone, in which 33,000 acres east of Sacramento burned.

Aggravating the problem is the number of urbanites who are moving to the country. "People moved to rural California from the cities and they expect the same level of services as they had before, but it's just not there," says Schell. "The tax base is less, services are fewer and it takes longer for the services to get to these remote areas."

While the Department of Forestry is worried about the loss of property, it is also concerned about fire fighter safety. "They put themselves in very hazardous situations — keep in mind that people die fighting fires," says Schell.

Moreover, "when we spend more time protecting homes then we have less resources to protect grass, brush, forest and other lands of California," contends Schell.

Technically, the state is responsible for wildlands and local government is obligated to protect structures. Both the state and property owners argue that the state has gotten into local fire protection matters because county government has dropped the ball.

Tougher local fire prevention policies would be a preferred alternative, because each rural area has peculiar problems that are unique to that location. The amount of water supply, for instance, varies dramatically from one part of the state to the other.

"How can one set of regulations solve everything state-wide in a cost effective manner?" asks Brock.

The 1987 legislation requires the new rules to be adopted by July 1 of this year, but Brock and other rural property owners plan to ask the legislature to delay the enactment of the new regulations. They hope this would give time to different regions of the state to adopt their own rules.

In the meantime, the disagreement over the proposed regulations won't go away because it's an emotional issue about self-determination on the one hand and human safety on the other.

"People aren't as concerned as they should be about this danger," claims Schell. "I guess it's the same reason people don't wear seat belts."

Country folks burning over new fire rules

CALAMITOUS fires in the wildlands of California have prompted the State Department of Forestry to propose tough new fire-prevention regulations for rural areas.

The draft rules, released late last year, have sparked controversy among rural homeowners who worry about the cost of following them. Also, they're concerned that the state is unnecessarily meddling in their rustic way of life.

Required under Senate Bill 1075, which passed in 1987, the proposed regulations would impose stiff requirements on current property owners. For example, the rules call for improving access to wooded areas where homes are located. In some cases, this would require clearing vegetation and increasing the turning radius on roads so that fire equipment can traverse narrow and winding country lanes.

Water supplies increased

In addition, the rules would increase the water supply for secluded areas by requiring new tanks and better access to ponds and lakes. But state officials say that under unusual conditions or hardship cases, a homeowner could be exempt from these requirements.

Still, rural homeowners are irate. They argue that the proposed rules would be costly. They estimate the cost of building a new water tank as high as $5,000.

Property owner Sandra Brock says, "Rural communities tend to be retirement communities, and these folks can afford nonsense the least — especially when it is nonsense that really will not do much good."

They doubt that fire safety will be substantially improved by enacting the rules. "Nothing can stop a Santa Ana wind," Brock says. "We aren't stupid; we don't want to burn."

The state says the regulations are necessary to prevent the growing number of property losses that wildfires cause.

"Since 1923, 4,500 structures have been destroyed by wildfires," says Rich Schell, division chief, Department of Forestry in Sacramento. "But 85 percent of those structures were destroyed since 1959 and 69 percent since 1970. The problem is getting much worse."

Last September, 148 home were destroyed by the "Off-49" wildfire alone, in which 33,000 acres east of Sacramento burned.

Adding to the problem is the number of urbanites moving to the country. "People moved to rural California from the cities and they expect the same level of services as they had before, but it's just not there," says Schell. "The tax base is less, services are fewer and it takes longer for the services to get to these remote areas."

The Department of Forestry worries about the loss of property, but it's also concerned about firefighter safety. Schell notes that firefighters "put themselves in very hazardous situations. Keep in mind that people die fighting fires. "When we spend more time protecting homes, we have less resources to protect grass, brush, forest and other lands of California."

Did counties drop ball?

Technically, the state is responsible for wildlands and local government for structures. Both the state and property owners say the state has gotten into local fire protection because county government has dropped the ball.

Tougher local fire prevention policies would be a preferred alternative, because each rural area has peculiar problems that are unique to that location. The amount of water varies dramatically from one part of California to another.

"How can one set of regulations solve everything state-wide in a cost-effective manner?" asks Brock.

The 1987 legislation requires the new rules to be adopted by July 1 of this year, but Brock and others will ask the legislature to delay enacting the new regulations. They hope this would give time to different regions of the state to adopt their own rules.

Meantime, the disagreement over the proposed rules won't go away. It's an emotional issue about self-determination on the one hand and human safety on the other.

"People aren't as concerned as they should be about this danger," Schell says. "I guess it's the same reason people don't wear seat belts."

State uses unknown law to force cities to offer affordable housing

A state housing agency worried about rising home prices, property owners who are upset with rent and growth controls and poverty groups which are concerned about the lack of affordable housing have all turned to an arcane state law to force local government to be more accountable.

Enacted in 1980 and often dismissed as irrelevant by local officials. Senate Bill 2853 requires municipalities to devise plans for meeting local housing needs by preparing and executing a housing element.

Prepared as a report that was often shelved and then ignored, the housing element is part of the community's general plan. It is intended to guide the amount and quality of development. Every five years, the state reviews local housing elements for-compliance with-state laws. That process just began this year.

Like it or not, an increasing number of communities are being forced to take the law more seriously.

In West Hollywood, the state Department of Housing is zooming in on various city policies including the city's rent control ordinance. "We caution the city to monitor ... the rent stabilization program to ensure it does not have an adverse impact on the maintenance and development of affordable housing." reads a letter from the state to West Hollywood City Manager Paul Brotzman.

Alameda, the Legal Aid Society is spearheading a lawsuit that says a 1973 city law that prohibits the construction of rental housing is in conflict with state housing law. The suit further claims that the city's housing element promotes housing discrimintion against low-income and minority residents.

Though state officials are reluctant to admit it, housing experts say the state Development of Housing and Community Development is getting tougher on cities and counties that don't comply with with the law. More than 25 percent of the 507 local housing elements are out of compliance, according to the most recently published HCD records.

In the past, cities have gone through the perfunctory exercist of preparing the housing element and submitting it to the state for certification, as is required by law. When that requirement was met, however, the law was too often forgotten.

Now, several of the communities that are out of compliance are being attacked by the state for substantive reasons. For instance, the state Housing Department and the county of Santa Cruz are wrangling over the county's housing element, which the state says it is out of compliance because of Santa Cruz's 1 percent limit on new development.

Santa Cruz officials claim they are being unfairly picked on by the state and argue that state housing personnel don't understand local conditions.

But state officials point to housing element law which says a community cannot turn its back on how land-use decisions — such as growth control rules — influence the larger regional housing market.

Without a certified housing element, the community's entire general plan is in limbo and the county is on loose legal footing when approving or rejecting other development proposals.

Though state officials say that they aren't out to bash rent or growth control, HCD Director Christine Reed says the normal five-year review of local housing elements may represent a "day of reckoning" for rent control and growth control in communities such as West Hollywood and Santa Cruz.

"We aren't rubbing our hands together saying 'oh here comes one with tent control,'" says Reed. But "a community may have to justify its policies."

The California Housing Council, and industry supported lobbying organization, is building a case that rent control violates housing element law. Specifically, they and other property owner groups cite the language in the state statue that reads, "potential and actual government constraints upon the maintenance, improvement or development of housing" must be analyzed.

While rent control advocates argue that rent control doesn't cause such problems, this new plan of attack is certain to find its way into court.

No Sausalito, this East Bay town moves to its own beat

Special to the Examiner

CROCKETT HOMEOWNER Ralph Wise has two things that dazzle. One is a 1963 red Corvette, a convertible in mint condition. The other is an awesome view of the Carquinez Straits from his home in the 6-year-old Vista Carquinez subdivision. Both are an eyeful.

Wise is helping to organize the 19th annual Vette-o-Rama. Scheduled for June 17 in Concord, the specialized auto event is a perfect showcase for his assiduously polished Chevrolet. However, the precious automobile is more than a material symbol; it's something special, as are his sweeping views.

"Here I feel like I have a real piece of California," boasts Wise, referring to the vistas from his backyard patio. "You just can't buy 4 his anymore."

From his perch you see a Little League baseball diamond, the Crocket Community Center and the town's main street. But that's not all. In the background there's the Carquinez Bridge to Vallejo, the slow-moving but determined tankers in the straits and the urban sprawl that is aggressively suburbanizing Benicia. Then there's the Bay.

On the warm and clear Sunday afternoon when I visited this Contra Costa County community, I felt lucky that Wise shared this privileged spot with me. Before I stopped to introduce myself, I was rubbernecking through the side yards of the once-affordable homes that line the streets of the subdivision. When they were built in 1983, they sold for $150,000. Today they're valued at $250,000.

But the views are the same: rarely obstructed and quite unbelievable, even though the wind often whips through the hills.

The only post-1950s subdivision in town, Vista Carquinez is new. Old Crockett, down the hill, isn't so fancy, clean and modern. From up high the rest of Crockett looks quaint; up close it is more funky.

"As soon as I drop off that freeway (Interstate 80), I feel like I go back 40 years," says Wise.

An 'exciting place'

Examiner Columnist Rob Morse rightfully argues that Crocket is the "most exciting place in the Bay Area." He's noted how they held the inspiring 60th anniversary party for the Carquinez Bridge for a lot less money than was spent on the parties for the Golden Gate and Bay bridges. A lot of offbeat artists live there (two had planned to shoot the first Barbie doll into outer space) and it's a biker destination.

Investors have had dreams of turning this small waterfront town into a Sausalito or some version of a popular bayside tourist hot spot.

It hasn't worked out that way. Crockett's tiny downtown has not been successfully transformed into awning-draped shops that hawk colorful kites or exotic and scented soaps.

But the fact that it has stayed the same is what makes it so appealing.

When I asked local merchant Pam Groot how the town had changed in the 14 years she has been living there, she shrugged and said, "It hasn't." With her partner, Pink, who owns a local antique shop, Groot is restoring a Crockett Victorian that she says was owned by John Strenzel, a relative of John Muir. They also peddle old neon signs out of a storefront at the main intersection of the three-block downtown district.

The center of commerce is an eclectic mix of eateries, antique stores and boarded-up buildings. : There are taverns everywhere.

With the C&H Sugar Refinery located there, Crockett was a bustling company town in the 1940s and 1950s. Dubbed "Sugar City," the downtown flourished. When the plant was automated in the 1960s, jobs were lost and the village population shrank.

Far fewer residents

The population is now down to 3,000. But there still appears to be a lively mix of young and old people living there.

Today the locals struggle with different schemes for attracting economic growth without destroying the town's flavorfulness. No community can afford empty storefronts, but a glitzy tourist scene might not be all good either.

One sign of reinvestment is the Valona Square shopping area, which is located in the old Valona Emporium building. In the pizza parlor there I had a hearty helping of spaghetti, half a loaf of french bread and a beer for less than $5. Service was great and people were friendly.

Crockett is only 28 miles from San Francisco, and if it weren't for the dreaded 1-80 commute, this place would gentrify in a blink. For now, the commute is a barrier to progress. And maybe that's not all bad.

On My Livable and Sensible Scale

Charming and a little stagnant, Crockett' is one of my favorite places.

Old law forces cities to take housing element seriously

IN RECENT months, each of three groups has turned to an arcane state law to force local government to be more accountable for its decisions.

The groups: a state housing agency worried about rising home prices, property owners upset over rent and growth controls, and poverty groups concerned about the lack of affordable housing.

The law they embrace is Senate Bill 2853, which was enacted in 1980 and often dismissed as irrelevant by local officials. It requires municipalities to devise plans for meeting local housing needs by preparing and executing what is known in planning as "a housing element."

The element was prepared as a report that was often shelved and then ignored. It's part of the community's general plan and is intended to guide the amount and quality of development. Every five years, the state reviews local housing elements for compliance with state laws. That process just began this year.

Communities put on the spot

Like it or not, an increasing number of communities are being forced to take the law more seriously.

In Alameda, the Legal Aid Society is pushing a suit that says a 1973 city law prohibiting the building of rental housing is in conflict with state housing law. The suit also says the city's housing element promotes housing discrimination against low-income and minority people.

In West Hollywood, the state Department of Housing is zeroing in on various city policies, including the city's rent-control law. "We caution the city to monitor the rent-stabilization program to ensure it does not have an adverse impact on the maintenance and development of affordable housing," says a letter from the state' to West Hollywood City Manager Paul Brotzman.

Housing experts say the state Department of Housing and Community Development is getting tougher on cities and counties that don't comply with the law, although state officials are reluctant to confirm this. More than 25 percent of the 507 local housing elements are out of compliance, according to the latest agency records.

In the past, cities have gone through the perfunctory exercise of preparing the housing element and submitting it to the state for certification, as the law requires. But then the law was often forgotten. Now, several of the communities that are out of compliance are being attacked by the state. The state Housing Department and the County of Santa Cruz are wrangling over the county's housing element, which the state says is out of compliance because of Santa Cruz's 1 percent limit on new development.

Santa Cruz officials say they're being unfairly picked on by the state. They argue that state housing people don't understand local conditions.

But state officials say the housing element law says a community cannot turn is back on how land-use decisions — such as growth control rules — influence the larger regional housing market.

Without a certified housing element, the community's entire general plan is in limbo and the county is on loose legal footing when approving or rejecting other development proposals.

State officials deny they're out to bash rent or growth control, but the agency's director, Christine Reed, says the normal five-year review of local housing elements may represent a "day of reckoning" for rent control and growth control in communities such as West Holly wood and Santa Cruz.

"We aren't rubbing our hands together saying, 'Oh here comes one with rent control,' "Reed says, "But a community may have to justify its policies."

To their liking

Nothing could make the housing industry happier. The California Housing Council, an industry-supported lobbying organization, is building a case that rent control Violates housing element law.

Specifically, it cites language in the state law saying that "potential and actual government constraints upon the maintenance improvement or development of housing" must be analyzed.

While rent-control advocates argue that controls don't cause such, problems, this new plan of attack is certain to find its way into court.

"I don't think they should just pick on rent-control cities just because they are under rent control" says Bill Fulton, former chairman of the West Hollywood Planning Commission. "A community like Thousands Oaks doesn't have rent control, but it is ignoring its obligation to affordable housing and what, if anything, is the state saying about that?"

Housing relief

In recent months, a state housing agency that is worried about rising home prices, property owners that are upset with rent and growth controls and poverty groups that are concerned about the lack of affordable housing have all turned to an arcane state law to force local government to be more accountable about its decisions.

Enacted in 1980 and often dismissed as irrelevant by local officials, Senate Bill 2853 requires municipalities to devise plans for meeting local housing needs by preparing and executing a housing element.

Prepared as a report that was often shelved and then ignored, the housing element is part of the community's general plan. It is intended to guide the amount and quality of development. Every five years, the state reviews local housing elements for compliance with state laws. That process just began this year.

Like it or not, an increasing number of communities are being forced to take the law more seriously.

In West Hollywood, the State Department of Housing is zooming in on various city policies including the city's rent control ordinance. "We caution the City to monitor...the rent stabilization program to ensure it does not have an adverse impact on the maintenance and development of affordable housing," reads a letter from the state to West Hollywood City Manager Paul Brotzman.

In Alameda, the Legal Aid Society is spearheading a lawsuit that says a 1973 city law that prohibits the construction of rental housing is in conflict with state housing law. The suit further claims that the city's housing element promotes housing discrimination against low-income and minority residents.

Though state officials are reluctant to admit it housing experts say the State Department of Housing and Community Development is getting tougher on cities and counties that don't comply with the law. More than 25 percent of the 507 local housing elements are out of compliance, according to the most recently published HCD records.

In the past cities have gone through the perfunctory exercise of preparing the housing element and submitting it to the state for certification, as is required by law. When that requirement was met however, the law was too often forgotten.

Now, several of the communities that are out of compliance are being attacked by the state for substantive reasons. For instance, the State Housing Department and the County of Santa Cruz are wrangling over the county's housing element which the state says is out of compliance because of Santa Cruz's 1 percent limit on new development.

Santa Cruz officials claim they are being unfairly picked on by the state and argue that state housing personnel don't understand local conditions.

But state officials point to housing element law which says a community cannot turn its back on how land-use decisions-such as growth control rules-influence the larger regional housing market.

Without a certified housing element the community's entire general plan is in limbo and the county is on loose legal footing when approving or rejecting other development proposals.

Though state officials say that they aren't out to bash rent or growth control, HCD Director Christine Reed says the normal five-year review of local housing elements may represent a "day of reckoning" for rent control and growth control in communities such as West Hollywood and Santa Cruz.

We aren't rubbing our hands together saying 'oh here comes one with rent control,' "says Reed. But a community may have to justify its policies."

Nothing could make the housing industry happier. The California Housing Council, an industry supported lobbying organization, is building a case that rent control violates housing element law. Specifically, they and other property owner groups cite the language in the state statute that reads, "potential and actual government constraints upon the maintenance, improvement or development of housing" must be analyzed.

While rent control advocates argue that rent control doesn't cause such problems, this new plan of attack is certain to find its way into court "I don't think they should just pick on rent control cities just because they are under rent control," says Bill Fulton, former Chairman of the West Hollywood Planning Commission. "A community like Thousands Oaks doesn't have rent control, but it is ignoring its obligation to affordable housing and what, if anything, is the state saying about that?"

Recession threat could end boom in state home prices

Rate of GNP growth is slowing and mortgage rates are rising

The $64,000 question about the latest surge in California home prices is, when will it stop?

In the last 36 months, most California homeowners have gotten spoiled.

With their annual home price gains exceeding 20 percent in urban markets and double digit rates of inflation in most other areas, property owners have been racking up record windfalls.

The price spiral seems to have no limits.

Nevertheless, evidence abounds that rising interest rates and the threat of at least a mild national recession could put an end to the radical run-up in California values arid curb expectations about rising prices.

The rate of growth in GNP is slowing and mortgage interest rates have been creeping up for more than nine months.

At nearly 11.5 percent for a fixed-rate mortgage, interest rates are more than two percentage points about where they were less than 12 months ago.

And with short-term rates continuing to climb, home loan rates are expected to go even higher.

While such economic forecasts are never certain, experts agree that the danger of a recession and rising rates will threaten future jumbo advances in real estate values like those of the last couple years.

While history has proven that it takes unusual economic events to jolt the steady spiral in California home prices, it has happened at least twice in the last 15 years — once in the early 1970s and again 10 years later.

Lessons can be learned from these two periods.

In the early 1980s, the California real estate market went into a tailspin.

Record high mortgage interest rates and an upswing in unemployment created havoc in the real estate market — putting the brakes on the wild home price inflation of the late 1970s.

When home loan rates topped out at 18 percent in 1981, demand for homes evaporated and prices began to slip.

While the median-priced home appreciated 8.2 percent in 1981, it only increased 3.8 percent in 1982, 2.3 percent in 1983 and actually fell slightly less than one percent in 1984.

During this four-year period, price increases were less than the overall rate of inflation.

In 1985, the median-home price began an upward march again and reached an all-time high in January of this year of $184,000, according to the California Association of Realtors.

Condominiums were even harder hit during the slowdown.

The median price of condominiums dipped 10 to 15 percent in the most overbuilt markets.

"The safety net of assumable loans just isn't there . . . Figures show the importance of assumable loans in the past. In 1982, loan assumption accounted for more than half of all home sales. Today, they represent less than 5 percent."

Joel Singer

With home buyers unable to afford a house or reluctant to make a major purchase in the middle of a deep recession, the once dynamic California real estate industry went into the doldrums.

The number of licensed real estate agents tumbled more than 25 percent and hundreds of builders were stuck with new homes that they couldn't sell Many were forced to bankruptcy.

Compared to the, go-go days of the late 1970s, real estate sales plummeted.

Home sales, for example, peaked at 605,000 in 1978 and fell to 234,000 in 1982.

In at least one way, a recession today combined with higher interest rates could be more damaging to home sales and appreciation than what occurred in the 1981-1984 period.

Then, state and federal law permitted home buyers to assume fixed-rate loans from home sellers.

Otherwise discouraged by rising interest rates, eager home buyers — though assumable loans — were able to buy houses at lower rates. Since then, federal and state laws have changed, now permitting lenders to call these lower Interest rate loans due when the property is sold.

It's true that many adjustable rate mortgages are assumable.

But the rate on these loans is increasing with the general rise in interest rates, 'and many lenders recast their loans at a new and higher rate when they are assumed.

"The safety net of assumable loans just isn't there," says Joel Singer, vice president of California Association of Realtors in Los Angeles.

"Figures show the importance of assumable loans in the past. In 1982, loan assumption accounted for more than half of all home sales. Today, they represent less than 5 percent," he said.

While experts aren't predicting as large an increase in interest rates as in the early 1980s, history provides proof that there are no guarantees that home prices will continue to climb.

Southampton respects both old and new

Special to the Examiner

First of two parts

WELL-INTENTIONED American city planners have spent decades trying to figure out ways to mix the historic elements of older communities with the growth and development that come with modern pressures. More often than not they fail.

There are no perfect models for such integration in the Bay Area, but high on the list of worthwhile experiments is the Solano County community of Benicia. Here, history and modern suburbia mix successfully. New and old get respect.

Perched at the edge of the Carquinez Strait, Benicia's shores are linked by the filigree of the Carquinez Bridge.

At one end of the town is "Old Benicia," which, thanks to a purposeful group of locals who were determined to rescue the town from its decaying waterfront past, is a tourist hot spot.

The 'new' Benicia

At the other end of town is the 2,300-acre, master-planned community of Southampton, which could be called "new" Benicia.

This subdivision is a living monument to the trials of California development in the 1960s, 1970s and 1980s.

There was a time, Marc Weiss notes in his book, "The Rise of the Community Builders," when developers got more respect. Before World War II, large-scale subdivides were the "guardians of a community's down-to-earth planning efforts through their role as private land developers," writes Weiss.

What people think

Although times have changed, that's' how people feel about Southampton.

Environmentalists, of course, would have preferred to keep the rolling hills of Benicia as virgin open space. Nevertheless, Southampton distinguishes itself from other residential developments for several reasons.

Although Southampton is just another suburban tract-home development, internal open space abounds. And it successfully mixes single-family homes with town homes, condos and apartments.

Southampton has grown from a dozen homes in 1971 to more than 4,000 today, but the development was designed carefully and, by today's standards, it was built out at a slow pace. Two hundred homes a year is not considered breakneck speed for residential construction.

The project was never syndicated to out-of-state investors and the same development team has been working on Southampton for nearly 20 years. It intends to stay until it's complete. One of the partners, Victor Freeman, lives there.

Until 1971, Southampton was a development disaster. The new town vision for this immense chunk of raw land was awash in problems. Then a partnership of the Southampton Development Group and Citizens Federal Savings came to the rescue.

Citizens, which is now First Nationwide Bank, provided long-term financing, while the development team began a long-term plan for building out the hilly site located on the north end of Benicia.

Two more houses

You can trace the history of Benicia through residents Lomax and Nancy Turner, who are in the insurance and real estate business. They have owned three houses there. First, they — like the community itself — were pioneers when they bought their first house there in 1969.

"Southampton Road was just a little gravel road. It was a country lane, where snakes used to sleep out in the middle of the road to get some sun," recalls Nancy Turner, "There were so few residents, PG&E wouldn't even turn on the street lights."

In 1976, the Turners bought their second home in Southampton.

Then in 1984, "we moved from our 3,000 square feet into a solar home with 1,372 square feet and gave the excess furniture to the kids," says Lomax Turner. "Now we're empty nesters."

When Southampton was first being built, prices ranged from $30,000 to $35,000. Today, homes sell for $160,000 to $298,000, with a long waiting list for each new one that is built.

"It's funny; no one thought of living out here in the boonies; now we can't build them fast enough," says Victor Freeman, one of the founders of Southampton.

In the last 20 years, Benicia has boomed. The population has tripled to more than 23,000; the old shipyards have been transformed into a prospering industrial park, and "Old Benicia" has become a bustling tourist showcase.

The town's rich past is the soul of the community, but Southampton gets credit for some of the town's success.

On my livable and sensible scale

New suburban tract homes have never been my favorite. But as the landscaping matures, the hills of Southampton are becoming more and more livable.

Despite voter approval, many counties won't accept Prop 90

At least ten California counties have rejected a voter approved statewide ballot measure which permits homeowners who are 55 or over to take there old and lower property tax bill with them when they move into another house in a different county.

Upset with how Proposition 90 might reduce their property tax revenue, the counties of Sonoma, Napa, Mendocino, El Dorado, Nevada, Monterey, Santa Cruz, Sacramento, Stanislaus and Tulare counties have already chosen to defy the voters wish.

The counties of Orange, San Diego, Kern and San Mateo have approved the rules, and the remaining 44 counties are currently deliberating the change.

Those voting to reject Prop 90 have done so even though the voters overwhelming approved the ballot measure in the November election.

When it placed Prop 90 on the ballot in 1987, the legislature was attempting to help out senior citizens who were stung by higher property tax bills when moving into a new home in a different part of the state.

Under the rules of the 1978 property tax cutting measure, Prop 13, those who stay put pay less and those who move pay more. When a home sells, the property is reassessed and the taxes change to reflect the homes current market value.

Because not everyone was happy with this procedure, the state legislature put Prop 60 on the ballot in 1987. Also approved by the voters by a wide margin, Prop 60 said a person over 55 who decides to buy a smaller house would not have to home pay higher taxes on their new home.

For retired people who want to move to a retirement community or a cabin in the hills, they can now sell the old house, buy another one and not worry about paying more in property taxes.

However, along with the age restriction, there were two caveats. First, the purchase price of the home couldn't exceed the selling price of the old house. Second, the senior couldn't transfer the tax bill when moving outside the county.

That restriction wasn't very popular among seniors, however. In 1988, Prop 90 was placed on the ballot, which permitted seniors to take their old tax bill when moving to other parts of the state.

There was one qualifier, however. The measure gave counties the option of rejecting or approving an implementing ordinance. Until the local county board of supervisors does so, eligible home buyer's can't benefit from Prop 90.

Strapped by shrinking tax revenue and rising costs, many county officials have been reluctant to do so.

"If someone from San Francisco sells a $300,000 house that is assessed at $100,000, they can come to Contra Costa, buy a $300,000 house and only pay propety taxes on that $200,000 difference," argues Claude Van Marter, Assistant Country Administrator, Contra Country, where one hearing has been held on the proposal.

"From a political point of view, we are (helping) people when don't live here yet, it does nothing for those who already live here "says Van Marter. This explain why some county officials are comfortable voting against the measure — despite the high level of voter approval of Prop 90.

On the other hand, some counties have rushed to implement the rules because they are predicting whether more people will be moving out of your county than moving in," says Van Martr. "If more people were going to move out then you can re-assess their property at a higher value; but if more people are moving in, then you are stuck with the lower tax bills that they bring with them."

Generally, senior citizens are more likely to move out of expensive urban areas into rural counties that are less expensive. This theory explains why large urban counties such as San Diego and San Mateo approved the measure and Tulare and Stnislaus counties have turned it back.

In the meantime, seniors determined to keep their low tax bills must find a county that has adopted Prop 90, stay put or find a place close by.

10 counties balk at Prop. 90; Officials: Tax transfer means less money

At least 10 California counties have rejected a voter approved statewide ballot measure which permits homeowners who are 55 or over to take their old and lower property tax bill with them when they move into another house in a different county.

Upset with how Proposition 90 might reduce their property tax revenue, the counties of Sonoma, Napa, Mendocino, El Dorado, Nevada, Monterey, Santa Cruz, Sacramento, Stanislaus and Tulare counties have already chosen to defy the voters' wish.

The counties of Orange, San Diego, Kern and San Mateo have approved the rules, and the remaining 44 counties are currently deliberating the change.

Those voting to reject Prop. 90 have done so even though the voters overwhelmingly approved the ballot measure in the November election.

When it placed Prop. 90 on the ballot in 1987, the legislature was attempting to help out senior citizens who were stung by higher property tax bills when moving into a new home in a different part of the state.

Under the rules of the 1978 property tax cutting measure, Proposition 13, those who stay put pay less and those who move pay more. When a home sells, the property is re-assessed and the taxes change to reflect the home's current market value.

Because not everyone was happy with this procedure, the state legislature put Proposition 60 on the ballot in 1987. Also approved by the voters by a wide margin, Prop. 60 said a person over 55 who decides to buy a smaller house would not have to pay higher taxes on their new home.

For retired people who want to move to a retirement community or a cabin in the hills, they can now sell the old house, buy another one and not worry about paying more in property taxes.'

However, along with the age restriction, there were two caveats. First, the purchase price of the home couldn't exceed the selling price of the old house. Second, the senior couldn't transfer the tax bill when moving outside the county.

That restriction wasn't very popular among seniors, however. In 1988, the Legislature placed Proposition 90 on the ballot, which permitted seniors to take their old tax bill when moving to other parts of the state.

There was one qualifier, however. The measure gave counties the option of rejecting or approving an implementing ordinance. Until the local county board of supervisors does so, eligible home buyers can't benefit from Prop. 90.

Strapped by shrinking tax revenues and rising costs, many county officials have been reluctant to do so. "If someone from San Francisco sells a $300,000 house that is assessed at $100,000, they can come to Contra Costa, buy a $300,000 house and only pay property taxes on a $100,000 assessment; and we lose the taxes on that $200,000 difference," argues Claude Van Marter, Assistant County Administrator, Contra Costa County, where one hearing has been held on the proposal.

"From a political point of view, we are (helping) people who don't live here yet; it does nothing for those who already live here," says Van Marter. This explains why some county officials are comfortable voting against the measure — despite the high level of voter approval of Prop. 90.

On the other hand, some counties have rushed to implement the rules because they are predicting that it will boost revenues. "It comes down to predicting whether more people will be moving out of your county than moving in," says Van Marter. "If more people were going to move out, then you can re-assess their property at a higher value; but if more people are moving in, then you are stuck with the lower tax bills."

23 April 1989 Page No 68
The San Francisco Examiner

It's one of the Best things happening there

Special to the Examiner

> *"A city's Chinatown is a monument to our ancestors' pioneering spirit. Those who excluded immigrants wanted to feel they had exclusive privileges: Chinatown now is a place represented by many ethnic groups. We can say this is a PanAsian Community where all people are included."*

—Rev. Frank C. Mar, Oakland Chinatown activist who died last month at age 66

UNLIKE SAN Francisco's Chinatown; Oakland's Chinatown isn't being squeezed by highrise development, isn't a tourist trap, doesn't suffer from deplorable housing conditions and isn't as densely developed. It also gets more sunshine and has many more trees and open space.

"You could say it's a more pleasant community to live in," says Ann Yee with the East Bay Local Development Corp. (EBALC), Oakland.

Sometimes referred to as Old Chinatown, this East Bay community is adjacent to downtown Oakland and is bordered by Broadway, Laney College, 14th Street and the Nimitz Freeway.

There are other differences between the two cities' Chinatowns. With the exception of the Kum Hay Teahouse at 8th and Franklin and a few small structures, the influence of traditional Chinese architecture is absent in Oakland.

Oakland's Chinatown also has some of the endearing qualities that make San Francisco's China-town so special. It is, like its counterpart in San Francisco, a close-knit ethnic neighborhood with definable boundaries and a buzzing street merchandising scene. It is inhabited by a purposeful group of citizens that care for their neighborhood.

But the term Chinatown may be a misnomer in Oakland. "A more appropriate name would be Asiatown," says Lynette Jung Lee, executive director of EBALC.

Along with a few thousand Chinese American residents, there are Korean storefronts between 12th and 13th streets on Webster. A handful of Vietnamese shops have opened around 9th Street. Then there are the Burmese, Cambodians, Thais, Japanese and Filipinos. Oakland's Chinatown is far less homogeneous than San Francisco's; it's an Asian melting pot.

Great place for locals

Without the glitzy gift shops and the traditional pagodas, the commercial scene is a hot spot for locals, and draws Asian Americana who now live in Walnut Creek, Concord, Fremont and Pleasant Hill. For folks in the East Bay, it has become a more convenient alternative than driving to San Francisco's Chinatown.

There is also a new, younger group of Asian Americana living near Chinatown. In the last few years, the most popular Oakland neighborhood for Asian Americans has been the San Antonio district seat of Lake Merritt. This area of older single-family homes is often referred to as New Chinatown and is favored by young families with children.

On the other hand, the elderly are partial to Old Chinatown.

For a while, though, the elderly faced a decline in available housing. Approximately 500 units of housing were lost when the Nimitz Freeway was expanded, BART was built and Laney College and the Oakland Museum were constructed.

"Most were lower-income rental units but some were single-family homes," complains Lee.

Community activists in China town are working to reverse that trend. They convinced the city of Oakland to approve an ordinance that controls the conversion of residential units to commercial use, and groups like EBALC are creating new housing opportunities.

Last year, the nonprofit group completed rehabilitation work on the historic Madrone Hotel, which has 32 low-cost single-occupancy rooms. The small rooms rent for $185 a month and have shared baths, kitchen facilities and social rooms.

Two of the residents are 75-year old Si Li and Wu Tai Chang, 81. Both are from Canton and have rooms adjacent to one another. They and other residents in the southeast wing of the second floor of the Madrone keep their doors open during the day which creates a spacious and airy living space.

Nearby, the Frank G. Mar Community Housing development is under construction; it will include 118 affordable rental units.

Low-cost housing isn't the only type of shelter making a comeback in Chinatown. The just-completed 42-unit Phoenix Plaza condominium development was sold out before construction was finished.

"We have mostly Chinese empty-nesters; some go back and forth from Hong Kong and others are retired people from the area," says local Realtor Ada Louie.

With vast window space in each unit, the one-bedroom condos average 700 square feet and sold for an average of $110,000. Two-bedroom units, 900 square feet,' sold for $145,000 and 1,000-square-foot, three-bedroom units fetched $160,000.

Louie notes, "There is tremendous demand to live in Chinatown; I have a waiting list of at least 200 people."

It's the same story at the 12-year-old, 318-unit City Center Plaza at Franklin and 9th, which rarely has vacant condos on the market.

Under construction is the Pacific Renaissance Plaza, which will occupy two city blocks at 9th and 10th streets between Webster and Franklin. The massive downtown project will include 250 condominium units, a cultural center and a library.

Beyond tradition and cultural familiarity, one attraction for seniors is a vast network of support services.

There are the 11 Asian family associations, several social clubs such as Wa Sung and the Chinese American Citizens Association, five churches and an array of nonprofit organizations.

This thick web of community involvement and neighborhood nurturing explains why the crime rate is low and why this place is becoming so desirable.

On My Sensible and Livable Scale

Though it is happening quietly, Oakland's Chinatown is expanding and growing, and what's already there is being preserved. It is the most remarkable and tangible sign of progress in downtown Oakland.

Prop. 13 fights off assault

Since it was approved by the voters in 1978, Proposition 13 has been protested, chided and rebuked by every conceivable interest group in the state. But until recently there was no evidence that critics of the 11-year-old revolutionary tax cutting measure might successfully turn their admonishment into a, serious assault on the Prop 13 rules.

To the chagrin of Prop 13 boosters, two recent events have shaken the political and legal framework that underlie the current system of property taxation in California. One is a U.S. Supreme Court decision handed down earlier this year, which addressed the constitutionality of certain methods of tax assessments like Proposition 13. However, it could be years before the decision affects property taxes here.

A more immediate threat to Prop 13 is a proposed statewide ballot measure that was filed with the California Attorney General's Office on April 21. If approved by the voters, it would dramatically restructure California property taxes by requiring commercial property owners to pay substantially higher taxes than homeowners.

Dubbed the Fair Share Property Tax Act of 1990, the measure calls for creating a "split-roll" property tax system, in which "non-residential property pays itsfair share by being taxed and re-assessed at a higher rate than residential property."

The proposed constitutional amendment was submitted by Los Angeles political consultant Bill Zimmerman, who has an impressive track record with progressive statewide ballot measures.

Along with consumer activist Harvey Rosenfield, Zimmerman heads up the non-profit Voter Revolt organization, which sponsored the controversial insurance ballot measure, Proposition 103. It was the only one of four insurance-reform initiatives on last November's, election ballot that was approved by the voters.

According to the 42-page proposal for the fair share property tax plan, the revenue windfall from the initiative would generate a tax rebate for homeowners and renters, provide a substantial infusion of funds for local government and earmark an estimated $1 to 2 billion for affordable housing programs.

Though some business and consumer organizations are already questioning the wisdom of the scheme, the sweeping measure didn't surprise many tax experts who are concerned about the growing inequities in the Proposition 13 property tax rules.

While neither the Realtors nor the Tax Reform Association has yet taken a position on the new measure, there is a good possibility that they may both oppose the Fair Share proposal.

"When similar bills have been put before the legislature, we have said that we don't believe one segment of society should be forced to pay a higher burden than others," says, CAR lobbyist Alex Creel. In the past, the Realtors have opposed the concept of split roll.

Goldberg is concerned that the proposal "doesn't deal with some of the real problems of Prop 13; it just raises taxes on some properties." However, Goldberg concedes that the measure "forces us to hasten what we are already doing to clean up the Prop 13 mess."

If this latest political ploy to undermine Prop 13 doesn't work, the courts may do the job. In the U.S. Supreme Court case of Allegheny Pittsburgh Coal Co. V. County Commission of Webster County, the high court decided that certain types of taxes may violate the Equal Protection Clause of the U.S Constitution's Fourteenth Amendment.

Detractors of Prop 13 charge that it is vulnerable to the same legal reasoning because of deep disparities between the property taxes that new and long time homeowners pay.

Legal experts claim the ruling is an important legal precedent for future California court cases that attempt to challenge the constitutionality of Proposition 13.

Under siege from the courts and the ballot box, Proposition 13 has never been on such shaky footing.

Prop. 13 looks shaky, for first time since '78

SINCE THE voters approved it in 1978, Proposition 13 has been protested, chided and rebuked by every conceivable interest group. But until recently there was no evidence that critics of the 11-year-old revolutionary tax-cutting measure might mount a serious assault on the Prop. 13 rules.

To the chagrin of Prop. 13 boosters, two recent events have shaken the political and legal framework of the current system of property taxation m California. One is a U.S. Supreme Court decision handed down earlier this year that considered the constitutionality of certain methods of tax assessments like Prop. 13. But it could be years before the decision affects property taxes here.

A more immediate threat to Prop. 13 is a proposed statewide ballot measure that was filed April 21 with the state attorney general's office. If the voters approve, it would dramatically restructure California property taxes by requiring commercial property owners to pay substantially higher taxes than homeowners.

Advocates new system

Dubbed the Fair Share Property Tax Act of 1990, the measure calls for creating a "split-roll" property tax system. Under it "non-residential property pays its fair share by being taxed and re-assessed at a higher rate than residential property."

Taxes on residential and commercial properties are at the same level.

The proposed amendment was submitted by Los Angeles political consultant Bill Zimmerman, who has an impressive track record with progressive statewide ballot measures.

Along with consumer activist Harvey Rosenfield, Zimmerman heads the nonprofit Voter Revolt organization, which sponsored the controversial insurance ballot measure, Prop. 103. It was the only one of four insurance-reform initiatives on last November's election ballot that voters approved. (The Supreme Court is reviewing the measure, which requires insurers to cut auto, homeowner and other property-casualty rates 20 percent from November 1987 levels.)

Funds for first-timers

According to the 42-page proposal for the fair share property tax plan, the revenue windfall from the initiative would generate a tax rebate for homeowners and renters, provide a substantial infusion of funds for local government and ear mark $1 billion to $2 billion for affordable housing programs.

Some business and consumer organizations are already questioning the wisdom of the scheme. But the sweeping measure didn't surprise many tax experts concerned about the growing inequities in the Prop. 13 property tax rules.

"There is an emerging consensus that there needs to be some major chances to how property taxes are levied in this state," says Lenny Goldberg, executive director of the California Tax Reform Association, which is supported by government agencies and labor unions.

A second look at Prop. 13

On the other end of the political spectrum, the California Association of Realtors recently issued a policy document that called for re- examining Prop. 13. The Realtors , are upset with the heavy property tax burden paid by new homeowners because it reduces affordability for first-time buyers and discourages real estate sales.

Californians owning comparable property face huge tax disparities, depending on when they bought the property. The measure set the property tax rate at 1 percent of assessed valuation and froze assessments for homeowners at their 1975 levels. These assessments may rise no more than two percent a year, unless the property is sold.

Commercial real estate is assessed using the same formula. But under Zimmerman's proposal, the tax rate would be set at 2 percent of assessed valuation and the assessment could rise by as much as 5 percent annually.

Opposition expected

While neither the Realtors nor the Tax Reform Association has yet taken a position on Zimmerman's measure, there's a good possibility that both will oppose it.

"When similar bills have been put before the Legislature, we have said we don't believe one segment of society should be forced to pay a higher burden than others," says CAR lobbyist Alex Creel. In the past, the Realtors have opposed the concept of split roll.

Goldberg is concerned that the proposal "doesn't deal with some of the real problems of Prop. 13.; it just raises taxes on some properties."

But he concedes that the measure "forces us to hasten what we are already doing to clean up the Prop 13; mess."

Court reviews case

If this latest political ploy to undermine Prop. 13 doesn't work, the courts may do the job. In the U.S. Supreme Court case of Allegheny Pittsburgh Coal Co. vs. County Commission of Webster County, the court decided that certain types of taxes may violate the Equal Protection Clause of the U.S. Constitution's 14th Amendment.

Detractors of Prop. 13 charge that it's vulnerable to the same legal reasoning because of deep disparities between the property taxes that new and long-time homeowners pay. Legal experts say the ruling is an important legal precedent for future California court cases that attempt to challenge the constitutionality of Prop. 13.

Under siege from the courts and the ballot box, Prop. 13 has never been on such shaky footing.

Wire reports: California's 1989 real estate sales off to strong start

COLTON — Led by strong March sales activity in both residential and commercial property categories, California real estate sales so far this year have significantly outpaced sales for the same period last year, according to TRW Real Estate Market Information.

An estimated total of $35 billion was spent on California property during the first three months of this year. While down 16.4 percent from last year's fourth quarter, the figure is 35.7 percent higher than first quarter of 1988.

"Although recent increases in mortgage interest rates have cooled the market somewhat since late last year, there is continued confidence in California's economy. The real estate market here is showing strength we're not seeing in other parts of the country," said Ed Setzer, vice president of TRW Real Estate Information Services.

"Several factors seem to be at work here. On the commercial side, a significant amount of overseas money is finding its way info property in California.

"On the residential side, home buyers remain confident that their property will increase in value. They seem to be willing to brave the recent rise in interest rates," Setzer said.

The number of properties that changed hands statewide was 260,421 for the first quarter, according to TRW. That was an Increase of 23.6 percent compared to the same period last year.

Of these, the number of homes was 130,969, up 1.3 percent from last year.

The average price paid for a home was $174,336 statewide, up 15.1 percent from last year.

The most expensive county to buy a home in was San Mateo at $280,967, homes are most affordable in Tulare County at $72,157.

The numbers include all homes: Single family residences and condominiums, new and existing homes. Apartment buildings are classified as commercial and are not part of the home statistics.

TRW's figures also show a high, although recently declining, level of building activity in California.

A total of $7.2 billion was made in construction loans during the first quarter, down 22.9 percent from last year's final quarter, up 15.3 percent compared to first quarter 1988.

TRW REMI monitors real estate activity in California, Nevada, Arizona, Texas, Illinois and Florida.

Marina Village in Alameda

A mixed-use neighborhood spruces up the Island
Special to the Examiner

THE MOST popular way to make a killing in the overheated Bay Area real estate market is to go but to the edge of the burbs and add another subdivision.

In these Bay Area communities where virgin land is being carpeted with scads of look-alike tract homes, this well tested formula works handsomely for well-capitalized and eager developers.

But there is another way.

Urban builders tear down old and "under-utilized" factories and replace them with slick high-tech mid-rises. They transform dated warehouses into attractive city office parks and squeeze in pastel-colored high-density condominiums on narrow infill plots in the heart of urban areas.

Real estate gurus call this "maximizing land value," and the trend explains why our built-up urban environment never stays the same. Sometimes it offends us; other times it is pleasing.

That's what Vintage Properties tried to do with 205 acres along the Oakland Estuary in Alameda.

At first, their vision for this run-down waterfront wasteland seemed like a flawed one. In the early 1980s, their condominiums were slow movers, and the business park broke ground just when the Bay Area commercial office market went to the dogs.

That was yesterday. Today, this tasteful mixed-use scheme called Marina Village is nearing completion and is a stroke of urban development genius.

Possibilities were endless

Just 10 years ago the windswept property was a waterfront ghetto with decaying shipyard piers and abandoned industrial buildings. But because it was located on a mile of waterfront property, the possibilities for a metamorphosis were tricky but endless.

With the help of the City of Alameda's redevelopment agency, Vintage has built 160 townhomes, a 1,000-berth marina, a 128,000 square-foot shopping center and several hundred thousand square feet of commercial space.

The commercial space has become a hot spot for computer software companies and the booming biotechnology industry. For example, Hana Biologics Inc. is located there. Among other things, the company is working on a cure for Parkinson's disease.

Marina Village is mixed up correctly

Before I visited Marina Village, I thought that living next to a new-age, gene-splicing research facility wasn't my idea of a desirable neighborhood. But for the 200 residents of Marina Village, it doesn't seem to matter.

"One thing that the developer definitely got right is scale," says resident Ron Rossi. "They packed up the low-rise office buildings farther away from the townhomes, and they are spending a fortune on landscaping," says Rossi, who is an architect with UC-Berkeley.

With rich detail, the rehabilitated 73-year-old Powerhouse building became the architectural standard for the rest of the commercial buildings. This and the unusual public art gives the office park appeal that you rarely find in other industrial settings.

The townhomes, which are separated into five courts, have a mix of old and young and very few children. Thirty percent of the resident have boats in the marina.

Successful investigation

"I had a lot of reservations about this condominium business, so I investigated the developers and hired a private contractor to inspect my unit and the property," says resident Deanna Osterberg-Schwartz.

She says she was more than satisfied and moved from Oakland's' Oakmore neighborhood (south of Montclair) in September, 1986, becoming one of the first residents in Marina Village. "I'm an Alameda cheerleader and I looked all over the Island, but I like it here," she says.

Many locals refer to Alameda as the Island, and the development of Marina Village has helped change a perception that this was the wrong end of the island.

With no plans for more residential units, the little community is a tight-knit group, brags Rossi, who is president of the Marina Village Homeowners Association.

"In other places, you are lucky if you know the guy next door," he says, "but here I know all my neighbors."

There is a nearby naval air station and flight noise can be bothersome. But residents say it is confined to the late afternoon hours when people are at work.

Cool winds also hit about then. Moving from San Francisco's Twin Peaks 10 months ago, Rossi says he isn't bothered by the "breezes." "Sure it can get cold, but there's no fog," he insists.

With a Lucks food store and a Long's drug store, the local shopping center draws customer from the entire region. It has a suburban feel to it, which makes it the only ho-hum piece in this otherwise clever mixed-use development.

On my livable and sensible scale

Marina Village is a place where industry, housing and recreation work well together.

State tries giving away housing aid

Spending a half-billion dollars is easier said than done. Just ask officials with the State Department of Housing and Community Development.

According to Propositions 77 and 84 which were approved by California voters last year, HCD was the state agency designated to issue $450 million in general obligation bonds and to spend the proceeds on solving the state's housing crunch.

Yet 12 months later, the bonds haven't been issued and none of the money has been spent.

"I think it's criminal that they have not gotten the money out faster," charges Marc Brown, attorney, California Rural Legal Assistance Foundation, Sacramento.

The two sweeping initiatives authorized aid for homeless shelters, assistance to first-time home buyers, loans for low-cost apartments and grants for earthquake proofing older housing projects.

Nearly one year after Prop. 77 was approved and six months after Prop. 84 was ratified, state housing officials are scrambling to recruit staff, set up programs, enact regulations, issue bonds, and decide which cities and non-profit organizations are entitled to the record level of housing aid, But critics charge that there is nothing to show for the flurry of activity.

Housing advocates, who thought that getting voter approval would be the biggest hurdle in pushing through the two ballot measures, have learned that the state bureaucracy can be an even more formidable challenge.

"You can't imagine the amount of time and personnel it takes to move a government organization in an entirely new direction," says Susan DeSantis, former director of the Department of Housing and Community Development and now a Newport Beach-based political consultant

Each element of the two ballot measures must be reviewed and approved by a confusing network of committees and agencies. For example, a special California Earthquake Safety and Housing Rehabilitation Finance Committee has been formed to oversee the $28 million set aside from Prop, 77 for earthquake proofing.

Because of inexplicable delays in issuing the bonds, this new committee had to seek a loan from the state's Pooled Money Investment Commitee before it could even get started.

However, this step was only the beginning in an elaborate bureaucratic maze. While the funding quirks were being worked out, HCD had to complete "development regulations" which now must be circulated among a "broad range of interested parties." Then the Director's Bond Advisory Committee must review and discuss the regulations before they go to the state Office of Administrative Law (OAL) for final approval.

Upon receiving a go ahead from the OAL, "A Notification of Funding Availability (NOFA)" will be mailed to government agencies and non-profit groups who are entitled to apply for the money. Then another HCD committee will review applications, decide who is eligible for the funds and disperse the money. Once the funds are released by the state, local groups must go through their own hoops before earthquake proofing ever begins.

"Let's hope in the meantime that we don't have a serious earthquake," snipped one housing advocate.

State officials argue that scrutiny by multiple committees and agencies insures that a myriad of outside interest groups has input into how these new programs will work.

But housing advocates claim that the entire process should be expedited. "I fault them for starting the planning process so late." complains Brown. He concedes, however, that "there have been some technical hurdles that had to be crossed in order to get this far."

The state, has decades of experience issuing bonds for parks, schools, roads and other government services, but "this is the first time that the state has issued general obligation bonds for housing assistance," explains Julie Nauman. deputy director, HCD, Sacramento.

Housing aid program mired in state red tape

SPENDING HALF-A-BILLION dollars is easier said than done. Just ask officials with the State Department of Housing and Community Development (HCD).

According to Propositions 77 and 84, which California voters approved last year, HCD was the state agency designated to issue $450 million in general obligation bonds and to spend the proceeds on solving the state's housing crunch.

Yet 12 months later, the bonds haven't been issued and none of the money has been spent.

"I think it's criminal that they have not gotten the money out faster," says Marc Brown, attorney for the California Rural Legal Assistance Foundation in Sacramento.

The two sweeping initiatives authorized aid for homeless shelters, help for first-time home buyers, loans for low-cost apartments and grants for earthquake-proofing older housing projects.

Nearly a year after Prop, 77 was approved and six months after Prop. 84 was ratified, state housing officials are scrambling to recruit staff, set up programs, enact regulations, issue bonds and decide which cities and nonprofit organizations are entitled to the record level of housing aid. But critics say there's nothing to show for the flurry of activity.

Election was the easy part

Housing advocates who thought that getting voter approval would be the biggest hurdle in pushing through the two ballot measures are learning that the state bureaucracy can be an even more formidable challenge.

"You can't imagine the time and personnel it takes to move a government organization in an entirely new direction," says Susan DeSantis, former director of the Department of Housing and Community Development and now a Newport Beach-based political consultant. "The red tape is overwhelming."

Each element of the two ballot measures must be reviewed and approved by a confusing network of committees and agencies. For example, a special California Earthquake Safety and Housing Rehabilitation Finance Committee has been formed to oversee the $28 million set aside from Prop, 77 for earthquake proofing.

Because of inexplicable delays in issuing the bonds, this new committee had to seek a loan from the state's Pooled Money Investment Committee before it could even get started.

But this step was only the beginning in an elaborate bureaucratic maze. While the funding quirks were being worked out, HCD had to complete "development regulations," which now must be circulated among a "broad range of interested parties." Then the Director's Bond Advisory Committee must review and discuss the regulations before they go the State Office of Administrative Law (OAL) for final approval.

Upon receiving a go-ahead from the OAL, a "Notification of Funding Availability (NOFA)" will be mailed to government agencies and nonprofit groups who are entitled to apply for the money. Then another HCD committee will review applications, decide who is eligible for the funds and disperse the money. Once the funds are released by the state, local groups must go through their own hoops before earthquake proofing ever begins.

"Let's hope in the meantime that we don't have a serious earthquake," snips one housing advocate.

State officials argue that scrutiny by multiple committees and agencies insures that a myriad of outside interest groups has input into how these new programs will work.

Ethical Problems abounded

But housing advocates claim that the entire process should be expedited. "I fault them for starting the planning process so late," complains Brown. He concedes, however, that "there have been some technical hurdles that had to be crossed in order to get this far."

The state has decades of experience issuing bonds for parks, schools, roads and other government services, but "this is the first time that the state has issued general obligation bonds for housing assistance "explains Julie Nauman, deputy director of HCD. "It's new territory for all of us."

Moreover, the state had to hire dozens of new professionals to administer the new programs, which caused further delays.

HCD says the first distributions — $6 million in homeless funds won't occur for many months although groups can start applying for the money in a few weeks.

Realtors flex their muscles on housing issues

This is the first of a four-part serial on the well-financed and powerful political action programs of Realtors. The first two parts deal with Influence at the national level while parts three and four address political action programs at the state and local level.

A number of disgruntled U.S. Congressional leaders used to snipe that the trademark letter "R" behind the word Realtor actually stood for Republican. Critics of the ultra-conservative political positions once taken by the National Association of Realtors (NAR) went further: the "R", they said, stood for reactionary.

In the early 1980s, "the NAR lobbying operation was an unmitigated living disaster in Washington, D.C.," says Rep. Robert T. Matsui, D-Sacramento.

Those days are gone, boast leaders of the nation's largest trade association, which represents 800,000 Realtors throughout the country.

"We are still the largest lobbying organization in the country," says Norman B. Flynn, President of NAR, which last year contributed more than $3 million to congressional candidates, making it the fattest political action committee in the country.

"But we have made a deliberate shift from staunch Republican flag-waving to bi-partisan pragmatism, where issues outweigh political party affiliation."

Former foes of the once highhanded real estate organization agree.

"Today, powerful but reasonable might be better words to describe NAR's political image in Washington, D.C.," says Ralph Neas, executive director of the Leadership Conference on Civil Rights in Washington.

Matsui notes that, "NAR has come full circle: it is a first-class organization today."

Last month, the Leadership Conference on Civil Rights gave NAR the "Business Community Award" at its annual Hubert Humphrey Civil Rights Award dinner. The Realtors were recognized for actively promoting the passage of the sweeping Fair Housing Act of 1988, which includes stiff new rules barring discrimination in housing.

"The Realtors have come a along way," says Neas.

Just eight years ago the organization was the pivotal force in blocking far less stringent fair housing laws. Then, NAR pushed conservative U.S. Senator Orrin Hatch, R-Utah, to filibuster a fair housing bill, which stalled the passage of the anti-discrimination legislation.

"We were thought of as the guys with black hats in white sheets," says Flynn.

Erasing such memories hasn't been easy.

In the past, "NAR fought each and every battle like it was the last one," says Steve Driesler, senior vice president for NAR. "With those bullying tactics, we had forgotten that today's foes may be tomorrow's allies."

There are dozens of examples in which NAR alienated members of Congress and an array of political interest groups.

During the early Reagan years, for instance, NAR ran full page advertisements in the Washington Post calling for drastic cuts in federal social programs. One such ad bitterly remembered by low-income housing advocate Barry Zigas stated, "There are pressing social needs in the country, but nothing is more pressing than the federal deficit."

Zigas observes that. "NAR was perceived as the most conservative organization in the Capital — frankly, the Realtors were told to change their habits, or else."

While President of NAR in 1985, California Realtor Clark Wallace remembers an embarrassing incident in which the problem was brought home loud and clear. In a meeting with leading California congressional Democrat Tony Coelho, "he ripped us apart for being so damned partisan and so carelessly conservative," says Wallace.

In a radical turnabout, "now we are seeing Realtors stand shoulder to shoulder with the NAACP and the Mexican/American Legal Defense Fund," says Neas. "Together, we created a legislative juggernaut that forced the House (of Representatives) to approve the fair housing bill 401 to zero."

In a coalition of unlikely allies, NAR used that same clout to help push through another major housing bill in 1987. Republicans came to the Realtors and offered to support NAR's pet program for improving FHA home lending, but with the condition that the Realtors back off supporting a part of the bill that increased federal funding for low-cost housing.

"NAR rebuked the Republicans and proved that it was serious about its new course," says Zigas.

Driesler sums it up, "We still fight hard; but we don't get personal, we try not to make too many enemies, we don't gloat, we don't pout and we no longer get vindictive."

State Realtors run bipartisan lobby in capital

The National Association of Realtors is the nation's largest trade group, and its policies impact significantly on housing, from the prices of homes to the availability of mortgage financing. This is the third of four parts on its political influence.

IN 1980 during the U.S. presidential campaign, a small group of staunch Ronald Reagan supporters within the California Association of Realtors proposed that CAR direct a large part of its 100-member professional staff to drop its current activity and work on the Reagan campaign.

The proposal never went anywhere, but the mere fact that the scheme came to light showed the partisan and conservative political direction of the 120,000-member real estate trade association just 10 years ago.

However, times have changed. Just as its national counterpart, the National Association of Realtors, has changed its political ways, the California Realtors now run a sophisticated bipartisan political operation. It prides itself on pragmatism, not ideology, and usually gets its way with the Legislature.

"I would definitely put CAR in the top tier of effective lobbying organizations in Sacramento," says Christine Minnehan, an aide to the majority leader, Sen. David Roberta D-Los Angeles.

Until a few years ago, the sizable CAR political action campaign fund "was seized by a right-wing element of the association," says Doug Gillies, a former Realtor lobbyist.

In 1981, for instance, a CAR-sponsored political affairs lunch reflected this sentiment when liberal Assembly Speaker Willie Brown was the speaker. In defiance, a number of the more conservative Realtors boycotted his speech.

Hard times for the old guard

Yet change was brewing and an internal brawl over CAR's political philosophy began to reshape the organization. As Republicans began to take CAR's support for granted and Democrats disdained the organization partisan record, Realtor leaders took stock and revamped their political donation program.

"Many old-time CAR members had a very difficult time coming to grips with the fact that they were going to be giving some of their money to Democrat, even though at the time leading Democrat like Mike Roos and Leo McCarthy were carrying major housing packages," says former CAR staff member Tom Bannon. He now heads the California Apartment Association in Sacramento.

Today, CAR's political war chest is divided evenly between Democrat and Republicans, according to public report filed with the Fair Political Practice Commission.

Doling out more than $600,000 to state legislative campaigns last year, CAR ranks as the second largest Political Action Committee in the state, second only to the California Medical Association.

"In terms of dollars, they are a significant force," says Brenda Robinson of Common Cause. "A lot of legislators are in (CAR's) political wallet."

"They have a lot of influence with the Governor, the Legislature, and face it, their people are all over the state," says Bill Powers of the Western Center on Law and Poverty.

Even when conservatives seemed to have a lock on the organization, CAR kept its reputation for having a skilled lobbying operation in the capital. Now retired for two years, Gillies get much of the credit for keeping CAR's legislative program on an even track.

What Gillies accomplished

During his 20-year tenure, the real estate trade organization got its way on dozens of issues affecting the industry. From programs that helped first-time home buyers to bills that reduced the legal liability of realty agents, CAR often over-powered the Legislature with it numbers, sizable political contributions and convincing argument.

Today, legislative aide Minnehan is impressed by signs that CAR plans to use its political muscle to help with affordable housing. Though largely absent from this debate in the last five years, the organization just released sweeping proposals to ease the housing crunch.

"They have begun to recognize the relationship between providing affordable housing and a healthy and functioning real estate market," says Arnold Sternberg, a progressive housing activist.

Although such observers as Bannon say CAR's new emphasis is "modernization not liberalization," conservative detractor abound.

"The Realtors have become a source of disappointment," says Gil Ferguson, a Republican Orange County assemblyman. "As people encroach more and more on private property right, the Realtors — instead of fighting it with all of their might have begun to acquiesce."

One source of conservative wrath is CAR's decision to back off from leading the charge to adopt state laws that would weaken local rent control.

"Our members recognize that there are dozens of important issues in Sacramento and rent control is only one of them," says CAR lobbyist Alex Creel "We have decided not to go down in flames over a single issue."

Report says condo suits increasing

Frustrated with construction defects, an increasing number of condominium and townhouse associations in California are suing builders to pay for expensive building repairs.

A 1986 study concluded that as many as 40 percent of the 16.000 common-interest associations in the state are involved in litigation. Experts say the number of lawsuits has increased in the last three years.

When an expensive construction defect is detected, associations often engage in painful and expensive lawsuits that are aimed at builders whose workmanship was in question.

The problems' are expected to worsen considering that an increasing number of Californians choose to live in a house, condo or townhome that is governed by a homeowners association. These volunteer organizations are responsible for the upkeep of common ground areas such as roofs, water drainage, landscaping and central plumbing.

When the roof leaks and the drainage system fails the association often turns to the developers for relief. Developers often argue that building problems are a result of poor maintenance practices such as not controlling tree growth that can cause foundation damage. But this "argument hasn't thwarted the number of lawsuits.

Homeowner association expert Linnea Scampini says associations seem to be more litigious than other businesses because of the high level of frustration and because they "aren't capitalized to take care of big ticket items like replacing a roof or fixing foundation."

San Francisco attorney Branden Bickel says "many of the people who buy condominiums are first time home buyers with limited resources." Faced with the alternative of a special dues association the board of directors will sue.

Consequently, "we have seen no let-up in the number of lawsuits aimed at developers," says Marc Fong, an Oakland attorney who specializes in homeowner association lawsuits. "It is a function of careless cost cutting; developers are looking for ways to economize, and if a cheaper product works they will say 'what the heck' and use it."

But lawsuits have risks that homeowner associations should consider before they contact their attorney.

For one, lawsuits are expensive. On average, "the attorney cost the association about $220,000 to bring-this stuff to a successful conclusion," says George Einfeldt of the Crow Canyon Country Club Homeowners Association.

When considering a lawsuit, Einfeldt recommends that association boards "review association documents to determine the right of the board (of directors) to commit to large unbudgeted expenses," such as a lawsuit.

It's true that contingency fees are a common way of financing a lawsuit today. In this case, the lawyer agrees to receive a percentage of the settlement as payment. This reduces the out-of-pocket expenses to the association.

But attorney fees aren't the only consideration; there may be hidden costs.

For example, "property often doesn't appreciate as fast," says Fong That's because, "lenders often pull out of financing the future sale of units when they get wind of a lawsuit," he says.

The Federal Housing Administration (FHA), for example, won't loan on condominiums when litigation is pending. And when lenders snub a particular project, resales' are more difficult and property values suffer. Lawsuits often last up to two years, which can tie up future sales for a long period of time.

Other problems begin when the lawsuit is settled. Einfeldt says associations often think that "all of their problems are solved when the cash comes in Ha!"

The awards or settlements are often smaller than the claim, .according to Fong. "Then the association must sort out how to spend the limited resources that they waited so long to get," he says.

Fongknows of cases where a faction of the membership threatens to sue the association for choosing to spend the legal award in a way other members don't agree with.

In the final analysis, litigation has become a way of life in California homeowner associations.

South Berkeley area coming back — slowly

Special to the Examiner

TWENTY-FIVE years ago, BART was planned as an intricate regional transportation network that would serve the needs of a commuter society. That vision succeeded: Every day the tentacles of the BART octopus whisk 215,000 workers to and from their homes. Though often chastised by its riders, BART remains a model for mass transit planning around the world.

But there have been damning side effects. The success of the system depended on building 34 BART stations in the middle of some of the Bay Area's most densely populated neighborhoods. In the beginning, community battles over the location and design of BART stops were often fierce.

It's true that many of the stations have since been woven into the community fabric. Fears about the growth and development that a BART station would purportedly unleash were unfounded, and construction disruptions were temporary.

Rockridge in Oakland and Glen Park in San Francisco are two examples where BART fits in well; Modest in scale, these stations complement a thriving commercial scene and haven't destroyed the stable single-family neighborhoods that surround the BART stops.

Then there's South Berkeley

In other instances, BART stations became a lasting menace, and some neighborhoods have never recovered. The Adeline-Alcatraz neighborhood in South Berkeley is a good example.

The area is located roughly between Sacramento and Shattuck. It's a middle- to low-income area in the early 1960s that wasn't growing and improving at the same pace as other Berkeley neighborhoods.

"The installation of BART was a coup de grace for the economy of the neighborhood," Christophe Girot wrote in his 1986 UC-Berkeley masters thesis for the school of architecture. "Serious decline in the neighborhood was accentuated in the late 1960s by the beginning of the BART construction."

Businesses closed, a horde of storefronts were left vacant and many nearby homes were poorly maintained.

A spawning ground for drugs

Commenting on this period, Mayor Loni Hancock said recently, "The underground construction of BART dealt a serious blow to the commercial viability of the neighborhood."

Today, the low-income community to the south of the Ashby BART station still struggles with deterioration. The neighborhood has become a spawning ground for drugs and dealers. Drifters hang out on corners along Adeline near the BART station. The median income of area resident is only 60 percent of the city average.

But there are signs that the neighborhood is on the rebound, although slowly.

"We have the infrastructure, the energy and the vision to make this neighborhood what it was before BART entered the picture, but it won't be easy," says Joe Brooks, who lived most of his life in the neighborhood. He now heads the Berkeley Rent Stabilization Board located in the neighborhood.

Berkeley is determined to turn the area around. The city's Office of Economic Development is pouring $1.25 million into commercial revitalization along Adeline.

"We have reached a critical point in our effort in the Adeline corridor," says Assistant City Manager for Economic Development Neil Mayer. "You can see concrete progress building by building and block by block.'

What some loans are doing

Berkeley's urban renaissance scheme isn't a bold plan to clear out the ugly and rebuild anew. Instead, the city is restoring and rebuilding existing buildings and giving a boost to current businesses. The strategy centers on a revolving loan fund that helps local business. For example:

J&B Fine Foods got a loan from the city to buy new refrigeration equipment.

Pride Home Care Medical is a minority-owned business that qualified for a .municipal loan to remodel and install a pharmacy.

Studio 5 Hair Design is using city funds to improve its business and buy new equipment.

In 1985, the South Berkeley Neighborhood Development Corp. was formed to help the revitalization plan. The community-based group bought a vacant lot at Adeline and Harmon and is building commercial office space and affordable housing there.

With a grant from the San Francisco Foundation, the Development Corp. is working with area people to plant trees in the neighborhood. It's also working with private investors to restore the old Wells Fargo building at Adeline and Alcatraz.

Years ago the neighborhood was a center for the East Bay blues scene. The clubs have closed, but the new Black Repertory Theater is there. So is the Guitar Center, a commercial retail business that will occupy what had been a neighborhood eyesore at the Northeast corner of Adeline Avenue and Alcatraz street.

With several popular black churches and many stable businesses, the Adeline neighborhood may yet survive the wrath of BART. But as local residents readily concede, it has a long way to go.
On My Livable and Sensible Scale:
South Berkeley was a victim in a mighty regional agenda. Healing the wounds hasn't been easy.

To grow or not to grow? That is the question

ATA UCLA conference on growth control last year, the discussion reached a stalemate when somebody asked whether it was time to slow California s population growth.

Invariably, any discussion about problems with growth and development ignite arguments. A grass-roots symbol of the anxiety about it is the popular bumper sticker that says, "Welcome to California — Now Go Home."

As impractical as it may sound, the idea of curbing the state's population goes beyond a cynical road [?] jest. In a statewide public opinion poll by the Field institute, 58 percent said they believe the state [?] growing too fast.

Upset with the expansion of the [?]'s economy that creates an [?]less wave of new jobs and attracts more than 1,750 new residents a day, people are asking: Are there limits to the state's population?

"Like any natural organism, a metropolis can grow so large that it ceases to function efficiently for the benefit of its inhabitants and their environs," says a new report published by the Greenbelt Alliance, one of California's most respected environmental organizations.

Dubbed "The Sustainable Metropolis," the report sidesteps how to about controlling the state's population, but the alliance's executive director, Larry Orman says, "This is a fundamental question."

Quality of lift declining

Compounding the fears are stories in national newspapers and magazines reporting on the declining quality of life in California. Newsweek this summer published a cover story on that issue.

The article and others like it point out that an endless wave of growth has damaged the coast line, added to pollution, put more cars on freeways and sent house prices soaring. In the minds of many Californians, merely reordering how and where development occurs ignores the larger question of population growth.

But bumper stickers and debates about the need to control the population defy a 20-year history of unprecedented migration. California is the most populous state in the nation with more than 28.3 million people. Forecasters predict that 35 million people will live here by the year 2000.

Los Angeles Times columnist Robert Jones recently referred to the state's growth rate as a "rush of civilization piling up on the Pacific slope."

A population explosion isn't the only demographic shift. In 1870, only one-twentieth of the foreign-born population in the nation lived in the West. Today, California is home to a fourth of the 14 million U.S. residents who were born in other nations.

Like it or not, California has become urbanized. One sign of this urbanization is the state's ethnic diversity.

A modern white flight

The far-reaching influx of minorities has prompted a modern-day white flight, according to some experts. They say the trend partly explains the rapid suburbanization of such areas as Contra Costa, Alameda and North San Diego counties and the growth in Riverside, Ventura and San Bernardino counties in the Los Angeles Basin.

Although the ethnic diversity has caused anxiety about the changing character of California, new immigrants have had many positive influences on the state.

For example, Southeast Asian refugees are fixing up abandoned store fronts in San Francisco's Tenderloin and Korean immigrants have upgraded Western Avenue in Los Angeles. In both cases, a thriving commercial scene has returned to these once dying communities.

Moreover, real estate values have been uplifted, which generates more property tax revenue and brings salvation to dozens of inner-city neighborhoods.

Twenty-five years ago, urban planner Jane Jacobs said, "A community's ethnic diversity can be used as an asset not a detriment — for encouraging neighborhood stability." For the most part, that has been the case in California.

And though we have become the most urbanized state, California enjoys expansive open spaces and natural beauty that can't be found in more congested parts of the country.

For the time being, we live in two worlds: one is urban and the other is pastoral. Record population gains may threaten the old California but it makes the new California possible.

Textile factory to open in Fresno

Special to the Examiner

If California economic development officials ever get around to printing a slick brochure on the merits of the state's 19 enterprise zones, a picture of the Nisshinbo plant in Fresno will be a likely candidate for the cover photo.

When the state Department of Commerce contacted Nisshinbo Industries, a Japanese textile manufacturer, about locating a new facility in California, the prospects of landing the first textile mill west of the Mississippi were bleak.

State economic growth boosters were all too aware of the obstacles: high labor costs, exorbitant taxes, expensive land and a political environment that was famous for shunning "dirty industries."

Nevertheless, when word got out that Nisshinbo Director of Operations Kaz Fujisaki was poking around Sacramento, Fresno, Riverside and Bakersfield for a new site, state officials put together a bundle of incentives that Fujisaki could not resist.

Part of the package was a suggestion to locate the Nisshinbo plant in Fresno, in the middle of one of the state's enterprise zones.

The strategy worked. Beginning in November, more than 150 workers will be spinning 1 million yards of fabric in Nisshinbo's new Fresno mill, which is a joint venture between Nisshinbo and Kanematsu-Gosho Ltd., a California trading company.

State officials are quick to point to the Nisshinbo success story as proof that enterprise zones work. However, the role of enterprise zones in Fresno and other places in California — including Pittsburg and San Jose in the Bay Area — may be exaggerated, experts say.

"The problem is that a considerable number of jobs are just moved like pieces of a chess board, when companies move or expand to take advantage of enterprise zones," says Peter Hall, a professor of metropolitan planning in the City and Regional Planning Department at UC-Berkeley. Hall conceived of the enterprise zone theory 10 years ago in England.

By waiving or reducing taxes, wiping out red tape and providing financing for new businesses, enterprise zones are hailed as economic development magic. With minimal government involvement, they promise to create jobs in depressed parts of the nation.

"My goal is to empower the people who live in ghettos and barrios and experience unconscionable levels of poverty, unemployment and despair by creating opportunities for employment," said U.S. Secretary of Housing and Urban Development Jack Kemp, a longtime cheerleader for enterprise zones.

A British 'reinvention'

Dubbed the free port zone by leftist Hall, the scheme was hijacked by Geoffrey Howe of the conservative Margaret Thatcher government in Britain, which coined the phrase enterprise zones.

They fit neatly into the Republican platform to deregulate American business, reduce direct economic planning favored by liberals and 6how concern for the vast pockets of economic failure. With Ronald Reagan as its champion in the 1980 election, enterprise zones were expected to spawn an urban metamorphosis.

For the most part, however, the scheme has been nothing more than material for well-waxed campaign speeches.

It wasn't until 1987 that the U.S. Congress approved the creation of 100 enterprise zones. Moreover, they have been largely meaningless, since no tax breaks were included in the bill.

When the federal government failed to deliver on the enterprise zone promise, states enacted their own legislation.

In California, the Legislature could not agree on one bill to create enterprise zones so it passed two in 1985. Assemblyman Patrick Nolan, R-Glendale, introduced a measure that created 10 enterprise zones, and a bill by Assemblywoman Maxine Waters, D-Los Angeles, created nine more that imposed local hiring requirements on companies locating in the zones.

Sales tax exemption

The biggest state incentive is an exemption from sales tax on equipment that costs up to $20 million. Nisshinbo expects to save $1.3 million in taxes on equipment for its plant in Fresno.

However, local government can no relief from environmental or labor regulations, and Proposi 13 prohibits any property tax abatement.

Nisshinbo negotiated a $1.2 million rate break, over five years, with Gas & Electric Co., but it was rejected by the state Public Utilities Commission. Then, the company discovered it had to pay a $50,000 development fee to the financially strapped West Unified School District.

To save time and money for growing businesses, the state calls for local governments to offer one-stop permitting for the approval of new plants in enterprise zones.

For Driz Knitting Mills Inc. in Los Angeles that was an impressive incentive, says developer Carlos Siderman. Working with Driz on a 35,000-square-foot expansion of its knitware plant, Siderman recalls that when he attended a function on enterprise zones in Mayor Tom Bradley's office, "The first thing (Bradley) said was, 'Eliminate red tape.' I said, 'great.' "

But would Driz have gone somewhere else without the enterprise zones? Probably not. Proximity to a vast pool of unskilled labor in south-central Los Angeles was too important.

Though the state Department of Commerce estimates that 137 new businesses and 6,000 jobs have been spawned in the state's 19 enterprise zones, not everyone is convinced that it's sensible public policy.

Senate legislative consultant Peter Detwiler notes, "We should make sure we aren't just giving tax breaks to businesses that don't need it."

Gimme shelter? — 'Not in my back yard'

Special to the Examiner

THERE IS something ugly going on, and it's going to get worse before it gets better. On the one hand, people bemoan the fact that the ranks of the homeless are mounting. In the cities and in the 'burbs they appear in almost every downtown sidewalk, and dozens are camped out in our municipal parks. No doubt about it — the open-air squatter population has mushroomed and it worries us all.

So let's build some housing and fix this problem.

That would be fine if Bay Area communities weren't stomping on proposals to build transitional housing for the homeless. In more than one case the proceedings have gotten downright nasty.

Take the 100 residents who objected to a 54-bed homeless shelter in Martinez. At a raucous hearing on the project last summer, a few of the angry opponents were waving American flags and called supporters of the shelter "un-Christian." Affixed to a wall at the rear of the meeting room was a banner that read: "Don't Tread on Me."

While all protests aren't this fiery or bizarre, the grim sentiment among residents about locating a homeless shelter in their neighborhood is a familiar one.

In Crockett, a plan to convert the old Crockett theater into a 30-bed homeless shelter died a quick death when 40 members of the Crockett Improvement Association voted in August to kill the proposal. The owner of the property backed off immediately.

Shelters can't find shelter

In Marin County, two homeless proposals were scrapped this summer after neighbors freaked out. One in the Canal District of San Rafael and another in the Santa Venitia area faced a storm of protest from next-door neighbors.

For two years, a group of homeless advocates in Concord has fought to construct a transitional homeless facility. Along with apathy from local officials, community resistance has played a big role in discouraging the worthwhile project.

Is this angst about homeless shelters a new development? Yes.

In 1986, our federal and state politicians began to fret about the number of people living on the streets. The fact their numbers were growing was well documented, and news stories about regular folks falling through the economic cracks ignited widespread concern about homelessness.

Money is now available

Aimed at offering relief, federal and state laws were approved, new homeless programs were launched and a pile of new funds were set aside for the homeless.

In California, voters approved two statewide ballot measures last year that will pump $400 million into building low-cost housing. In the next several years, state, federal and local programs will unleash more than $100 million for homeless solutions in the Bay Area alone.

After years of blue-sky jawboning about the homeless problem, the resources are finally trickling down to local nonprofit organizations, church groups and municipalities.

Here comes the rub: Who wants a homeless shelter in their back yard? For some, helping the homeless is all well and good when it is being treated at some ethereal public-policy level, but when it comes to 20 units next door, forget it.

"Often, the concerns expressed publicly are a mask for deeper feelings of prejudice against people of different income, race or lifestyle and frustration about loss of control over the neighborhood's makeup," says a new report by Home-Base, a regional support center that promotes programs and policies for the Bay Area's homeless.

'A huge problem'

"It's a huge problem," says Karen Klein, HomeBase's associate director. "There are too many instances where you have the funding, political will and the technical expertise but you can't find sites that are acceptable to the surrounding community."

Where community angst prevails, homeless shelters risk losing government assistance and landowners sometimes get frustrated and choose to sell the property to far less controversial buyers.

Public education about poverty is the long-term solution, but this idealistic strategy does nothing for shelters embroiled in nasty disputes today.

HomeBase recommends old-fashioned community organizing as the best cure for diffusing neighborhood anxiety.

A good example is the work of the nonprofit group Shelter Network, which diffused a community time bomb in Daly City when it proposed 17 units of transitional housing for the homeless in 1987.

The group spent a year wooing the community. That included putting 30 trained volunteers on the streets who went door to door talking to neighbors. "We fought all of the stereotypes head on; we had to convince the community that these weren't wino bums, but people like the rest of us who came on some back luck." says Christina Sutherland, executive director of Shelter Network.

The HomeBase report notes that "popular misconceptions about homeless people portray them as an unsavory population that manifests all of society's ills." To soften these perceptions. Shelter Network packed a city hearing with more than 300 church volunteers who showed up to praise the project.

The development opened in January, 1988. It's still operating with no complaints from its neighbors.

Unfortunately the success stories are overshadowed by the passions of the opponents. And you haven't heard the last of it. According to state law, every community in the Bay Area must identify acceptable sites for homeless housing. Yes, that includes Piedmont, Ross and Hillsborough.

As far as I am concerned, that's the way it should be. Homelessness isn't someone else's problem. It's society's problem and, therefore, we all share the burden. NIMBYs (not-in-my-backyard) are becoming a worse problem than the homeless themselves.

Real Estate Newsletter Folds

THE WASHINGTON POST

Western Exposure, an irreverent, insiderish Oakland, Calif.-based publication that explored facts and foibles in the real-estate industry, is shutting down, according to publisher Bradley Inman.

The subscriber-supported newsletter, which was read by top executives at many national real-estate firms, was operating in the black, Inman said, but he decided to fold the publication after consulting with an attorney because of his mounting fears over potential liability in the event of a lawsuit.

"The industry does not have a lot of critics," Inman said. "While our purpose was not to criticize the industry, at times it was critical, and we found the industry to be very sensitive."

The monthly publication took aim at numerous sacred cows — both people and issues — during its year of operations. Those included self-righteous neighborhood activists who oppose worthy projects, avaricious developers and brokers, political wheeling and dealing by industry insiders, and windbag real-estate coverage by some newspapers.

In one recent issue, Inman compiled information on what he called the "big-time" political contributions given to state legislators by real-estate companies and trade groups in California in 1988, which totaled about $2 million. The California Association of Realtors took top billing, passing out $611,400 to California legislators in 1988, according to Inman.

"The industry does not have a lot of critics. While our purpose was not to criticize the industry, at times it was critical, and we found the industry to be very sensitive."
—Publisher Bradley Inman

The newsletter rubbed the National Association of Realtors the wrong way by reprinting a form press release the trade group had distributed to member organizations with instructions that they retype it and mail it to local newspapers. It provided local real-estate boards with a fill-in-the-blank pitch designed to demonstrate grassroots opposition to proposed changes in the income-tax deductibility of home mortgage interest. The sample release even provided a quotation, with a blank space left for local organizations to insert the name of a local person who could pretend to say what the central organization had dictated.

Inman also took himself and other journalists to task at times. In the publication's final issue, he discussed the failure of the media to examine the problems within the Department of Housing and Urban Development. "... Those of us in the housing journalistic industry blew this one in a big way," the newsletter said.

The final newsletter ended with a joke:

Three real-estate developers on a hunting expedition chartered a plane to the backwoods of Canada. After landing deep in the woods, the pilot warned the developers about how much game he could transport back. "Now remember, this plane will only handle one deer. Anything more will be too heavy and make the plane unable to fly," said the pilot.

In two weeks, the pilot returned to the backwoods only to find the developers ready with three deer to transport back to the States. "No way," the pilot said. "We'll crash. It's too much weight and it will make the plane much too dangerous."

The developers chimed in, "Oh, come on, we can strap one deer to one wing, one to the other wing, and the third on the top. ... We'll be fine."

Finally, after some arguing, the pilot agreed. The plane sputtered down the runway, made it up about 100 yards and crashed into the woods. With no one hurt, one developer brushed himself off and yelled over to his partner, "Hey, we made it 50 feet farther than last year."

Defeated bill would have funded water and sewers in communities that offer affordable housing

At the end of this year's legislative session, Governor George Deukmejian sent a surprising message to local government: ignore the problem of high housing costs and the state won't do much about it.

While he put his pen to a package of housing bills that aid the homeless, provide government assistance for low-cost housing and help the plight of California first-time home buyers, the governor vetoed the most noteworthy housing bill that was approved by the legislature.

Introduced by Orange County Senator Marion Bergesen, D-Newoport Beach, Senate Bill 966 would have directed state funds for water and sewer expansion to those communities that are "making substantial progress in meeting their share of regional housing needs," according to language in SB 966.

Housing advocates were hopeful that the measure would spark municipalities to do more io approve low-cost housing developments.

State won't help with water and sewers where affordable housing not offered

"Get them by their wallets, and their hearts and minds will follow," says Senate Local Government Committee consultant Peter Detwiler. He points out that several other slates routinely link state funds to what local government is doing to support affordable housing. Though California has been reluctant to interfere with local control, the legislature showed with the passage of the Bergesen measure that it was willing to break with tradition. Deukmejian wasn't as eager.

In his veto message, the governor said, "I do not believe that the apparent failure of local government to meet housing needs is a good policy reason for altering safe drinking water, groundwater recharge and water conservation programs in a way that may interfere with their unique pruposes."

The governor wasn't necessarily consistent in his defense of local control, however. For example, to make it easier for builders to produce more affordable housing, Assembly Bill 1863 was signed by Deukmejian. The bill forces local government to offer higher zoning densities to developers in exchange for building more low-cost housing.

Using a similar approach, Assemblyman Dan Hauser, D-Eureka introduced AB 1274, which was also signed by the governor. This measure ties future state housing aid to what cities are doing to encourage or discourage affordable housing. However, local government won't feel any pressure from this bill until next year when the legislature must decide which local government policies hurt or help the cause of low-cost housing.

The governor and the legislature saw eye to eye on the need for relief for first time home buyers.

Deukmejian signed a bill that lifts the ceiling on Cal-Vet home loans. The state agency can now offer mortgages to California veterans for as much as $125,000.

"The current lid of $90,000 on Cal-Vet loans is unrealistic in a housing market where the medium home price is more than $200,000" says Realtor lobbyist Alex Creel.

More help was delivered to new home buyers by senator John Seymour, R-Annaheim with the passage of Senate Bill 1283. Signed by the governor, Seymour's measure will clear the way for the California Housing Finance Agency to provide Mortgage Credit Certificates (MCCs) to first time buyers.

MCCs provide new home buyers a lucrative federal income tax credit to offset the costs of sky-high mortgatge payments. But local governments must first implement the MCC program and most municipalities have been reluctant to offer the aid.

To compensate for the lack of local interest, the Seymour bill permits the state to make the tax credit available directly to the consumer.

"There are families who, without these mortgage assistance programs, will be unable to achieve the American dream of owning a home," says Seymour.

Low-income families will get a boost from state ligislation that discourages local government from demolishing low-cost housing in urban redevelopment zones. Introduced by Los Angeles Democrat Maxine Waters, Assembly Bill 2080 requires local government to replace 75 percent of the housing that is destroyed to make way for urban renewal projects.

Though new legislation was a priority, housing advocates spent time this year pressing the state to spend money appropriated in earlier sessions of the legislature.

"We made modest gains in the legislature," says Marc Brown of the California Rural Legal Assistance Foundation, Sacramento. "But spending what we got in previous years is just as important."

Developments uneven depending on health, income, services needed

Special to the Examiner

SURE MARIN County is an exclusive kind of community; but it's also exclusionary. For example, there are at least two groups that are shut out of this expensive region: young families looking to buy their first home and poor people who need low-cost rentals.

With virtually no new reasonably priced housing being built in Marin, the trend seems irreversible. That's because the satisfied majority seem eager to defend the status quo.

It's too bad because there are consequences. Because entry-level service workers are completely priced out of the market, for instance, everyone feels the pinch with higher wage contracts for essential services like child care.

And then there's the other end of the age spectrum: the over-55 crowd. Many empty nesters reach a point where they no longer look forward to managing the headaches of their single-family homes. Like seniors in other parts of the Bay Area, many become nervous about their long-term health care needs, and they begin to look for smaller places nearby to plop their home equity.

They are house-rich but cash-poor. On fixed incomes, they have piles of equity but are stuck with fixed-incomes that can't even afford them a studio apartment in an undesirable neighborhood.

'Things go haywire'

"As long as they can live in their homes, they are sailing. But once they can't drive or they lose a mate, things often go haywire," says Elizabeth Moody, director of community relations for the Ecumenical Association for Housing in San Rafael. "What we need most is modestly priced senior housing project with a full range of health care and social services."

Senior developments can offer up to three levels of care: independent living, extended care or skilled nursing. Those that offer all three are dubbed life-care communities, of which Marin County has several.

In San Rafael, there is the Aldersley Retirement Home, which is a small nonprofit Danish life-can community. Residents pay a $70,000 to $80,000 one-time, upfront charge for individual units, three meals a day and extended care. Skilled nursing is extra.

Another life-care facility, the Redwoods, is located in Mill Valley. Greenbrae has a project called Tamalpais, which is more upscale.

Also at the high end are Villa Marin and the new Smith Ranch, which are both located in San Rafael.

Completed in 1985, Villa Marin sits atop Quail Hill with spectacular Bay views. Unlike some senior developments that offer lifetime care with a lump sum payment, Villa Marin is organized more like a typical condominium development. Residents own their units and are entitled to the appreciation that their homes realize. A monthly fee that ranges from $867 for a single person up to $2,000 for a couple covers comprehensive medical care, one meal a day, weekly house-keeping, transportation and common ground maintenance.

'Good life is yours'

Scheduled to open in January, the 37-acre Smith Ranch makes it very clear in its sales brochure which market it is aiming at: "The good life, the life you worked so hard for is finally yours. You've provided for your family. You've planned for your financial independence."

Smith Ranch *general manager John Lombardo: He has more than 11 years of experience in four-star resort and hotel management.*

Stalled several times over the years, Smith Ranch is being developed by Tishman Speyer Properties, which bought controlling interest from founder Dr. Henry Grausz. Grausz remains a limited partner and active in the sprawling Lucas Valley property.

In the center of five residential buildings, the clubhouse, which is still under construction, can be reached by covered walkways and includes a lap pool, putting greens, dining facilities and lawn bowling.

Included in the monthly fees are 20 meals a month. The chef is Heidi Krahling, who previously had stints at two restaurants well known among the gourmet see, Butler's in Mill Valley and Square One in San Francisco.

The dining is consistent with the resort-styled ambiance the developers tried to create at Smith Ranch. The general manager, John Lombardo, has more than 11 years of experience in four-star resort and hotel management.

The 100-bed extended care facility planned next door to Smith Ranch will be an independent entry, also built by Tishman. Monthly assessments will range from $1,39 to $2,595 and includes a basic health care policy.

For seniors without big buck there are several modestly price senior developments including Tamalpais Creek and Deer Park in Novato and Drakes Landing in San Rafael.

Fixed incomes

For seniors on fixed incomes there's the 83-unit San Rafad Commons, Parnow Friendship. House and Bennett House in Fairfax.

One of the only low-cost senior projects with services is the 61-unit Kruger Pines in Mill Valley. Thanks to a Housing and Urban Development demonstration project, it is able to offer meal service housekeeping, personal care and community health nursing.

Specialists in senior housing have dubbed this type of facility "enriched housing."

However, most affordable senior developments lack a full range of health care and social services. Unfortunately, federal and state housing programs provide subsidy money for senior housing, but very little for companion social services.

Moody sums up the situation well. "If you have income and equity, you are fine; if you own a house and you have your health, you are OK; but on a limited income and failing health, there just isn't much around."

On My Livable and Sensible Scale:

Marin seniors have options, but they depend on economic status. I guess like everything else in Marin, there is a certain unevenness.

Quake-proofing law finds most cities lagging

IN THE earthquake aftermath, questions arose about the effectiveness of a state law designed to prod cities to quake-proof older masonry buildings in California.

More than 1 million people live in 40,000 unreinforced masonry buildings in California. They were built before the passage of strict seismic safety building codes.

Reports indicate that hundreds of them suffered severe damage in the quake. Five people died when a masonry building's facade collapsed at Sixth and Bluxome streets in the South-of-Market area.

Fears about this type of building prompted the Legislature to pass a law in 1986 requiring cities and counties to identify all potentially hazardous masonry buildings. Of the state's 450 cities, the law regulates 354 because they're in what's known as a Seismic Hazard Zone 4. Communities located in Zone 4 are in the most earthquake-prone regions of the state.

The Legislation also required cities and counties to establish a program for improving the risky structures by Jan. 1, 1990.

Fifty-one percent of the affecting governments have begun taking building inventories. But only 9 percent have met all of the law's requirements, according to the California Seismic Safety Commission.

Oakland lagging on survey

For example, Oakland — with more than 2,000 unreinforced masonry buildings — hasn't completed its survey or submitted a plan on how these buildings will be improved. San Francisco has finished its inventory but not its mitigation plan.

Los Angeles has satisfied the law's requirements and approved a tough law for improving unreinforced masonry buildings. People there are debating the expense of earthquake-proofing all unreinforced masonry buildings, which could cost as much as $1 billion.

Tom Tobin, executive director of the California Seismic Safety Commission, recalls a discussion with a leading proponent of low-cost housing.

"He said upgrading all of the buildings would put many low-income tenants out on the streets, while I argued that we were risking lives."

But Tobin concedes that "important social questions must be resolved and the discussion always comes down to finding the necessary public resources."

To partly overcome this problem, voters approved a statewide bond measure last June. Proposition 77 allocates $80 million to lend for seismic retrofitting of unreinforced masonry buildings.

Funds not released

The state Department of Housing and Community Development will administer the funds, but none has been distributed.

"It's a crime that the funds have been sitting there for 18 months," says Donald Terner, president of BRIDGE housing, a nonprofit Bay Area developer. "We now know that putting those funds to use can save lives."

Housing officials defend the delay. It takes time to start a complicated new program, they say, and Prop. 77 funds can be released only to those cities that have complied with SB 547. Also, the only community to apply for Prop. 77 funds is Los Angeles.

Even though executing the law seems to be a problem, previous warnings about heeding the law have gone unheeded. Soon after the 1987 Whittier earthquake, a special study conducted by the Governor's Office of Emergency Services and the Federal Emergency Management Agency recommended that "the state take steps to strengthen the effectiveness of SB 547."

The study concluded that "unreinforced masonry structures . . . pose the greatest life-saving concern in future earthquakes."

Analysis of the San Francisco quake will undoubtedly decide the same thing.

S&L bailout's low-cost housing provisions won't help California

After President Bush signed the savings and loan recovery bill in August, analysts pointed to the legislation's affordable housing provisions as the silver lining in the $168 billion thrift bailout cloud.

But a close examination of the legislation shows that the benefit to low-cost housing in California is likely to be much less than it will be in other parts of the country.

The primary purpose of the Financial Institutions Reform, Recovery and Enforcement Act (FIR-REA) is to re-capitalize the near-bankrupt Federal Savings and Loan Insurance Corporation (FSLIC), which provides federal insurance on savings deposits.

With the support of several consumer groups, Congressmen Henry Gonzalez, D-Texas and Joe Kennedy, D-Mass., pushed through amendments to the controversial legislation and the bill now contains a handful of affordable housing provisions.

For example, the legislation has special requirements for selling off $100 billion in troubled real estate deals that were controlled by insolvent S&Ls. Before peddling the properties to private bidders, the federal government must first offer them to public agencies or nonprofit housing groups. They in turn must rent the units to low-income families.

Ceilings too low

But this provision isn't expected to work in California because of sales price ceilings on the foreclosed properties. The legislation calls for a $67,000 cap on single-family homes and $20,000 per unit on apartment building. At these prices, the government isn't expected to unload too many projects in California where market prices are so much higher. "In this state, there will be virtually no opportunities for properties being sold for affordable housing," says San Fran Cisco housing consultant Rick Devine.

Federal Home Loan Bank Vice President Jim Yacenda points out that even if the limits better reflected California's high housing costs, there would be a short supply of properties. "Most of the thrift problems in California involve some commercial real estate loans, not residential," says Yacenda.

Another provision of the law requires the nation's 12 district Federal Home Loan Banks to set up community investment programs, which provide low-cost financing for affordable housing projects.

Again, the legislation offers no added benefit to California because the 11th district Bank (which covers California) has had a similar loan program for more than six years. In fact, the California community investment fund was a model for the new federal legislation.

Minority loans

Unpopular with some financial institutions is a provision in FIR-REA that should increase the number of loans to residents in depressed neighborhoods and mortgages made to minorities.

Beginning next year, detailed information about to whom and where lenders make loans will be published and made available for public scrutiny. Moreover, federal regulators will rank financial institutions based on their track record for loans based on sex, race and neighborhood.

The law beefs up existing regulations on home loan disclosure requirements. The current rules require lenders to keep track of the location of mortgages, but institutions only make the information available on request. And, for the most part, federal regulators have ignored the data.

"The glare of publicity will now be on all lenders," says Ann Winchester, First Vice President, First Nationwide Bank, San Francisco, which has a distinguished record on urban lending. "I can assure you that some are not looking forward to the exposure."

In an article for the American Bankers Association's Banking Journal, associate editor Phil Hall wrote, "If they ever held a contest for the most unpopular law among bankers, the (home loan disclosure requirements) would be an odds-on favorite."

Eager to lend

Despite the sentiment. Winchester predicts that lenders will be bending over backwards to improve their community lending programs by working more with local housing groups.

Importance of disclosure

Last week before Bakersfield dentist Dr. Robert Reed put a three-unit apartment project on the market, he filled out a Real Estate Transfer Disclosure Statement.

The two-page legal form required Reed to attest to the condition of the furnace, foundation and hundreds of other features in the building that he is trying to sell in Bakersfield.

When Reed bought the property several years ago the seller wasn't required to provide such a document. But thanks to a three-year-old state law, all property sellers in California must complete a detailed disclosure statement on the condition of their property before putting it up for sale.

According to a new report commissioned by the Department of Real Estate, the law is working.

"The study shows that consumers are getting much better information about what they are buying," said Real Estate Commissioner James Edmonds. "The disclosure statement also prompts home buyers to ask the right questions, which protects them later on."

The California Transfer Disclosure law was approved by the Legislature in 1986 and took effect in January of 1987. Triggering the legislation was the California Appellate Court decision in the case of Easton vs. Strassburger, in which a home buyer successfully sued a home seller and real estate agent for failing to disclose defects in a home.

The legislation gives explicit instructions to home sellers on how to make disclosures. They must make a detailed listing of the working condition of the house and report any significant defects.

"It only took him (Reed) about fifteen minutes to complete the form," said realty agent Jim Antt, who is representing Reed in his sale. "And now everyone will have a better idea about the condition of the building, especially prospective buyers."

Otherwise, "the home itself can become a major unanticipated financial burden, if the roof leaks or the foundation requires extensive work, for example," reads the soon to be released study which was conducted by U.C. Berkeley research fellow Carol Silverman.

The report is based on mail surveys of home buyers and real estate agents and concludes that the law is achieving its intended result:

Home buyers who received the disclosure form were 'more likely to be satisfied with their purchase than those who failed to receive disclosures.'

Buyers surveyed said that the disclosures were useful and that they took the time to review the reports.

The cost of meeting the disclosure requirements was inexpensive for the real estate agents involved. 'Most agents said it took between one and two hours to comply with the law,' reads the study.

Agents felt that the disclosures helped to educate home buyers and sellers. Moreover, "real estate agents are recommending more home inspections which contribute to people being more satisfied," said Silverman.

The report also showed that compliance with the law was the highest when the transaction involved a real estate agent. Widespread industry education about the new disclosure law explains this finding, according to Edmonds.

"Owners who are selling the property by themselves, who are not using an agent, need to become more aware of the law," concludes Edmonds. The Department of Real Estate only regulates licensed real estate agents; and, therefore, the commissioner isn't sure which state agency should take on the task of broader consumer education.

Researchers did conclude that the disclosure law has not reduced litigation, which was the main reason the California Association of Realtors pushed through the legislation in 1986.

The DRE study also examined other disclosure laws, including a statute that requires sellers of condominiums to provide governing documents and financial statements of the condo association.

'A place where everyone knows everyone else'

Special to the Examiner

UNTIL I talked to a handful of community leaders from the tiny Contra Costa County hamlet of Port Costa, I figured there wasn't a place in the Bay Area where local residents weren't gnashing their teeth about the threat of growth.

But as Port Costa Town Council member Frank Jurik puts it, "We don't have developers to hassle with anymore."

The town folks in this little village on the Carquinez Straits have made certain that their rural way of life will never be stomped on. After fighting a string of development proposals over the past 25 years, they convinced the East Bay Regional Park District in the early- to mid-1980s to buy up the land on the brown hillsides that surround the town.

With the property on all sides in public ownership, it is impossible for daring developers to slap up anything new to the area that might add more people or create congestion.

I can think of dozens of Bay Area neighborhoods that would die to be in such an enviable position. Because of the dynamic regional economy, urbanization seems enviable in the most far-flung Bay Area locations. Port Costa is a refreshing exception.

"This is a throwback to an old kind of Americana," says Mary Powell who has lived in Port Costa since 1945 and heads up the Port Costa Conservation Society. "It's a place where the dog still lies in the street and where everyone knows everyone else."

With 91 members, the Port Costa Conservation Society has been working to preserve the abandoned historic Port Costa School. Since the school closed, children attend classes in nearby Crockett. The Town Council meets in the old school, and it serves as a community center.

Crockett is the big city

To put the town's size in perspective, Powell says Crockett is almost like a big city compared to Port Costa, which has a population of 250. "Crockett has 10 times as many people," she says. Crockett, which is four miles from Port Costa, has a grocery store and a gas station and other amenities that Port Costa doesn't enjoy. Which is just fine with Port Costa residents.

Local Postmaster Teresa Jurik laughs when she brags that there are "no lines in the post office and no one has to take a number waiting their turn." However, there is no local delivery, residents pick up their mail at the post office.

Rampant rusticity

Wetting my appetite for the rural ambience was the road into Port Costa off Highway 4, west of Martinez. It's a weaving, two-lane road with cattle paths running parallel to the lane. Watching cows amble up and down hills can force the swiftest drivers to clip their pace.

The only other way into town is from Crockett, a four-mile trip along Carquinez Strait Road. Again, there are very few signs of civilization.

Contributing to the charm is the town's history. At one time, it was a thriving railroad destination for freight and passengers.

"When I was a little girl, we used to take the train to Richmond and ferry into San Francisco," recalls Powell.

More than 100 years ago, grain was shipped to every country in the world from Port Costa, she says. Then the buildings in the small downtown — which now include two restaurants and a couple of antique stores — were built over the bay. Ships from around the world dumped stone into a small the town's public affairs and serves as an advisory board to the Board of Supervisors.

"We hope to hold an election some time," says Jurki, head of the council, "but no one seems in too big of a hurry."

That's how it should be in a small town that isn't on the edge of change like so many other Bay Area communities.

On My Livable and Sensible Scale:

Port Costa is a hidden Bay Area treasure that in all likelihood will stay that way.

Emeryville, Fillmore Street and Rockridge revisted

Special to the Examiner

IN HIS book, "Looking at Cities," Alan Jacobs examines the cycles of neighborhood change. Over 20 to 30 years, ethnic neighborhoods dissolve when minorities are assimilated, he says. Industrial areas are transformed when factories become obsolete, and areas made up of single-family homes change when older residents die or move out.

But if you think such changes are always a slow and predictable process, visit Emeryville in the East Bay or San Francisco's Fillmore Street.

With a jump start from big redevelopment schemes, these two marginal neighborhoods have seen a surprising turnaround. Garbage-strewn vacant lots now have slick new mid-rises. Instead of abandoned cars on the streets, you see late-model German autos zooming in and out of newly paved parking lots. Boutiques have replaced check-cashing store fronts, and popular bars and restaurants outnumber package-liquor outlets.

If you haven't visited these two places in the last few years, see for yourself. You may be in for a shock.

EMERYVILLE

Two years ago, I described Emeryville's reputation this way: "Like a bad little boy with no friends, this industrial rust patch on the bright side of the Bay has been the victim of mockery for years," ("Living in Emeryville, Oct 4, 1987). Today, the city's bold redevelopment effort isn't finished, but anyone who still pokes fun at Emeryville is woefully out of touch.

The transformation began in the early 1980s with a small group of artists who took advantage of the cheap rents in vacant warehouses. Where heavy industry once thrived, bio-tech companies were gobbling up space in retrofitted brick buildings.

But these changes weren't noticeable at first. It was the arrival of new apartments, a slick new shopping center, glitzy office buildings and a public market, which opened in 1938, that got people talking about the changes in the town.

The biggest surprise is Emeryville's night life. You can dine at one of several new restaurants, including the Emery Pub, a "micro-brewery" in the Emeryville Public Market complex near the Powell Street exit off I-180. (Micro-breweries brew their own brand of beer). Then there's a choice of 10 movies at the largest movie complex in the Bay Area. Or, there's entertainment at Kimball's East jazz club, which opened in March 1988. It isn't North Beach, but what a change from the old Emeryville. And there's parking.

FILLMORE STREET

Two years ago, I said gentrification along Fillmore Street from California to Geary was unstoppable ("Living in the New Fillmore," Aug. 16. 1987). But I didn't expect the changeover to happen so quickly.

After piles of thick plans, thousands of hours of political bickering and loads of unrealized dreams, the Fillmore area finally awoke from a long slumber.

Chance there was inevitable. With Japan town to the east, Laurel Heights to the west and Pacific Heights to the north, the community was being squeezed from all sides.

The final chapter in this revival is the construction of the controversial 1,100-unit Fillmore Center apartment project south of Geary. It anchors the Fillmore strip and guarantees this community will never be the same.

Neighborhoods, towns are reborn

When I first wrote about Fillmore Street, the community had a mixed-up identity, which explains its many names: Upper Fillmore, the New Fillmore, Baja Pacific Heights, Western Addition or Lower Pacific Heights.

The fact that many locals now simply refer to the area as Fillmore Street is a sign that the neighborhood is stabilizing. The big changes are over.

ROCKRIDGE

In sharp contrast to what's happened in Emeryville and to Fillmore Street, consider my Oakland neighborhood, Rockridge.

Emeryville and Fillmore are in flux and acquiring new identities. But once a community has a strong identity, the slightest change in neighborhood character arouses community passions. That's certainly the case in Rockridge where I feel like the odd man out on the issue of neighborhood chance. ("Living in Rockridge," Nov, 20, 1988).

Many of my neighbors get alt worked up about small in-fill developments that I think are just fine. For example, they have been acriping with Dreyers Ice Cream over its expansion on College Avenue for years. Before that they gave fits to the Wilson family who put up the Rockridge Market Hall, which has become a popular neighborhood landmark.

When two colorful and eccarfic buildings designed by Ace Architects were proposed south on College Avenue, Rockridge residentialists objected. Now these buildings are up, and I can't figure what-ev-eryone is complaining about.

But I concede that I am out of step with the kind of neighborhood change that some of my more vocal neighbors prefer. I like billboards and I don't get turned on by earth tones.

Environmentalists, developers clash over gas tax funds

A controversial proposal to increase the state's gasoline tax has opened up wounds between environmentalists and developers about where to spend a projected $18 billion revenue gain for relieving traffic congestion.

Both sides agree that more money needs to be spent on the state's overburdened and decaying transportation system, but the harmony ends there.

The dispute centers on a constitutional amendment that is scheduled to be on the California ballot in June of next year. If approved by a majority of the state's voters, the 9 cents per-gallon gas tax will increase to 14 cents beginning August 1990, and after that will swell one penny per year for the next four years.

The gas tax bonanza will finance local transportation improvements including new highways and mass transit.

Herein comes the rub. The environmental community doesn't want the money to be arbitrarily distributed to communities that ignore the pressures growth and development have on traffic. Instead, they favor putting restrictions on how and where gas tax revenues can be spent.

Developers, on the other hand, fret that enacting a gas tax with such requirements will become the latest tool for stopping unpopular developments.

So far, developers are losing the debate.

Approved by the legislature and signed by Gov. Deukmejian, Senate Constitutional Amendment 1 (SCA 1) will be on the ballot in June of next year and calls for the gas tax increase. To implement the statewide ballot measure — when and if it passes — the Governor also signed Assembly Bill 471 which offers specific language on which communities are entitled to receive transportation funds.

The idea is to award those cities that are taking steps to reduce traffic congestion and plan for growth and penalize those who fail to analyze the influence new development has on choked roadways.

"Planned growth is the only way for the state to grow," says Assemblyman Richard Katz, D-Panorama City, who introduced AB 471. "The alternative is flash and burn, and we know from experience that approach doesn't work."

Builders are worried SCA 1 will become a Trojan horse for stopping development.

"It creates a dangerous form of statewide growth control," says Don Collins, general counsel for the Building Industry Association in Sacramento. "This trendy planning gimmick has been tried before and it doesn't work."

As an example, Collins points to a measure approved last year in Contra Costa County which links an increase in the local sales tax for transportation funding with a plan to manage growth. While Collins is quick to find fault with the Contra Costa plan, other experts say it may be too early to evaluate its shortcomings.

"We aren't saying you should or shouldn't grow, but we are saying that you must plan and mitigate for growth so that our traffic situation doesn't get any worse," argues Katz.

Because of the strict standards in AB 471, real estate industry representatives also claim that some of the most traffic-prone areas in the state won't qualify for the funds. The legislation sets up specific traffic levels a community cannot exceed — or face losing state transportation funds.

Katz readily admits that there are consequences to inaction. "There are developers who want to be able to do whatever they want no matter what, and that just isn't reality in California anymore."

Building industry lobbyist Owen Waters complains that the Katz measure is "a political deal." "People who could figure out how to make such a program work weren't even consulted," says Waters. He says industry leaders weren't advised about details of the plan until late in the legislative session.

Katz discounts such claims. "As long ago as August of 1988 I held meetings that included builders to discuss the elements of what a statewide transportation program should be — those meetings became a framework for this plan."

"Does anyone have a better way of fitting 8 million people into the state by the year 2000 without total gridlock?" asks Katz.

Chaparral/Rogers Ranch

A return visit to Albany, El Cerrito, Richmond Annex

Special to the Examiner

IN A recent article in Vanity Fair, writer Stephen Schiff predicts that the trend to watch in the 1990s is "proletariat chic." He points to TV's blue-collar heroine, Roseanne Barr, as proof that "imperfection is in now."

But you don't have to stare at the tube to find an anecdote to support Schiff's opinion. Here in the Bay Area, home values in working-class enclaves such as El Cerrito, Albany and the Richmond Annex provide ample evidence. These are plain houses on plain streets for big bucks.

I first wrote about these three neighborhoods just as home prices were beginning to go haywire. ("Living in El Cerrito," May 8, 1987; "Living in Albany, Feb. 7, 1988; and "Living in the Richmond Annex," June 12, 1988.) Back then I figured it was only a matter of time before these new areas would become yuppie havens.

Wrong. Now I have a new theory: People bidding $200,000 to $300,000 for houses along this stretch of the Interstate 80 corridor in the East Bay are like baseball owners offering million-dollar contracts to middle-rate players. In other words, there appears to be no relationship between price and actual value. I'm not sure what craziness has invaded baseball, but I can explain what has happened to home prices. The reign of home-inflation terror that struck the region in the last two years has upset the pattern of Bay Area home buying.

When sky-high housing prices closed off traditional entry-level neighborhoods such as San Francisco's Sunset district, Burlingame on the Peninsula or North Berkeley in Alameda County, young first-time home buyers sought refuge elsewhere. It explains why vanilla-wrapper East Bay neighborhoods became so popular.

And so expensive.

Take one home now for sale on Carmel Street in El Cerrito. It's advertised as a "charming Albany MacGregor," which refers to a local, architectural style (MacGregor was a local contractor from the 1920s). It's on the market for $205,000. For that price, you can get a tiny two-bedroom house on a little 2,500-square-foot lot that 10 years ago would have sold for less than $85,000.

But while the home price spiral has ridden roughshod over neighborhood change in many areas, the buildings and the street-scape in the Richmond Annex, El Cerrito and Albany look the same as they did a decade ago. You won't confuse them with Palo Alto or Tiburon.

"The neighborhood hasn't really changed much but, oh brother, have the values ever soared," says Art Sullivan. He paid $125,000 for a house in El Cerrito in 1986 that is now worth more than $250,000.

Still, a less visible generational and economic shift is occurring. Instead of an older crowd of blue-collar retirees, you see young white-collar and pink-collar owners.

Out with the old-timers

Replacing the older residents who at one time commuted to their industrial jobs at the Richmond refineries or the West Berkeley and Emeryville foundries is a generation that takes BART to San Francisco's Financial District or drives to nearby bio-tech facilities or health-care jobs.

They are nothing at all like the fast-track crowd, the ones who figure out how to move from Pacific Heights or the Marina District as renters to Noe Valley or Mill Valley as homeowners.

In the new high-tech service economy, the stake-holders along the 1-80 corridor represent the modern working middle-class. The only reason they can afford neighborhoods that are priced for the upper class is the borrowing power of two incomes.

Don't be fooled by the home prices — these are still middle-class neighborhoods. The houses and the commercial strips look the same. Besides several new condominium projects along 1-80 and the addition of the Richmond BART line along San Pablo Avenue, nothing much has changed in the last 30 years.

It's true that Albany had a spurt of second-story additions that blew up some of the tiny homes in this bay-front city north of Berkeley. But this activity ended when uptight neighbors complained about losing their views.

Still the same old avenue

Along San Pablo Avenue, you still find an eclectic mix of stores and services. There's not a shopping mall in California that can duplicate the rich variety found on this lively Avenue. And on-street parking is no real problem.

Anchoring the Avenue at the edge of the Richmond Annex is the dated El Cerrito shopping center. The city of El Cerrito has hashed over great plans for improving the old center but made no visible progress.

Farther down San Pablo, another vestige from a different era is a drive-up window at Mechanics Bank with a human being on the other side of the glass. And the franchise outlets that dot San Pablo Avenue are mixed in with such traditional store fronts as Alex's Cafe, the Idaho Motel and Pastime Hardware.

Albany's Solano Avenue offers a more intimate shopping experience. With trendy hot spots like the Solano Grill & Bar, this is where change seems eager to occur. But the classic Albany Theater nearby is proof nothing radical is about to happen.

Just like the entire area, everything stays pretty much the same — except the price to get in.

State Realtors Survive 'news' from back East

CALIFORNIA REAL estate bashing was one of the more popular games played in the financial pages of newspapers over the holiday.

Beginning with a New York Times article on Dec. 10 about the possibilities of a demise in the state's home prices, a gaggle of writers from major newspapers and magazines ominously predicted tumbling California housing values.

The final blow came from a Barron's article Dec. 18 entitled "A Slowing Home Market in the Golden State."

A band of California real estate experts lined up to dispute claims of a crash. But was it too late to avoid a self-fulfilling prophesy?

"I worry that this type of negative publicity can manufacture a consumer confidence problem." said Ron Wilmot, a San Francisco real estate broker. "The press is not only contributing to a chill, it may be creating it," he said.

The repercussions from the Barron's article were immediate on Wall Street with construction stocks taking a beating the week before Christmas. But opinions conflict about how unfavorable press may affect the behavior of the home-buying public.

"The economy is too strong in California for a little bad publicity to undo," said John Savacool, Vice President, WEFA, an economic and real estate consulting firm based in Bala Cynwyd, Pa. "Sure, evidence is out there to support a weaker housing market, but it's unlikely that consumers are going to react to a spate of adverse publicity."

Other analysts are less quick to dismiss the role of the news media. "When the press started this barrage of stories, a certain amount of confusion was created," said Stan Ross, Co-Managing Partner, Kenneth Leventhal & Co., Los Angeles.

He points to one example in Southern California in which home buyers benefited from the publicity. A couple in L.A. were prepared to bid $250,000 for a house that was on the market for $275,000, according to Ross. After reading a 'gloom and doom" real estate story, the buyers lowered their offer to $220,000 and got the house for the lower price.

"What you start to see is home buyers looking for opportunities to take advantage of the situation," said Ross. "They begin to push for lower prices and they seek concessions from the sellers. Then home sellers get nervous and decide to move quickly."

"Anti-housing stories" have hurt the real estate market in the past, according to Jack Reed, publisher of Real Estate Investor's Monthly, in Danville.

He remembers an instance in the middle 1970s when mortgage interest rates shot up. "The press jumped all over the fact that rates were rising, which bruised consumer confidence. But later on the press didn't report that home loan rates fell."

Reed blames "the herding effect of the media," but said the number of real estate crash stories have a short life because they are responding only to a single report that "makes a big splash."

"It's like Jean Dixon, who became famous after predicting Jack Kennedy's assassination," said Reed. "After that, dozens of unknown psychics made dire predictions, but how many of them ever came about?"

According to Reed, some real estate specialists operate the same way. "They get a lot of attention for making a wild prediction and become famous if it happens. But it rarely does."

One example was a report out of New York two years ago that foresaw a nationwide crash in home prices. Published in the Comstock Investment Strategy Report, the study became big news for a few weeks in California but was soon forgotten as home prices soared in much of the state.

This time the news media are responding to more mainstream forecasts from industry groups that have a stake in keeping the market hopping. The California Association of Realtors showed a 4.2 percent drop in home sales for the third quarter, and the National Association of Realtors reported that home sales began to slip this fall.

But the cautionary news has been balanced with more optimistic reports. Three days before the Barron's article appeared, Century 21 Real Estate Corp. sent out a press release with its forecast for the new year. The headline-grabbing lead predicted that "home buyers can anticipate continued appreciation and lowered mortgage rates in 1990."

In the Hiller Highlands, life is looking up

SPECIAL TO THE EXAMINER

I'll bet 95 percent of East Bay residents have never heard of Oakland's Hiller Highlands, and that a higher percentage have never been there. But for those who have driven on Route 24 up the hill leading to the Caldecott tunnel to Orinda, the 336-unit development has probably entered your peripheral vision.

It's that rambling condominium complex that hangs atop the hills above the Claremont Hotel.

I once heard a UC-Berkeley urban planning student describe it is "a worst-case example of permitting development in the wrong place."

But exactly what the young planner didn't like about Hitler Highlands — its location — offers local residents some of the most spectacular views in the Bay Area, and comfortable isolation from the bustling urban scene below.

"I used to live down in Rockridge and I remember in the 1960s looking up here wondering 'what are they doing to that scarred hill,'" says Hiller Highland resident Robert Ploss. Ten years later, Ploss moved to the community and has become one of its most vigorous boosters.

The first phase of the development began in 1966 after various schemes for the site fizzled At one time, there was a plan for 800 homes and a large shopping center.

A very livable community

The scale was eventually modified and the retail extravaganza never panned out. Now with the community built out and the landscaping mature, Hiller Highlands has become a very livable community. It explains why Oakland A's outfielder Ricky Henderson and Reggie Jackson, a former As player, own property there.

The architecture is conventional 1960s wood-frame California garden-apartment style. But the site plan for this hilly location works well. In addition to a few single-family homes, the two-, three- and four-unit buildings are tucked into the interior of the hill.

The design scheme creates a bowl effect with one of the best-kept secrets in the East Bay at the bottom: the affordable and well-maintained Highlands Country Club.

Country club is a misnomer because the golf course is a near miniature, a pitch-and-putt place. But the pool, tennis courts, a huge spa and men's and women's lockers — and saunas — are a bargain at only $45 a month. You don't have to be a resident to join.

The country club is one of several things that gives this place a keen sense of community. Unlike many condo developments where detachment among neighbors is common, the folks at Hiller Highlands seem to enjoy one another's company.

Take the Hiller Hymners. On Dec. 18 a band of Hiller Highland residents walked from building to building singing Christmas carols.

'A positive community event'

"It turned into a real positive community event," says Ploss. He and his wife, Peggy, have lived in Hiller Highlands for 12 years.

Then there's the travel club, the spring home tour, the Hiller Highlands Music Disc Jockeys Cooperative and the Hawk Hill Investment Club, which earned its members a return of 10.6 percent last year.

Along with the social activities, the six homeowner associations that govern the complex have an assortment of committees that tend to the community's business. They represent the six phases of the development, and each has its own board of directors. Occasionally, they cooperate on community-wide projects.

For example, a Disaster Preparedness Council was recently formed to develop a plan in response to natural disasters. While Hiller Highlands survived the earthquake with minor damage, it "literally shocked (us) into an awareness that we had better begin serious community preparedness for natural disasters," said a recent Hiller Highland monthly newsletter.

Eight years ago, Ploss began the popular publication, dubbed the Shriek. It has a "circulation of almost 500" and at times is controversial. The four-page newsletter keeps residents posted on neighborhood issues and has helped to build community identity.

One-time resident Ollie Hammerel says the age of the populace accounts for the level of community participation. "A younger group is moving in, but for a long time it's been primarily the 55 crowd with a number of retirees who have time on their hands," says Hammerel, a real estate agent active in the area.

Volunteers run the place

He referred to them as "people leaving Piedmont who don't want to move through the tunnel (to Contra Costa County) — the empty nesters."

Most developments of this size would hire a professional property manager, but volunteers run Hiller Highlands.

The spirit as well as the responsibility for a rich community life in Hiller Highlands are captured in a line from this month's newsletter: "The smallest (and most important) governmental organization we deal with is our own community. Let's help each other to guard it well."

In Hiller Highlands, they do just that.

On My Livable and Sensible Scale:

Many homeowners associations have become like dysfunctional families, but high above the urban fracas, Hiller Highlands stands out in more ways than one.

Redevelopment is for blighted areas — period

A TARECENT State Senate hearing, critics gave legislators an earful about the .state's 40-year-old Community Redevelopment Law. They say cities are abusing the powers of redevelopment by offering government subsidies for private construction in areas that aren't blighted.

Redevelopment is being used to subsidize suburban shopping centers and other glitzy commercial buildings in areas that have no recognizable urban problems, say experts who testified in Los Angeles last month before the Senate Committee on Local Government.

According to one report from the state controller's office, dozens of cities an violating a state law that requires redevelopment zones to be located in run-down areas.

The concerns haven't curtailed the number of redevelopment projects. No financial formula since the creation of junk bonds has done more to attract private investment as redevelopment — billions of dollars in California alone.

Though not always welcome, the results are often impressive, with new apartments, hotels, office buildings or convention centers, nearly every city in California has expanded its slice of the economic pie through redevelopment subsidies.

Even in decrepit areas redevelopment is controversial. It's an aggressive municipal game plan that often displaces small businesses, bulldozes older affordable housing projects and offers deep tax subsidies to developers and businesses who wouldn't ordinarily be interested in investing in marginal areas.

It "has literally changed the way California looks," says a new report by the Senate Committee.

To the chagrin of its adversaries, redevelopment isn't confined to the state's largest and most depressed metropolitan centers. Tiny communities have a redevelopment zone. They include Monterey County's Sand City with a population of only 205 and so do resorts. South Lake Tahoe and Indian Wells tap the powers of redevelopment to spawn new construction.

At the center of the debate is the definition of blight.

When redevelopment was introduced more than 100 years ago, it was designed to clear slums. In the late 1890s, "tenements with high rates of tuberculosis or other supposedly contagious diseases could be leveled; officials saw the problem only in terms of dangerous environments," wrote Gwendolyn Wright in her book "Building the Dream: A Social History of Housing in America."

But cities have strayed from the original goals of health, safety and eliminating pockets of poverty, according to citizen activist Sherry Passmore-Curtis of Arcadia.

"Now we have a situation where government is subsidizing private investment in places that just don't need it," complains Passmore-Curtis, one of several witnesses who lambasted local redevelopment programs at the state hearing.

This isn't the first time the Legislature has been pressed to police redevelopment. To prevent abuses, it approved legislation in 1983 saying that for an area to be considered blighted, it must be located in a "predominantly urbanized" part of the community.

According to the law, one measure of a blighted area is how much land is vacant in a redevelopment zone. If more than 20 percent of the property has no buildings on it, it may violate state law. Thirty-five cities in the state now have redevelopment zones that don't meet this limit, according to a report by the state controller's office.

"We thought we were shutting the door on abuses with the 1983 bill, but we left the door ajar," said Peter Detwiler, principal consultant to the Senate Local Government Committee.

One community identified in the controller's report is Antioch, a Bay Area suburb. It has a 130-acre redevelopment district that was created in 1984 and is 90 percent vacant.

While he concedes that the land isn't built up, Antioch City Manager Lee Walton defends the city's action: "The site was an old abandoned quarry and there was no way the project area could be developed without some sort of public financing — that's why we turned to redevelopment."

That type of reasoning doesn't satisfy critics of redevelopment. It's time we "cut the B.S. on the criteria for what is and what is not blight," David Diaz, an environmental planner, said at the state hearing.

Residents have learned to fight environmental degradation

Editor's note: In this article, Examiner columnist Bradley Inman takes a look at a "hidden" Bay Area neighborhood: an area not well known but interesting because of a unique history, a hot community debate or unusual goings-on. If you think you live in or know of a community that Inman has never heard of and is noteworthy, mail in the coupon on Page F-9. Inman will select several to write about in the future.

OF THE EXAMINER STAFF

STAND ON the spot where John W. Ott was laid to rest 93 years ago, and the assorted nuisances that afflict the Blum Road neighborhood in central Costa County become abundantly clear.

Ott's skewed tombstone rests atop a small mound of dirt in an unkempt cemetery along Blum Road. The first thing you notice from his grave site is the noise. Blum Road is situated a few hundred feet from the intersection of two congested East Bay freeways. Highway 4 moves traffic east and west, while the busy Interstate 680 goes north and south. It cannot be easy to rest in peace here.

Pushing up the decibel level is the clamor from a stream of trucks that rumble down Blum Road to Pacheco Boulevard onto the freeways. Every few minutes a load of petroleum, gravel or toxic waste travels from the industrial sites that surround the neighborhood.

Anyone who reads this column regularly knows that I have little patience for uppity neighborhood groups that become unglued about slight changes in the status quo.

Unbending in their demands, they freak out when a small affordable housing project is proposed or an infill retail center is planned in their too precious neighborhood. I dubbed these folks "NIMBYs" — Not In My Back Yard activists.

But along Blum Road, the NIMBYs deserve to be heard. This neighborhood has been unfairly singled out as a dumping ground for unwanted land uses.

All through the '60s and '70s, "Oh well, put it on Blum Road" seemed to be the common refrain by Contra Costa County officials. Blum Road was like a punished serf in the hierarchic planning system. When the county scrambles to find places to hide the waste that is generated by luxurious high-end growth and commercial and industrial development, Blum Road is an easy mark.

There's the County's Animal Control Center, the County Spay and Neuter Center, a class-A toxic waste dump, the park-and-ride commuter lot, the Central Contra Costa County Sanitary Treatment Plant, the Southern Pacific petroleum tanks, the toxic burners, a recreational vehicle storage lot and scads of unfriendly warehousing and industrial uses.

"To live in this neighborhood is a challenge," says Bob Gabriel, a resident.

Now the public works department wants to add a county equipment storage yard.

Which might not be an issue, except next door to this tortured landscape live a couple hundred people. And they have learned to fight back.

"Our favorite expression today is, 'Don't mess with Blum Road,'" says local resident and community activist Paul Macchia.

In the early '80s, acting through a neighborhood group called the Blum Road Alert, local residents stopped plans to put a prison in the area. Since then, they have successfully opposed a commercial truck stop, a garbage transfer station and the expansion of a toxic-burning facility.

"We stick together," says Macchia. "The county is beginning to figure out that 230 people make Blum Road home."

The Blum Road Alert was formed 25 years ago when it convinced the county to form the Mountain View Sanitary District so that antiquated septic tanks could be replaced. Since then, the group has become so sophisticated about planning issues that "we could job ourselves out as community consultants," boasts Macchia.

"People thought this neighborhood was full of a bunch of Okies, but we have an attorney, an environmental engineer (who live here) and an organization that in a moment's notice can mobilize the 120 families that live here," says Macchia.

"We aren't NIMBYs," he adds. "But why concentrate it all in one neighborhood? We were here before the toxic waste came along."

Indeed, one of the ironies of Blum Road is that the area is zoned as a residential neighborhood. Seven units of housing are permitted for every acre.

The homes are nestled along the streets that jut off Blum Road. On the north side, vast open spaces begin the climb up Mt. Diablo.

A Highway Patrol office is located at the gateway to the community, which helps keep the neighborhood safe. With single-family homes for less than $150,000, it's also affordable.

For all its stubborn activism, the neighborhood has learned to compromise. To stop the proposal for a county truck storage yard, Blum Road Alert accepted a plan for new office development.

The backlash along Blum Road provides some interesting lessons. When I asked Macchia where in the county the undesirable land uses should be located, he offered "a global alternative."

"Reducing the output of hazardous wastes is the only solution. Nobody wants these uses in their back yard, so steps must be taken to reduce the toxics," he says.

Another lesson is that communities are often found where you least expect them. What impressed me about Blum Road is that at first glance the area appeared to have little going for it. Yet, that's not what the people who live there would have you think. They banded together to better the quality of life in their neighborhood.

"Remember, we chose to live here," says Gabriel.

As a result, the county can no longer count on Blum Road to roll over and simply take environmental abuse.

On My Livable and Sensible Scale:

The folks who live along Blum Road aren't selfish reactionaries; they are a concerned group of citizens that deserve better.

Rediscovering former glitzy S.F. hot spot

OF THE EXAMINER STAFF

SEVERAL WELL-KNOWN neighborhoods epitomize the trend of urban gentrification: Newberry Street in Boston, Melrose Avenue in Los Angeles and the SoHo district in lower Manhattan.

These were once plain and nondescript neighborhoods that suddenly became tony urban hot spots in the 1970s and 1980s.

Mom-and-pop stores were squeezed out by stylish designer boutiques and the local blue-collar pubs were converted into chic wine bars and high-end eateries.

San Francisco's Union Street is the Bay Area's most notorious example of an area that became too cute for its own good.

But look again.

There are signs that the glitz period is over for this celebrated stretch of Union Street between Van Ness Avenue and Lyon Street in the Cow Hollow District of San Francisco.

On a recent jaunt down Union Street, I spotted several soiled awnings and was surprised to see a number of vacant storefronts. Don't get the wrong impression; Union Street is far from being a run-down neighborhood.

But its heyday as San Francisco's leading yuppie haven appears to be over.

Scads of upscale restaurants and boutiques still thrive on Union Street, but "the hippest of the hip hang out South of Market," says KGO radio personality Ronn Owens.

Rediscovering Union Street

Owens and his wife, KCBS talk show host Jan Black, own a condominium on Union Street. Dubbed the "unofficial mayor" of Union Street, Owens is one of the neighborhood's oldest and most vocal cheerleaders.

"FOR A while, (Union Street) started to look a little like Rodeo Drive," says Owens, a 15-year resident. "That's when the double-decker buses were unloading tourists at the corner by Prego."

Today, the tour buses are gone; and signs posted up and down the street forbid them.

Market changes have modified the face of the Union Street commercial strip. The razzle-dazzle "ran its course when rents went through the ceiling — now its personality is becoming more of a neighborhood that serves the residents who live in the Cow Hollow," says Owens.

Union Street also is no longer the only trendy game in town. It faces competition from areas like Chestnut Street in the nearby Marina District and from the emergence of Van Ness Avenue as a popular hangout for the evening crowd.

And the mood has changed as the street's loyalists get older and more utilitarian in their habits.

OWENS POINTS to the changing clientele at erstwhile Perry's as a good example. In the 1970s and 1980s, this popular San Francisco watering hole symbolized the fun and frolic that Union Street was famous for. It was a familiar scene with freshly scrubbed Financial District types lined up six and seven deep at the 25-foot bar.

"I used to go there as a single guy in the late 1970s," says Owens, "Now I go to the back of the restaurant with my little girl."

The occupancy history of 2100 Union St at the corner of Webster and Union streets is another example and typifies the turnover trail of retail shops. Union Street Groceries was located there for years but closed when rents soared in the late 1970s. Then came the New York West apparel shop.

Now The Athlete's Foot occupies the space.

Today, several franchises thrive in the neighborhood. But instead of designer fashions, the trend is toward more basic goods and services like bakeries and coffee shops. And sports fashions seem to have replaced diamond-studded blouses.

For affluent outsiders, the exotic is still available.

You can get cosmetic dentistry, a European tan or a "thermo-trim" (rubber heat wrap for weight loss) on Union Street. Several galleries and antique shops continue to tout collectibles.

SOME THINGS will never change. Stalwarts along Union Street include A. Valente & Sons Plumbing and Heating, the Metro Theater and the Northern Lights Bookstore. There's also Madame Rose's psychic, palm and tarot card readings. For $10, she promises a glimpse into the future on your love life, your marriage and business.

Plus, you can still get an inexpensive haircut at Lombardo's Barber Shop, get your car repaired and buy fresh produce.

The party crowd shouldn't be completely discouraged by the more subdued mood at Perry's. They can still enjoy libations at the Blue Light Cafe, the Bus Stop, Margaritaville, the Deli Restaurant and several other drinking and eating establishments.

Union Street may no longer be the trendiest spot in San Francisco, but it is alive and kicking.

On My Livable and Sensible Scale:

The eclectic mix of shops that currently do business along Union Street is proof that this area is in flux. That's probably a good sign for anyone who has a long-term stake in the neighborhood's future.

Report shows Bay Area worst place to be poor

SPECIAL TO THE EXAMINER

WE DON'T need a dry statistical report from an East Coast think tank to figure out that Bay Area housing costs create economic havoc for the poor. But maybe the microscope of an outside group will get the attention of lethargic local officials who choose to ignore our wretched housing mess.

The Washington, D.C.-based Center on Budget and Policy Priorities is scheduled Monday to release a comprehensive look at the Bay Area poor and housing. Housing sources familiar with the report provided me with a preview of some of the conclusions.

The report is dubbed "A Place to Call Home: The Crisis in Housing for the Poor," and it paints a depressing picture of the Bay Area's housing predicament for renters, homeowners, minorities, older people and single-family parents.

The Bay Area is already known for its lack of affordable housing for middle-class residents. Now, according to the report, the Bay Area has earned the dubious distinction of having the least affordable housing in the nation for its poor as well.

"While the affordable housing crisis for the poor is national in scope, it is particularly severe in the San Francisco-Oakland area," a draft of the report says.

The study covers the counties of San Francisco, Alameda, Contra Costa, Marin and San Mateo. Much of the data comes from the Department of Housing and Urban Development and U.S. Census Bureau figures, combined with local statistics on the housing market.

The report provides some insight into how the housing climate has changed in the past few years.

For example, the only piece of good news is that while the median family income in the Bay Area went up 26 percent from 1985 to 1988, rel2verty.

Unfortunately, the study makes no recommendations for improving our muddle.

I read a study like this and I want to throw up my hands. That, also unfortunately, is exactly what our political leaders have been doing for too long.

Low-income housing groups are turning to the courts

IN 1988, a lawsuit that forced the city of Yonkers, N.Y., to accept low-cost housing made national news. At first, the city defied a federal court order to move forward with a housing desegregation plan that involved building an affordable housing project. It finally acquiesced after a federal judge threatened to bankrupt the city with court fines.

Charges of racism were leveled against stubborn municipal officials, and the city accused the court of righteous judicial interference.

The Yonkers case may appear to have been an isolated tiff over where low-cost housing should be built — an incident far from the borders of California.

Not necessarily.

A similar legal confrontation is shaping up in California that rivals the events in Yonkers. The only difference is that the controversy here will likely erupt in several cities at one time.

In at least two communities — the city of Alameda in the Bay Area and Hidden Hills in Southern California — a Yonkers-styled legal brouhaha is already unfolding. And more cases are expected to follow in the coming months.

Leading California low-income housing groups and legal aid organizations indicate they are ready to sue recalcitrant local officials who won't accept affordable housing.

At a major gathering of low-cost housing advocates in Sacramento earlier this month, legal strategies for lawsuits were mapped out. When introducing the results of a new study on affordable housing, Stan Keasling of the California Right to Housing advocacy group warned communities that exclude low-cost housing: "You will hear, from our attorneys."

City of Alameda targeted

The city of Alameda knows that such comments aren't idle threats.

The Legal Aid Society of Alameda County late last year filed a lawsuit which argued that the city of Alameda's policy of barring multi-family housing construction was discriminatory.

The court suspended the city's right to issue any new building permits until it completed an acceptable local housing plan, and the judge put the burden on the city to defend its policy of only permitting single-family development.

City officials in Hidden Hills reluctantly agreed to build a senior housing project under the direction of a controversial court order. But the decision has deeply divided this affluent community in West San Fernando Valley, which currently has no affordable housing. Two weeks ago, a new city council majority was elected that pledged to fight the housing project.

In response, Los Angeles Superior Court Judge R. William Schoettler Jr. said he would summon local officials to compel them to adopt a plan for lower-cost housing if the senior project is turned back by the new council.

Legal scholars say there is no shortage of federal and state laws, including civil rights statutes, to make a case against exclusionary housing policies. However, the debate over where to build low-cost housing in California has largely stayed out of the courts until recently. Community groups, homeowners associations, environmentalists, housing groups, developers and state and local officials have chosen to duke it out in the legislative arena: at zoning hearings and planning meetings.

Seeking a different arena

But housing advocates have begun to realize that they are losing these battles. Communities have turned down or delayed hundreds of low-cost housing projects in the past few years. A recent survey showed that California cities have only met 11 percent of the overall i housing need in the past five years.

This lackluster response comes at a time when resources for housing are becoming more plentiful. Two recent state ballot initiatives provide more than $450 million for low-cost housing construction and another measure is planned for the November ballot.

Moreover, in recent weeks, several major California banks have announced plans to pump more than $3.4 billion into affordable housing.

But these funds are useless when communities choose to turn their back on the problem. This explains why housing advocates are turning to the courts to make their case, and why California has the potential for a Yonkers-style donnybrook.

Correction: In my April 8 column, a description of SCA 2 introduced by Sen. Bill Leonard, R-Upland, had an error. The bill would allow local agencies to levy a property tax of 0.05 percent on the fair market value of real and personal property.

Still doing right thing: History's converted to affordable housing

SPECIAL TO THE EXAMINER

IN THE last month I have been reminded twice about the value of old buildings. At a meeting of California preservationists, a member of the group challenged me to recognize that "saving historic structures is more than preserving valuable old architecture: It's also about keeping the spotlight on important symbols and significant events in our history."

I was impressed enough with the words that I wrote them down — even though I wasn't exactly sure what they meant.

I recently got the point. It took a visit to the Center for Afro-American History on San Pablo Avenue in Oakland. There, I chatted with the center's director, Lawrence P. Crouchett, and an Oakland resident and retired policeman, Hadwick A. Thompson.

We met to discuss the historic California Hotel, which is located along San Pablo Avenue between 34th and 35th streets at the center of the Oakland freeway maze only 40 feet away from Interstate 580. You may have seen it while traveling on the freeway. It's being rehabilitated into 150 affordable rental units and is covered with scaffolding.

Crouchett and Thompson aren't involved in the latest improvement to the 63-year-old hotel, but they know the building's history. More important, they understand why its past is so important.

"That old building represents a breakthrough for integration in the Bay Area," said Crouchett, who plans to write a history of the hotel.

Until 1949, African-Americans couldn't stay, eat or party at the California Hotel, which for decades was an entertainment hot spot. The segregation extended to black entertainers who performed there.

A lawsuit that year by a railroad porter forced integration, and blacks were no longer stuck at the clubs and the hotels along Seventh Street in West Oakland.

Desegregating the hotel "showed that money could be made from us, and it showed we were civil," said Thompson, who patrolled the hotel for the Oakland Police Department in the 1950s. After the segregated doors to the California Hotel were unlocked, other commercial establishments began to drop their barriers as well.

The hotel itself became a popular hangout for famous jazz, blues and rock entertainers. Over the years, hotel guests or entertainers there included B.B. King, Joe Turner, Fats Domino, Ike and Tina Turner, James Brown, Big Mama Mabel Thornton, Sam Cook and dozens of others.

'It was the place to go'

"It was the place to go," said Crouchett. The hotel had an all-night restaurant, and "we would just go in hopes of seeing someone famous."

Celebrities played at the hotel's Club Zanzibar, while others stayed as guests and played at nearby nightspots such as Slim Jenkins along Seventh Street or Sweets Ballroom downtown. Big-band dances were held in the hotel's Gold Room.

Dancer Ruth Beckford had a penthouse Apartment in the hotel all through .the 1950s and remembers it during that period as a "class act."

"Make sure you mention the Latin mambo dancing on Sunday afternoons," she told me. "That place was always going, but it was safe for ladies to come to by themselves."

Hotel built in 1927

When it was built in 1927, the hotel was the first major commercial building to be constructed outside downtown Oakland. Even today, the imposing edifice with its twin towers stands out among the low-rise commercial and residential uses in the area.

But for decades it turned out to be an ideal location. The hotel was only four blocks from the central railroad station for the old key system at 40th Street and San Pablo Avenue. Trains arrived there from The City and all over the East Bay.

The Oakland Oaks baseball team played nearby and always drew a big crowd to the area. The hotel was also next door to Emeryville where gambling and burlesque thrived.

El Rey Theater across the street

The El Rey Theater was just across the street. Tempest Storm, among other strippers, often danced there in the '50s. She purportedly met singer Herb Jefferies at the' hotel; they later married.

In the 1960s, the hotel began to lose some of its luster, but the stars continued to entertain there. By the late '60s and early '70s, it went completely downhill and became a center for prostitution and drugs. It finally closed in 1972 and became a victim of vandalism.

A couple of years ago, East Bay nonprofit Oakland Community Housing Inc. came to the rescue with a plan to convert the hotel into affordable housing with monthly rents of $250 for a single room that includes a bath and access to a communal kitchen.

With grants and loans from public and private groups, the $7.5 million restoration began last year. Construction should be completed by the fall of 1990.

"It's the rebirth of a great Bay Area landmark," said Crouchett.

Thompson summed up the California Hotel best: "That hotel has gone through a lot of changes, and it's responsible for some important changes as well."

At a Glance

California Hotel

Registration: The hotel has been listed on the National Register of Historic Places.
Architect: The architect on the restoration is James Vann of Oakland.
Style: The lobby has 22-foot ceilings and is 1920s period revival style architecture.
Size: The hotel is five stories high with a 214-foot-long facade an San Pablo Avenue.

Legislators take a critical look at Prop. 13

Under the current rules, homeowners who stay put enjoy low and stable tax bills. According to Prop. 13, property is assessed at 1 percent of market value at time of sale, and then tax payments can only go up 2 percent a year.

When the property is sold, however, the property is reassessed at the sales price. Because California housing values have skyrocketed, recent home buyers pay a higher and disproportionate share of the total property tax burden.

This inequity has spawned at least three court cases that could eventually force the legislature to revise Prop. 13.

In the case of Norlinger v. Lynch, home buyer Stephanie Nordliner is suing the Los Angeles County tax assessor on the grounds that Proposition 13's system of property tax assessment discriminates against recent property owners in favor of longtime land owners, and, therefore, violates the equal protection clause of the California and U.S. Constitutions. The suit claims that there is as much as a 15 to 1 disparity in tax assessments on homes with comparable value.

R.H. Macy & Company is making a similar claim in a lawsuit filed against Contra Costa County, where the assessor upped the retailer's property tax bill 250 percent when a corporate restructuring caused a change of ownership in a Macy's store in this Bay Area suburb.

In the case of Northwest Financial v. State Board of Equalization and San Diego County, Northwest sued when it was forced to pay a property tax bill four times higher than the previous owner did on a home the company purchased in La Jolla.

In 1979, the California Supreme Court considered the issue of equal protection in the case of Amador Valley Joint Union High School District v. State Board of Equalization. At the time, the state's high court ruled that Prop 13 was constitutional. But some legal experts argue that the disparity in tax bills eleven years ago was not enough to alarm the court. Today, the gap is much wider.

A recent U.S. Supreme Court decision has compounded the anxiety in Sacramento. In the case of Allegheny Pittsburgh Coal Company v. County Commission of Webster County, the high court held that a Virginia property tax system was invalid.

A proposed statewide ballot measure has also contributed to the political stirrings in Sacramento. The "split-roll" initiative would create a higher property tax rate for commercial property than residential.

Treasurer's Campaign Comes Calling on the Investment Banks

For the past few months, state Treasurer Tom Hayes has been wearing two hats—one as campaigner, the other as guardian of the state's public purse. That can't be easy for a button-down guy who is a novice on the campaign trail and who is just beginning to master his current job.

Hayes—a 43-year-old ex-Marine who was appointed to the job in January, 1989, and won the Republican primary earlier this month—is portrayed by his supporters as a fiscal taskmaster and a steady hand at the helm of the state's vast financial empire. During the general election campaign, voters will be reminded of his credentials as a champion of the competitive bidding process and as a trustworthy custodian of California's AAA credit rating.

But with a formidable opponent in Democrat Kathleen Brown, Hayes faces an expensive statewide campaign that depends on a lot of big contributors.

Recently, campaign fund-raising and the state's financial affairs have crossed paths, illustrating what a wobbly tightrope Hayes must walk.

On April 26, Hayes solicited proposals from 16 of the nation's largest investment banking firms on issuing $150 million in revenue bonds for construction of the California state prison in Madera. Companies such as Smith Barney, Harris Upham & Co.; Goldman, Sachs & Co.; Lazard Freres & Co.; Morgan Stanley & Co.; Prudential-Bache Capital Funding, and First Boston Corp. were contacted. Their proposals were due back in the Treasurer's office May 4.

On May 16, the investment bankers were notified that all of the firms invited to submit proposals had done so but that the Treasurer's office would delay a decision on which firm would manage sale of the bonds.

During this time, many of the same firms or their employees were invited to campaign fund-raising luncheons for Hayes. A $1,000-a-plate affair was scheduled for May 10 at the executive dining room of Security Pacific Bank in Los Angeles and a $500-a-plate gathering for May 24 at the Bankers Club in San Francisco.

Critics see a conflict of interest. "You should not be raising funds from those people who you are soliciting [state business] from," argues Ruth Holton, legislative advocate for Common Cause. "Even if it wasn't a deliberate attempt to coerce a contribution, there appears to be a conflict of interest."

Thomas Hayes

Hayes was not available for comment, but spokespersons for his campaign and the Treasurer's office denied a link between his fund-raising activities and decisions in the Treasurer's office.

"We can't just stop the business of the state because Tom has a campaign to run," said Donna Lucas, of the Treasurer's office.

Assistant Treasurer Russell Gould said his office's guidelines prohibit the staff from getting involved with Hayes' campaign. Campaign manager Brian Lungren said lists used for the fund-raisers were not obtained from the Treasurer's office and that campaign officials had no knowledge of the Madera prison project.

"We are no different than any other campaign," Lungren said. "We rely on local fund-raising consultants, and they often have developed lists from other campaigns, such as Bush, Reagan and Deukmejian."

The Hayes campaign also taps a "house list," which is made up of 6,000 contributors who have previously donated to him. Lungren said there's little doubt that some names on the Treasurer's bidding list would also show up on fund-raising rosters. In fact, all of the firms on the bid list for the Madera prison project have previously contributed to the Hayes campaign or have key employees who contributed. In 1989, Hayes received at least $80,000 from these companies or their employees.

Moreover, there is nothing illegal about an elected state officeholder soliciting political contributions from the same groups that do business with a state agency—unless there is a *quid pro quo* between candidate and contributor.

What about the *appearance* of a conflict of interest? "We are going out with RFPs [requests for proposals] all of the time. This is no different," Lucas said.

One investment banker, who asked to remain anonymous, had a different view. "It was breathless timing," he said. "Never have I seen such a hurried attempt to issue a bond and then have everything be put on hold—all right before the [primary] election."

'You should not be raising funds from those people who you are soliciting [state business] from. Even if it wasn't a deliberate attempt to coerce a contribution, there appears to be a conflict of interest.'

Ruth Holton

Common Cause

But Gould cites other reasons for delaying the Madera prison bond sale; "Just about the time we were making plans to go to market, the governor announced the $3-billion budget deficit. That's not a good time to make investor decisions of this magnitude."

The investment banking community has a mixed view of the matter. "This is an example of how politicized the process can get," complained a banker who asked not to be identified.

"I don't see any relationship between the two [fund-raising and the bids]," said a representative from Prudential-Bache. "Maybe it's because I receive so many fund-raising requests this time of year. I've got seven on my desk right now."

First Boston apparently felt that attending the San Francisco fund-raiser would hurt its chances of doing business with the state, so it didn't attend. "It may sound odd, but we were worried that appearing on the list of attendees might hurt us in the long run, given Mr. Hayes' widely proclaimed divorce between policy and politics," managing director Michael George said.

Campaign manager Lungren declared flatly that contributors won't get special treatment when it comes to awarding state business.

"Tom has been up front about his commitment to competitive bidding and open about his fund-raising philosophy," Lungren said. "If contributors want to demonstrate their support of open and competitive bidding, they can contribute to the campaign, but all they can hope for in return is that they will be treated fairly."

30 June 1990
The Desert Sun

California grapples with growth issues

Unhappy with the state's lackluster response to regulating California's burgeoning growth rate, several state lawmakers are looking north to Oregon for counsel on the best way to manage the pace of development here.

Recently, a handful of legislators played host to a delegation from an Oregon citizen's lobby that oversees the state's 19-year experiment with statewide growth management.

Unlike California where growth decisions are largely made at the county or municipal level, Oregon has one of the most comprehensive statewide systems for managing growth.

The trip was timely: the California legislature is considering more than a dozen bills that would tighten up rules that govern growth.

Moreover, state policy makers are grappling with how to implement the "congestion-management" program that is part of the Proposition 111 gasoline tax increase.

Approved by a narrow majority of the state's voters last week, the $15 billion tax hike calls for allocating transportation funds to those communities that take steps to tie future development to acceptable traffic levels and other actions to manage growth.

This latest citizen mandate forces California to consider a plan for how much and where growth will be concentrated in the next decade.

The last major legislative initiative that was aimed at corralling growth came almost 20 years ago with the adoption of the California Coastal Act.

This far-reaching measure changed the rules for development along the coast and is credited with opening up public access to the beaches and curtailing construction up and down the coastline.

Today's debate isn't confined to the coast, but the desire to do something about growth is just as strong as it was in the early 1970s.

In the last several years, most California communities have been embroiled in a fight over growth. Wrangling about increased traffic, lost open space and the lack of affordable housing is common in urban, suburban and rural communities throughout the state.

The debate isn't confined to a few developers and environmentalists bickering over where to build another condominium project. Indeed, the growth issue has become a mainstream political issue, and the friction is forcing the California legislature to grapple with the quandary.

Although local control continues to be a coveted value of governance in California, a consensus seems to be evolving that some sort of statewide growth management plan is desirable.

And a growing number of land-use experts in California are eyeballing the Oregon system as a model for what should be done here.

In 1971, the Oregon state legislature created the Urban Growth Management plan for the metropolitan Portland area, which is where more than 80 percent of the state's population lives. Under this recipe, an urban growth boundary was created, which covers three counties, 24 cites and more than 60 special service districts.

With an elected board but no taxing authority, the Portland Metropolitan Service District manages the growth plan and has the legal muscle to approve and veto local building plans.

"They have the power to shut off state funds and cut off building permits — so, yes, it does have real power," said Robert Liberty of 1000 Friends of Oregon, the citizen group that serves as a watchdog for the state planning program.

Though it was hotly debated in the 1970s, the plan has widespread support today.

For example, "home builders are some of our strongest supporters," said Henry Richmond of 1000 Friends of Oregon.

He points to an attempt to repeal the plan a few years ago in which "developers were the biggest financial backers in the campaign to preserve growth management."

For real estate developers, the Oregon plan offers certainty.

"They know where they can build and where they can't," said Liberty.

Moreover, within the urban limit line, builders are encouraged to construct high-density housing projects, and local moratoriums that temporarily halt development are illegal. In California, high densities are frowned upon and communities frequently put a stop to development altogether.

The Oregon growth management plan isn't just a model for improving the quality of development, it may also be a blueprint for forming a new coalition.

30 July 1990
The Los Angeles Times

Nonprofit Groups May Ease Dearth of Affordable Homes

Housing: Organizations dedicated to building high-quality, low-cost units are emerging as a second-tier real estate market.

Like a disease with no cure, finding solutions to Orange County's and California's affordable-housing mess has baffled policy-makers for at least a decade.

The consequences of the breakdown are grim. The homeownership rate in the state has fallen below 50%, more than 700,000 Californians live in overcrowded conditions, and 1 million residents pay 40% or more of their income on rent.

The problem has a simple explanation: Personal incomes can't keep up with the cost of housing. Solutions are more elusive.

In 1989, California residential real estate values increased by nearly $75 billion. But incomes only grew an estimated $12 billion. Include $1 billion in state, federal and local housing aid, and $62 billion was added to the state housing deficit last year alone.

Fat with equity, homeowners benefit from this trend, but finding solutions for people who are stuck renting is one of the state's most pressing challenges. This gap is dramatic in Orange County, where the median home price is $250,000.

Historically, remedies to the housing malaise involve taking one of two tacks: increasing the supply of housing, or forcing developers to offer affordability.

At real estate industry conferences, "supply, supply, supply" is proffered as the panacea for high housing costs. The build-your-way-out-of-the-problem approach holds that increasing supply to meet demand will stop the price spiral and wipe out the affordability gap.

Another scenario mandates that private property owners and developers come to the rescue. The theory says that since real estate interests benefit from property inflation, it's fair to require developers to include a certain percentage of affordable homes in every new project. Rent control also fits into this strategy.

However, neither of these two approaches—leave it to the free market or redistribute the wealth—have done much to solve the state's housing ills.

In the meantime, a third approach is taking shape that may hold out hope for long-term solutions to the current muddle.

With government aid and corporate philanthropic contributions, nonprofit groups are popping up all over the country with a mission to produce high-quality, low-cost housing. A second-tier real estate market is emerging that specializes in affordable homes and apartments.

Nationwide, there are now between 1,500 and 2,000 community-based housing development groups. Organized as tax-exempt, public-purpose groups with special access to government funds, they have built nearly 125,000 housing units.

These grass-roots organizations have become the darlings of state and federal lawmakers. Every major housing bill approved in the last several years has targeted money for nonprofit housing groups. In the coming years, they will have exclusive access to more than $1 billion in state and private funds that are earmarked for housing in California.

"It's a very political, palpable way to privatize the job of building and managing low-cost government housing," says Michael Yaki, an aide to Rep. Nancy Pelosi (D-San Francisco). "By letting community-based groups do it, you eliminate layers of bureaucracy, and they tend to humanize the design of the units and give the residents more control over their homes."

One of the most successful residential developers is a nonprofit corporation. Bridge Housing Inc. of San Francisco has no stockholders, no earnings and no profit, but its developments suffer few vacancies, frequently win design awards and are affordable to entry-level home buyers and low-income renters.

Credited with building 3,000 units in the last seven years, Bridge ranks as the 37th largest builder in Northern California. The organization is expanding its operation to Southern California with projects planned in Irvine.

By vowing to use government funds exclusively for the production of low-cost housing, nonprofit groups also promise long-term affordability. They own and maintain the units that they produce, guaranteeing that they remain affordable.

In the past, government aid programs were used to give incentives to private developers for building low-cost housing. But requirements on affordability often lasted no longer than 10 to 15 years. Nonprofit groups, on the other hand, often guarantee permanent affordability.

These new organizations don't replace the private market. Home builders will continue to build to the middle and upper income groups, and private firms will often join in ventures with nonprofit groups for the part of the market that is too often ignored.

All remains quiet in this coastal village

Special to the Examiner

MUIR BEACH – Some neighborhoods are museum pieces. The West Marin community of Muir Beach is close to being one of them.

This tiny seaside village almost seems too fragile, too beautiful and too pristine to be lived in.

My city-numbed senses wake up when I visit a place like this. Sparsely laid out over green hills facing the Pacific Ocean, the small collection of homes in Muir Beach is wedged between pines, wildflowers and Monterey cypress with idyllic views of sand, cliffs, hillside meadows, breakers and San Francisco.

There are plenty of spots in Marin County that should be developed, but this 16-acre gem should never be blemished with plazas, malls or condominiums. People make messes, and this is the kind of place that doesn't deserve to be messy.

So far, no real damage has been done.

In fact, there is so little here that residents must drive five miles over Mount Tamalpais to civilization to get groceries, haircuts, pizza and anything else. There isn't a single store in this unincorporated village. The only commercial establishments are the Pelican Inn and a horse boarding stable.

Near the stables is a row of community mailboxes and the volunteer fire department office.

Muir Beach, with an estimated 400 people and 200 houses, has 226 families listed in the Muir Beach Community directory. The directory concedes that "some residents have requested that their names should not be published."

Listed in the directory is resident John Buttress who moved to Muir Beach from Mill Valley in 1974 because "it smells good and feels good." He built the house he currently lives in and owns another property nearby.

A challenging commute

Like many other Muir Beach residents, Buttress works out of his house and doesn't have to face a commute. However, many of the locals make the 30- to 45-minute trek to San Francisco every day along a challenging and curving two-lane road.

Today, access to Muir Beach is even more encumbered because of the closing of Highway 1 between Muir Beach and Stinson Beach. Most residents to whom I talked don't complain about it because there are fewer visitors passing through.

People in Muir Beach "aren't as privacy conscious as they are in Bolinas, but they're close," said former resident and local real estate agent Loretta Ferraro. Bolinas is north along the coast and is famous for its efforts to keep visitors out.

The day I was in Muir Beach a band of teen-age tourists was frolicking on the beach, which sits on the edge of the Golden Gate National Recreational Area.

From the sand, you can view the homes on the hills with their modern California rustic exteriors and loads of windows. A closer look shows that there is an eclectic mix, even though the community has a local design review board that keeps gross building schemes out.

Also from the beach can be seen a large letter "R" adorning Joe Rodrigues' house on Pacific Way.

Portuguese original settlers

One of the last remaining Portuguese residents who originally settled this area, Rodrigues said that the "R" was found on the beach by a neighbor, and he figured his house was as good as any place for the letter.

Rodrigues, who moved to Muir Beach in the 1940s when he worked in the shipyardsin Sausalito, lives in the older part of the area along Sunset. More contemporary-styled homes have been built in an area referred to as Sea Cave. All the street names come from Herman Melville's "Moby Dick."

While Muir Beach remains relatively quiet, an occasional controversy erupts over use of the community center, costs for funding the water system (each homeowner has a septic tank, and a community service district pays for water tanks) and just "small town politics," according to Buttress.

"But things never get too serious," he said.

I asked Rodrigues why he lived in Muir Beach. He replied, "I have the best view in the world."

It's hard to argue with him.

On My Sensible and Livable Scale:

Muir Beach is an idyllic seaside village with few people and no commercial amenities but limitless natural beauty.

Lawmakers Take Some Shots at Prop. 13

SACRAMENTO-State lawmakers are skittish about modifying the Proposition 13 property tax rules, but in the absence of state leadership, the voters have shown a willingness at the ballot box to make selective adjustments to the regulations.

For example, over the last several years, special exemptions to the revolutionary tax-cutting law have been approved for elderly homeowners, the disabled and children who acquire property from their parents.

This November, California voters will have another shot at watering down the rules of Proposition 13. Approved for the ballot in the upcoming general election, Proposition 127 proposes to exempt earthquake-proofing from increases in property taxes.

Under the current law, a homeowner's tax bill is reassessed when the property is sold or when major improvements have been made to the home. A reassessment usually triggers a higher tax bill because of higher home values.

Under Proposition 127, "installation of seismic improvements that increase structural safety," would not be subject to a higher assessment and a stiffer property tax bite.

If the measure is approved, the Legislature is expected to define specific improvements that are eligible for property-tax relief.

The Senate voted in May to place Proposition 127 before the voters. The bill authorizing the measure was introduced by Sen. Don Rogers (R-Bakersfield) and faced no opposition when it was approved.

Voters are likely to be sympathetic to the change as they have been to other targeted modifications to Proposition 13.

Sen. John Seymour (R-Anaheim) would like to further expand the list of Proposition 13 exemptions to low-and middle-income tenants who buy homes that they are currently renting.

In 1986, the electorate approved Proposition 60, which permits Californians who are 55 or older to retain the lower property tax liability on their existing homes when they sell and buy elsewhere in the same county.

Two years later, the voters approved Proposition 90, which permits older Californians to carry forward the lower tax tab to other California counties. Ordinarily, property tax assessments are based on 1% (not including voter-approved indebtedness) of the actual sales prices of a home and, therefore, increase when property is sold.

In 1986, the voters also extended special property tax benefits to people who inherit or acquire property from their parents. When property is transferred from parent to child, the property taxes are not adjusted upward.

Last year, the voters approved another exception to the Proposition 13 rules when they voted in Proposition 110, which gave the state's disabled population the same property tax relief as people over 55. Moreover, when disabled homeowners pay for improvements that make their homes handicapped-accessible, tax increases are waived.

Sen. John Seymour (R-Anaheim) would like to further expand the list of Proposition 13 exemptions to low- and middle-income tenants who buy homes that they are currently renting.

Approved by the Senate and pending in the Assembly, Senate Constitutional Amendment 37 would permit a group of low-income renters who collectively purchase their existing apartment buildings or mobile-home parks to assume the lower property tax rate of the property seller.

This measure is aimed at low-cost housing developments where the property owner may be motivated to evict the tenants and rent to higher-income renters.

Nearly 80,000 low-cost units are in this situation, according to Seymour. His office estimates that more than 22,000 units will be lost this year and another 57,000 will be threatened by 1994. The vast majority are subsidized by the federal government and will no longer receive the government aid. Without the subsidy, landlords have no economic inducement to keep the rents affordable.

To qualify for the tax exemption, 50% or more of the tenants would have to agree to purchase the building or the park. When the building was sold, there would be no reassessment, and the old tax bill would be carried over.

To sweeten it for the owner, a companion bill would defer capital gains tax on property that is sold to the tenants.

"With this bill, both the tenant and the property owner win," Seymour said. "The owner of a housing project has incentives not to displace the residents, and the tenants have an opportunity for a piece of the American dream."

Preservation falls from state agenda

In the past decade, support for restoring historic buildings in California has waned.

As the preservation movement struggles to recharge its mission to save older structures, it faces a decline in government funds and a dearth of political leadership.

The historic preservation crusade peaked in the 1970s. Then, federal and state lawmakers rushed to support local grassroots efforts to save older neighborhoods, preserve historic landmarks and encourage homeowners to rehabilitate their older homes.

When public awareness of the value of reclaiming older neighborhoods reached an all time high, "it was very glamorous" to refurbish historic buildings, according to Elizabeth Morton, program associate with the California Preservation Foundation in Oakland.

A historic home even graced the cover of Time magazine during that period.

But today preservation has slipped in importance.

"Preserving the housing stock was a national priority in the 1970s," said Clarence Cullimore, executive officer of the State Historic Building Code Board. "Then funds began to dwindle in the 1980s. Now, it's nothing like it was 10 or 15 years ago — maybe everyone thinks we got the job done."

A significant blow was federal tax reform, which in 1986 removed lucrative tax benefits for investing in the repair of older structures.

"There has been a tremendous decline in interest to rehabilitate historic buildings since tax reform," said Kathryn Gualtieri, a state historic preservation officer.

Also, federal grants for historic rehab work on California buildings plummeted. At its peak in the late 1970s, $1 million was appropriated for California, but today less than $500,000 is spent, according to Gualtieri.

Though California has as many as 100,000 structures that fall into the historic category and deserve to be restored preservation struggles for attention in a state that is enamored with new growth and development

For example, the Legislature in the last few years has approved or considered seads of bills that earmark funds for new infrastructure to accommodate more development. But during that period state lawmakers authorized no new funds for historic preservation. Even a proposal for a modest state tax credit for private investment in historic preservation failed to muster serious legislative consideration. In 1984 and 1988, California voters approved two ballot measures that provided $21 million for preserving older buildings, and in November another measure could add to this fund. Stacked against the need and the cost of rehabilitating older structures, however, the bond measures are considered a meager public investment.

Members of the preservation movement must accept part of the blame for the weakening enthusiasm for saving older buildings.

For example, preservationists are criticized for encouraging gentrification of older neighborhoods and pushing out the poor.

It's nice to honor buildings and put plaques on them, but saving a building is not enough unless you tie that agenda to social needs such as housing," said Gualtieri. "We can't afford to be elitist anymore."

Morton added, "Preservationists have had to reconfigure their dogma and become a little more responsible. Many are beginning to realize that preservation is a seismic safety issue, a growth management issue and a housing issue."

Part of the movement's challenge is to ignite renewed public interest in saving older buildings.

The California Preservation Foundation is trying to do just that with workshops the non-profit group is sponsoring this month in northern and southern California.

Dubbed "What's In It For You," the sessions offer information of special, property tax breaks that homeowners who rehabilitate may be entitled to. Also, the state's historic building code will be discussed, which can supersede local codes and can give homeowners more flexibility when making improvements to historic structures.

With some of the old magic gone, the preservation movement is hoping to achieve a new wave of interest by appealing to people's economic bottom line.

Massive rental complex that's big on amenities

Special to the Examiner

GIVEN A choice between home ownership and renting, most people would prefer to own their own place.

Of course, there are the lucky few who don't need or want to make major sacrifices to attain the American dream. These are the folks who enjoy a charming rent-controlled apartment in North Beach, Pacific Height or North Berkeley. For them, inflation is never an issue.

Or there are the ones who find a quaint little second unit behind a widow's home in Sausalito — a spot where the landlord never increases the rent because she just wants a quiet and reliable tenant.

For many people, these choices are preferable to a $1,500-a-month mortgage on a new tract home in Martinez. Also, they don't worry about property taxes, maintenance headaches or homeowners insurance.

But these kinds of nifty rental units are never listed in the want ads and they're nearly impossible to find. In a hot rental scene such as the Bay Area, where vacancies are tight and the pressure on rents is relentless, it's a landlord's market. For 10 years, renters have been scrambling to find value.

Don't despair. Occasionally something comes along that has respect for the tenant and is available to the general renter population.

I would put the massive Fillmore Center in The City in that category.

Located in the Western Addition on Fillmore Street, the sprawling apartment complex is only 50 percent complete and it's still a construction-in-progress eyesore. But underneath the development rubble, a community is emerging that offers its tenants real value.

It's not tiny

Don't get me wrong. This isn't your quaint little walk-up. Bounded by Fillmore, Steiner, O'Farrell and Turk streets, it's a 1,113-unit monster with two 19-story highrise towers, two mid-rise buildings, five low-rise structures, 73,000 square feet of commercial space, a 1,260-space underground parking garage, four acres of open space, a 22,000-square-foot community center and a jumbo-size health club.

And it has the advantage of being close to services and transportation, a good construction scheme and great amenities.

The health facility is what attracted Richard Carlini to Fillmore Center. He just moved from the Castro into a two-bedroom unit and uses his second bedroom as an office for his marketing business.

"I work, I sleep and I go to the health club — all in one central location with indoor parking," said Carlini, who pays $1,400 a month for his new apartment.

Most new rental projects today brag about having a health facility. Whenever I tour these places, it's the first thing the developer shows me. But it's usually a single room with a few stationary bicycles and some universal equipment that I don't understand because I don't work out. I'm rarely impressed.

A healthy sized health club

Fillmore Center is an exception. This is a health club with a capital "H." The 34,000-square-foot facility has a regulation lap pool, racquetball and squash courts, saunas, spas, juice bar, aerobics room and a gym for basketball and volleyball.

It also has a fully equipped nautilus and weight room.

One drawback: Tenants must pay $45 a month to use the facility.

It wasn't the health club that attracted 75-year-old Mildred Thayer who moved to the Fillmore Center from an older apartment in Laurel Heights that "was getting moldy."

"This place is brand new and the climate is better around here," she said.

Thayer also likes the neighborhood because "you can roll out of bed, go shopping, get your shoes fixed, get keys made and your clothes cleaned — and it's convenient to two bus lines."

A direct line to downtown

The bus lines include a direct route to downtown and other major points. Within walking distance is San Francisco's vibrant Fillmore Street, with its many retail shops, Japantown and the AMC Kabuki movie house complex.

Unlike most new apartment projects, sound isn't a problem at the Fillmore Center because the walls are concrete. Originally planned as a cost-saving feature, this turned out to be expensive for the developer.

In fact, the development at Fillmore Center has been a tale of confusion and controversy. The project got into serious financial problems after cost overruns nearly stopped construction. But because it's a redevelopment project, city leaders kept the development moving. Surprisingly, the developer has kept most of its original deadlines for completion.

The Fillmore Center is still a sore subject with many long-time residents. They remember how redevelopment's bulldozer mentality ruptured a once lively black community with single-family homes mixed in with the small-scale apartments.

When things were going haywire, some people argued that the Fillmore Center was too ambitious. Plopping down 1,000 units in a city that has problems building anything had to be a high-risk venture.

As things turned out, it was. The investors and lenders who are $210 million deep into this deal are still scratching their heads. The average per-unit cost is $175,000, which is unheard in the apartment business. Multifamily projects are expected to come under $100,000 a unit to make any financial sense.

But for tenants, Fillmore Center ended up offering a lot of value — something many of them aren't used to getting in the expensive Bay Area rental market. Because the project received government financing, 20 percent of the units rent for as little as $637 a month, up to $999 for a three-bedroom apartment. But only those people who meet specific income guidelines qualify.

Of the 520 units that are open, 490 have been leased.

On My Livable and Sensible Scale:

After a messy birth, Fillmore Center may actually fulfill its grand promise of providing reasonably priced rental apartments with loans of amenities.

Why not build homes instead of boutiques?

Special to the Examiner

AT A recent real estate powwow, surrogates for California gubernatorial candidates Pete Wilson and Dianne Feinstein agreed that future housing growth in California should be at higher densities and directed along transit lines.

Commentary

Despite the property rights advocates, most elected officials, policy makers, en vironmentalists and major developers see the wisdom in this strategy. Putting housing close to rail and bus lines reduces auto use and saves open space by steering growth into built-up areas. Moreover, higher densities are more likely to achieve entry-level prices and rents.

Unfortunately, execution of this plan has fallen woefully short. Like peace in the Middle East, everyone is for it but no one knows exactly how to achieve it.

What's been missing in the high-density along-transit vision is an aggressive game plan. Rezoning a little land here and there doesn't work. Writing the idea into community plans gives lip service but nothing happens. Calling it a goal of statewide importance sounds impressive, but so what?

How to make strategy work

One controversial way to put this growth strategy into action is to redirect the multibillion-dollar California redevelopment apparatus: Make its primary goal the creation of high-density infill housing near transit.

State redevelopment law permits local communities to establish independent public agencies that act like developers, but with special government powers. Using public funds, they can assemble property for development by using eminent domain to buy land, even when the seller is uncooperative. These local agencies can issue bonds for financing development and use the property tax code to create special financial advantages that induce the type of development local officials desire.

The time is right for shifting the redevelopment agenda. For the last 40 years, its mission has been to wipe out blight with an emphasis on commercial development.

The results have been impressive. With new hotels, office buildings and convention centers, every major city in California has expanded its economic pie through redevelopment. Dozers of downtowns have been brought back from the ashes of neglect through redevelopment. Until the junk bond was conceived, no financial formula has done more to attract so much private investment.

Wrong kind of redevelopment

It's true that in a few cities such as San Francisco thousands of housing units have also been built through redevelopment. But in the last 20 years, redevelopment emphasized retail, hotel and office projects.

Now, the commercial revitalization mission needs to wind down. We have an oversupply of hotel rooms. Every city with more than 100,000 people seems to have a civic center or convention facility and the office market is glutted.

Also, California doesn't really have blight anymore. Sure, we have urban problems such as expensive housing, crack-infected neighborhoods, teen-age unemployment and a scary crime wave. But it's not a problem of blighted buildings or blighted neighborhoods. There aren't more than one or two areas in the state that have a string of boarded-up buildings.

Left with nothing else to do, some redevelopment agencies are stretching the definition of blight to fit their needs. Redevelopment is being used to subsidize suburban shopping centers and other glitzy commercial buildings in areas that have no recognizable urban problems.

Bad use of public funds

Smaller suburban towns that should be building affordable housing are using redevelopment powers to build little boutique shopping centers.

This is an abhorrent use of public funds and government powers.

According to a report from the State Controller's Office, scads of California cities are violating a state law that requires redevelopment zones to be located in rundown areas of the state.

So, for two reasons, restructuring redevelopment makes sense.

First, the old agenda is outdated and bordering on scandal. Most important, redevelopment is a perfeet way to create affordable high-density housing opportunities along transit lines.

More than 75 percent of the cities in California have redevelopment agencies, which employ thousands of people who could be cut loose on the housing shortfall. The redevelopment infrastructure includes civil servants who specialize in land assembly, finance and development.

These agencies could buy up property near transit lines and grant approvals to private and non-profit developers who would build housing. Bond funds and tax incentives could be used to make the housing affordable and high density would be a prerequisite.

Current state law calls for 20 percent of the public revenue earned from redevelopment to be set aside for affordable housing. Is it time to change the formula to 80 percent for housing with requirements that the housing be located near transit with a mix of market-rate and low-income units?

The rest could be spent on infrastructure and commercial projects.

It's time for a debate

Such a proposal would certainly spark criticism from redevelopment specialists who are comfortable with their niche and from city officials who often shun housing. But a debate should begirt.

Even in older cities such as Oakland where nearly $50 million is targeted for new retail shopping projects, a shift to housing makes sense. Permanent residents add to the retail base and make private investment in commercial enterprises more promising.

Not all Communities will accept this new redevelopment mission. Cities such as Orinda will be uncomfortable with the agenda. There, local officials seem to view the BART station as its pet public limousine service. Fearful of community outcry, they are taking no action to encourage housing on vacant parcels that surround the rapid transit station.

But in other places, redevelopment agencies are equipped to take on stubborn community groups that don't want affordable housing. In the 1960s and 1970s, redevelopment agencies got criticized for their aggressiveness. In the 1990s, we could use some of that grit to do what we all know is right.

Feinstein: 'We have never built enough housing'

Third in a four-part series examining the records of Gov. Deukmejian and gubernatorial candidates Pete Wilson and Dianne Feinstein on housing issues.

WHEN DIANNE Feinstein talks about housing, she sounds like an economist.

"High housing costs are a problem of supply and demand," said the Democratic candidate for governor. "We have never built enough housing to meet the demand."

This isn't a new theme for the former mayor. Ten years ago, San Francisco earned the dubious distinction of having the most expensive housing in the country, and Feinstein concluded that the problem was a lack of supply. Moreover, she believed that The City could do something about the imbalance.

In the spring of 1981 while she was mayor of San Francisco, Feinstein asked her planning director, Dean Macris, and her housing chief, Bill Witte, to come up with a program to produce more housing.

They came back with a six-point plan that became the back-bone of Feinstein's effort to tame the housing price spiral. It called for rezoning hundreds of acres of land, increasing the amount of city funds that were spent on housing programs and offering mortgage help for middle-income, first-time home buyers.

Feinstein's national reputation

While the San Francisco real estate market was never brought under control and the imbalance persisted, Feinstein earned a national reputation for her efforts to produce and finance affordable housing.

For example, Feinstein pushed through a fee on office construction that requires developers either to donate funds to affordable housing programs or build housing elsewhere in The City. Other U.S. cities have emulated the plan.

Other parts of her housing program took much longer to take shape. She envisioned housing on older industrial locations such as Rincon Point and South Beach in the South of Market district.

But it took years to rezone the sites from industrial use to housing, and several major apartment projects in these areas weren't complete until after she left office in 1987.

The proposed development of the 300-acre Mission Bay site was Feinstein's most controversial housing scheme. After a five-year debate, she pushed the Santa Fe Pacific Co., which owned the property, to increase the amount of housing from 4,000 to 8,000 housing units. She also persuaded Santa Fe to reduce its plan for office space on the site.

Rent control showed the way

Still, some community activists criticized Feinstein for not insisting that the railroad company do even more for housing. Today the project still languishes in The City's approval process.

Rent control was another issue that tugged at Feinstein and prompted her to push for more housing.

"It (rent control) made me realize that we needed to increase the supply of housing," said Feinstein. "You either put everything under strict price controls or you increase the housing supply so that you don't need the regulations."

As mayor, Feinstein was often criticized by tenant leaders for rejecting proposals to tighten The City's rent-control ordinance, which was first enacted by the Board of Supervisors in 1979. With support from the real estate industry, she stubbornly fought to keep the rules flexible so that landlords could raise their rents to market levels when units were vacated.

"She absolutely would not change her position on this issue," said Faye Lacey, chairwoman of the Old St. Mary's Housing Committee, a San Francisco tenant rights group. "I think that she honestly believed that [not allowing unlimited rent increases when units were vacated] would stop people from building in San Francisco."

Home-ownership help was another important element to Feinstein's housing strategy as mayor, and something she espouses today.

"We can't give up on home ownership in this state for those families earning $20,000 to $40,000," said Feinstein. "Even if people have to buy a garage the first time and fix it up and sell it to move up, home ownership is the best savings plan and economic lift that we can give people."

Expanded state mortgage plan

Some housing activists encouraged her to make low-cost rental housing the centerpiece of her recently announced housing program. Instead, she chose to highlight a home-ownership proposal to expand a state mortgage program that offers low-down payment home loans to civil servants such as firefighters, police officers and teachers.

A memo from one of Wilson's housing advisers that criticized Feinstein's housing platform attempted to paint her proposal as an expensive liberal program. But most housing experts agree that Feinstein's plan is a mainstream blueprint that requires no major infusion of public funds.

Based on her record as mayor and based on the fact that she addressed the housing issue with a detailed proposal during the campaign, Feinstein can be expected to make the problem of high housing costs a priority if she is elected governor.

"She was one of the first elected officials to see the problems associated with high housing costs," said, Witte, now a Newport Beach developer. "She understood the housing market and she thinks that she can do something about making it work better."

Everybody won because the city scattered units

SPECIAL TO THE EXAMMER

BERKELEY — While I was waiting to interview Arnold Perkins about a public housing project built in his Berkeley neighborhood, his 6-year old son Darryl offered a fresh perspective.

"First it was a plain old ugly lot and then they started building and they looked better and better and now there are some pretty houses over there," Darryl said of the new duplexes on the corners of Dwight Way and Valley streets.

A few years ago when Darryl was still in diapers, his adult neighbors weren't as excited about the city of Berkeley's plans to build simple but attractive public housing on the vacant Santa Fe right-of-way.

"People were in an uproar" said Arnold Perkins.

Perkins, who had hoped for a park on the site, admits: "For a hot minute, I was just as mad as my neighbors. And then I realized that people need affordable housing."

In the end, that view won out in one of the most cantankerous low-cost housing battles to hit the Bay Area. The four units on Dwight Way were part of a larger 61-unit public housing plan that scattered the homes throughout Berkeley. The city put the plan in motion more than six years ago.

After more than a hundred public hearings, an expensive lawsuit and two decisions by the state Supreme Court, the family-oriented projects were finally built. Some say the controversy was so divisive for the political scene in Berkeley that it rallied support for a system of district elections, later approved by the Berkeley voters.

The concerns were familiar ones: drugs, crime and property values. Also, some community leaders were upset that public land such as schools and government right-of-ways were being used for housing and not for open space or for future education needs.

The last building was occupied last year, and most of the apprehension has subsided. Based on what I heard from some of the neighbors, the Berkeley experiment with public housing has proved to be a success.

John and Kathy Porter rent a house across the street from the development at Channing and West streets. They weren't even aware of the controversy or that the two units were public housing.

"There's such a mix of people around here you wouldn't even notice," said John Porter. "And we don't know of any problems with vandals or anything like that."

Carrie Adams and Tim Arai live in an old Victorian on Francisco Street right next to the 12-unit development that was built on the site of the old Franklin School playground. They have no complaints about their neighbors.

"The people are real nice and they do a good job of maintaining the lots — just look at that lawn," said Adams, pointing to a meticulously kept front yard next door.

Adams and Arai just recently bought their house for $230,000.

Berkeley's success with public housing

The previous owner had paid $170,000 only three years before, which suggests that the project hasn't hurt property values.

There have been a few problems with tenants and at least two evictions, but "there's only been a few complaints that I am aware of," said Assistant City Manager Eve Bach. "The worst fears never materialized."

One of the units on Dwight Way was occupied by a suspected drug dealer, Perkins said, but "the community got together with the city and the problem was taken care of."

Not everyone has been won over, although many of the original opponents apparently are slowly learning to live with their new neighbors. "Most of us are elderly on this block and we weren't very happy," said homeowner Kaiko Kawakami, who lives across the street from the units at Ward Street and Martin Luther King Boulevard. "But it's not dirty or anything. I guess it's OK, if it stays that way."

When Berkeley officials decided to use government funds to build public housing, the idea was to scatter the units throughout the city so that the poor wouldn't be concentrated in one area. With three- and four-bedroom town homes, the projects were built on 10 sites with two to a dozen units at each location.

Dispersing the developments

"We dispersed the developments, which was more expensive, but the idea was to allow people to blend into the community," said former project manager Sharon Brown, who now works for a property-management company in San Francisco.

By not concentrating the units in one development, city officials also hoped to prevent opposition to the project.

"We figured people wouldn't get that upset about one or two units in their neighborhood," said Brown. "We were wrong."

On the other side of the original controversy are people for whom the affordable units weren't a problem — they were a solution.

"I was on the (Section 8-low cost housing) waiting list for two years, then this came along," said Lynetta Taylor, who pays $148 a month for her three-bedroom unit on West Street. "I don't think we are bringing the area down," she added, noting that she has made friends with people across the street.

Part-time student Ngoc Hoang lives in a three-bedroom unit with his two sisters. "With this rent, we can afford to stay in the area."

Though the issue was often clouded, this is the reason the housing battle in Berkeley was worth waging.

On My Livable and Sensible Scale:

Berkeley's new public housing units weren't easy to produce but they offer 61 needy families livable relief from the region's high housing costs.

Trade Groups Say State Laws Are Best Way to End Local Regulatory Spats

For years, proposals to ban smoking in public places have incensed the California Restaurant Assn. Then, this summer, the 3,000-member trade group came out with a surprise announcement: It would support a ban on smoking in all public places.

But there was a catch: The support would come only if "such regulation is rendered on a statewide basis."

Frustrated trying to fend off different regulatory schemes at the city and county level, restaurant owners are asking the Legislature to approve a bill that would adopt state standards and overturn dozens of local laws that regulate smoking in restaurants.

The effort is part of a growing movement among business trade groups of asking state lawmakers to intercede in local regulatory spats.

The real estate industry persuaded the Legislature to curtail local laws that limit the use of for-sale signs in open houses. Banks and thrifts wouldn't support a bill to make automated teller machines safer until the legislation was amended with a provision that prohibits local communities from enacting their own rules.

Commercial property owners are turning to state lawmakers for relief from local smoke detector rules, and legislation on rent control and pornography is also being pushed by special interests that don't want to deal with local regulations.

"You see more industries pushing for state legislation because cities are more interested in regulating business," said Fred Main, vice president of the California Chamber of Commerce.

Main said business first turned to state legislation in the 1950s, when it lobbied for a uniform sales and use tax. "Business has always liked uniformity," he said.

In the case of the restaurant lobby, its stance is a concession that regulation is necessary.

"We have always taken a position that government should stay out of our way," said Stan Kyker, executive vice president of the California Restaurant Assn. "But after much soul searching, we decided that the pattern of local regulation that was evolving wasn't serving anyone, including our industry."

Restaurant owners admit that economic self-interest is behind their new position. Fearful of suits about secondhand smoke and worried that a patchwork of local ordinances is hurting some of its members, the association decided that a statewide ban was the best way to go.

"The reversal was smart politics, California-style," Kevin Farrell wrote in a restaurant trade magazine. "CRA, with its announcement, was able to get into step with the public, which has clearly indicated its preference for a smoking ban."

But Kyker conceded that it will be difficult to persuade the Legislature to adopt the smoking ban. "The tobacco industry isn't happy with us at all, and we don't have the resources they do," he said.

Also, the restaurant association has taken an all-or-nothing position. It wants a ban in "all public places," which Kyker said might be interpreted as Dodger Stadium and even open-air patios. "Our position is that restaurants should not be singled out, which is what happens with many of these local ordinances," he said.

Because the restaurant association has not come up with specific recommendations for legislation, some charge that its change of heart was a public relations ploy. Kyker denies that. "We intend to see this through," he said.

Industries besides restaurants are also turning to the Legislature to try to obtain relief from local regulations.

The California Assn. of Realtors was troubled by homeowner associations and cities adopting laws that regulate placement of for-sale signs. Twice in three years, the industry has pushed through state laws that permit signs to be placed anywhere they don't pose a safety hazard.

This trend concerns the League of California Cities.

"Unfortunately, it has become too easy for a special interest to come to the Legislature and pass a bill that waters down local laws or eliminates them altogether," said Executive Director Don Benninghoven. "When several cities consider the same issue, it probably means that there is a legitimate problem out there. Then we permit state lawmakers to squelch the local responses to these concerns."

Business lobbyists see the trend as a practical response to a proliferation of regulations at the local level.

"I don't think this is a case of business lobbyists getting together and deciding that we are going to take away local control," said real estate lobbyist David Booher, who has been pushing for statewide rules on rent control. "Business sees 450 municipalities and 58 counties coming at them with different regulatory schemes, so they look to the state Legislature to better manage the problem."

State lawmakers must decide what is best left to local leaders and what is of statewide significance. "I try to resist marching out and telling local officials what they should be doing about all of these issues," said Tom Hannigan (D-Fairfield).

Tough U.S. Plan Irks State Bank Regulator

California Superintendent of Banks James E. Gilleran wants L. William Seidman, chairman of the Federal Deposit Insurance Corp., to tread carefully when he pushes for tougher banking regulations.

When Gilleran heard about an FDIC proposal to prevent banks from underwriting insurance and making real estate investments, he fired off a letter to Seidman.

"California offers a textbook example of how to conduct real estate and insurance powers in a prudent and profitable manner," wrote Gilleran, who is responsible for regulating state-chartered banks such as First Interstate, Union Bank and Sumitomo Bank of California.

He encouraged Seidman "to reject any broad and sweeping changes."

"We too are concerned about the condition of banks in an economic downturn," said John Paulus, deputy superintendent of banks. "But when regulators do something from Washington, they shouldn't paint everyone with the same brush."

According to Paulus, the state superintendent carefully examines banking activity and closely monitors real estate investment and insurance activities.

To prove his contention that California banks aren't in serious trouble with their real estate and insurance portfolios, Gilleran will soon release a report that analyzes these investments and their performance.

Another study that supports Gilleran's position was released last week by the California Mortgage Bankers Assn. It shows that less than 0.8% of the 8,208 commercial property loans in California are delinquent 30 or more days.

Nestled below Mt. Davidson is the suburb in The City

SPECIAL TO THE EXAMINER

HARRY WALRAVEN, 72, doesn't remember anyone complaining about the housing affordability crisis in 1953. That's when he bought his house in the San Francisco neighborhood of Miraloma Park at the top of Portola Drive below Mt. Davidson.

Thirty-seven years ago, he put $1,000 down for his $15,500 three-bedroom house on Molino Drive. With an FHA loan at 3.5 percent interest and a monthly mortgage payment of $58.59, he burned his 20-year mortgage in 1973.

Earning $400 a month as a bookkeeper at the old San Francisco Bank, Walraven only needed to set aside 14 percent of his income for house payments when he bought the home. Today, first-time home buyers often spend 35 percent of their earnings on house payments.

"We can thank Franklin Roosevelt for a lot of things," said Walraven, referring to the FHA program that made home ownership possible for millions of Americans after World War II. Today, FHA loans don't work in pricey San Francisco because the loan limits are too low.

Walraven can also thank the resolute political will of local officials who readily responded to the need for .housing during that period. After the war, the demand for housing was overwhelming, developers were eager to build and city officials let it happen. Many of the neighborhoods in the Miraloma Park area were built in the 1930s, 1940s and 1950s in response to this pressing need.

Today, we have the same challenge, but we dismiss the solution as encouraging growth. We spend the same amount of time debating plans for more housing as it took to build out the entire Miraloma Park neighborhood.

Though the housing was built quickly, the simple designs in this close-knit neighborhood endure.

Today, the home prices in Miraloma are high: Single-family homes start at $250,000; but the neighborhood's livability is found in its austerity. On wide and curving streets that follow the contour of the Mt. Davidson slopes, the simple, two-story gems are stacked right next to one another on zero lot lines. There are five-, six- and seven-room floor plans.

The homes reflect the emergence of production building techniques. A brochure at the time bragged that the houses are priced "to reflect the savings made possible by quantity buying and building."

The homes that were built in the '30s are quaint Mediterranean style with Spanish tile roofs. The homes constructed in the 1950s are more boxy with straight lines and shingle roofs.

'Better homes for less money'

Marketed as "better homes for less money," they have individualized exterior designs with two and three bedrooms. Some of the houses have additions on the rear. But because there are no side yards, Miraloma Park doesn't have the remodeled-big-house problem that some communities face.

The utility poles are in the rear yards — an early innovation used to hide wires. In the 1960s, developers began burying them underground.

The small front yards have shrubs instead of trees, which gives the area a well-groomed look. The back yards are packed with tall trees and foliage.

The local garden club offers residents tips on landscaping. At the Oct. 15 meeting of the club, resident Rose Gelardi presented a slide show on roses at the Miraloma Park Improvement Clubhouse, which is located on Del Vale Avenue. Miraloma Park resident Eric Norland recently won the "best small garden" award in the 1990 Bay Area Garden contest.

The clubhouse was donated to the community by the Meyer Brothers, who built Miraloma Park and referred to it as a "controlled-development subdivision."

Tucked off busy Portola Drive, the neighborhood is insulated from the rest of the urban scene. San Francisco student Rosalie Kuwatch did a history of the neighborhood in 1984 and described Miraloma Park as "a suburb with in a city."

This explains why "it's so quiet," said local resident Sue Kirkham, who moved there from the East Bay in 1987. "We aren't crime-free, but it's one of the safest neighborhoods in this part of The City," she added.

The neighborhood has more fog than the Mission and Noe Valley but less than the Sunset and the Richmond. "We are in between when it comes to weather," said Kirkham, who paid $179,000 for her two-bedroom home.

When Miraloma Park was built, The City lost scads of trees, acres of open space, a spacious valley and pristine views. But the trade-off was worth it: San Francisco got a livable neighborhood of 2,400 affordable homes that local residents now bend over backwards to preserve.

On My Livable and Sensible Scale:

Simple and well-maintained, Miraloma Park is a neighborhood worth repeating today.

A 25-year-old neighborhood dies, painfully

Special to the Examiner

SUISUN CITY — This story is about a Bay Area neighborhood that is dying.

The 25-year-old Crescent neighborhood in Suisun City has been ill for more than a decade. Drugs, crime, poverty and neglect have been the shame of this multifamily neighborhood for a long time.

Now, officials in this central Solano County community have decided to put the tiny four-block area out of its misery. The city is buying and demolishing all of the low-cost units in the area.

Once the bulldozing is done, the ground will be prepared for a slick new "neo-traditional small-town suburban subdivision." Instead of 450 apartments, there will be 116 single-family homes selling for $160,000 to $240,000 with a marina and retail shops right next door.

So far, only a handful of buildings have been razed, but another half-dozen are boarded up and await the wrecking ball. The remaining units stand in various states of neglect.

Amid this mess is a community of people who await city action to relocate them to other parts of the county.

Some will be moved to Old Town Suisun across the Suisun Channel, but most will find places in Fairfield. For their trouble, the city will pay moving expenses and a monthly housing subsidy if residents can't find an apartment at the same rent they're paying in the Crescent.

The Crescent neighborhood exists in a high-density, barrack-like setting. It's a "melting pot of old and young, working-class and fixed-income people," said Sheila Figaniak who has lived in the neighborhood for 13 years.

The city estimates that 97 percent of the residents in the area are low-income, but "a lot of us are working people," said Figaniak who lives on Florida Street with her husband, Larry.

People become invisible

The economic and social strategy here is a familiar one: Move out the indigent and move in the middle class. Concentrate the disadvantaged and they are considered a threat to civilized society; disperse them and they become invisible.

Slum clearance isn't a new idea, but it still makes me uneasy.

On the one hand, it's another example of public money — in this case, redevelopment funds — being used to wipe out low-cost housing without any real plan for how to replace it.

It's also a way to enrich the city's tax rolls, clean up its image and help make a community with a troublesome eyesore more tidy, more upscale and more homogeneous.

But I admit that there aren't any simple alternatives.

For example, before the bulldozer strategy was settled on, the city made an attempt to rehabilitate some of the units and save the affordable housing that was there. But before long the improved buildings fell into disrepair. Today the rehabilitated structures don't look much different from the rest of the neighborhood.

"That's when we realized that the problems in this area couldn't be solved with some design gimmicks and new paint," said city redevelopment project manager Steve Baker. "There were other social problems that we couldn't deal with adequately."

The community is understandably wringing its hands and feels inadequate to deal with problems in the Crescent. Before the big clearance project began, 50 percent of the city's budget was spent on police services and half of that was spent policing the Crescent area, according to local officials.

Keep in mind that 75 percent of Suisun City's 20,000 population lives on the other side of Route 12 in a tract-home-style bedroom community.

A lot of folks will be happy to see the word Crescent disappear from the Suisun City map. The area has such a bad reputation that a year ago neighbors in a nearby government subsidized housing development removed the word Crescent from its name. It was called the Crescent Village and now it's simply the Village.

Why the Crescent declined

There are reasons for the Crescent's decline. To begin with, concentrating people in poorly-designed, stacked and shabby apartments in an area with no landscaping, parks or social services is often a formula for disaster. Disinvestment by the city and neglect by some private property owners also contributed to the area's decline. Then tenants begin to treat the property with the same disdain that everyone else seemed to have for the area.

After that, drugs, crime and a heavy police presence crept into the neighborhood, and you had an unlivable mess.

But don't blame the folks who live in the Crescent.

Referring to numerous local newspaper articles about crime and drug problems in the area, Figaniak said, "The people that live here are good people — despite what you hear about the Crescent." She added, "just because we aren't terribly affluent doesn't mean we aren't worth anything."

She also said some of the stories about the area being a frightening suburban ghetto may be exaggerated. "When I picked up the paper and read all of these things I wondered where they were talking about."

But Figaniak concedes that drug dealing "got out of hand a couple of years ago." Then, "the police came in here and did a good job of controlling it."

Despite the problems, some people in the community are reluctant to leave. For the most part, however, the Crescent is a transitory area and the relocation benefits will give many of the people a fresh start.

But watching a neighborhood die still isn't easy.

On My Livable and Sensible Scale:

Crescent City is on its last breath and I'm not sure how I feel about it.

Highly unusual: Official may cut property taxes

ONE OF the best kept secrets about tax law in California is that the county assessor can single-handedly reduce property taxes. When housing values slip, the assessor has the choice of adjusting property assessments and rolling back the annual tax tab for thousands of homeowners.

That's exactly what Sonoma County Tax Assessor Jim Gallagher did in 1987 and 1988 and is considering doing next year.

Three years ago, he knew that condominium values in Sonoma County like other places in the state had suffered from a seven-year downturn. Gallagher surveyed condos in the county to prove that they had lost value. He then turned to a 10-year-old California law and lowered the assessments on 1,350 condominiums. His actions reduced the value of the units by $21 million and shrank the average tax bill by about $186 a year.

This is the only major rollback in property taxes since the passage of Proposition 13 in 1978.

Gallagher is an admitted non-conformist among county tax assessors around the state. "They like to see increases in the rolls and the revenue, not declines," said Gallagher.

It's one reason — despite the downturn in the housing market — that most Californians will see a slight increase in their annual property tax tab next year.

According to the rules of Prop. 13, property taxes are limited to 1 percent of the market value of a house. The tax measure also limits increases in the taxable value of property to 2 percent a year but allows property to be reassessed at its market price when it is sold.

In 1979, voters approved Proposition 8, which permits the assessor to lower property assessments after considering "reductions in value due to damage, destruction, depreciation or other factors causing a decline in value."

For example, if a couple bought a house for $300,000 when prices peaked in 1989, they pay 1 percent or $3,000 a year in property taxes. If identical homes in the vicinity begin to sell for less than $300,000, the owners can try to persuade the assessor that the "fair market value" or the price they paid for the home — which is the basis for tax assessment — doesn't reflect the real value.

As the market softens, Gallagher is "now preparing to do a county-wide market (housing) analysis to determine if the timing is right for an adjustment." But he conceded that it will take a thorough analysis of housing conditions to reach such a conclusion.

Most county assessors only consider reducing property assessments on a case-by-case basis, according to Gallagher. "Talk of county-wide adjustments isn't very popular in the halls of government," he said.

But it can sure make 1,350 condo owners happy.

Proposition 13 wins one

The legal assault on Prop. 13 stumbled earlier this month when the state Court of Appeals ruled that the 12-year-old tax-cutting measure was constitutional.

In the Nordlinger vs. Lynch case, Baldwin Hills homeowner Stephanie Nordlinger protested the property tax bill that she received from the Los Angeles County Tax Assessor on the grounds that it violated the equal protection clause of the U.S. Constitution. Nordlinger argued that her tax bill was five to six times higher than her neighbors' merely because she owned her home for less time.

Prop. 13 requires property assessments to be based on the sales price of a house, so home price inflation has caused tax bills for newer buyers to be much higher than for long-time homeowners.

The Nordlinger case is one of three property tax cases pending before California courts. Legal scholars predict that one will overturn Prop 13. Each case challenges the current taxing system, which rewards long-time owners and penalizes new buyers.

"This is a victory for Prop. 13 and all taxpayers in the state," said attorney Anthony Caso of the Pacific Legal Foundation, which is working to uphold the measure.

The Nordlinger case will be appealed to the state Supreme Court, according to attorney Ann Carlson who represents Nordlinger. "We expected this decision from the lower court, but we are hopeful that either the state Supreme Court or the U.S. Supreme Court will examine the problems with 13," said Carlson.

www.ingramcontent.com/pod-product-compliance
Lightning Source LLC
Chambersburg PA
CBHW082010190326
41458CB00010B/3139